Arts in Earnest
North Carolina Folkli

G000122359

Arts in Earnest

North Carolina Folklife

Edited by Daniel W. Patterson and

Charles G. Zug III

Duke University Press   Durham and London 1990

© 1990 Duke University Press
All rights reserved
Printed in the United States of America
on acid-free paper ∞
Library of Congress Cataloging-in-Publication Data
Arts in earnest:
North Carolina folklife /
edited by Daniel W. Patterson and Charles
G. Zug III.
p.   cm.
Bibliography: p.
Includes index.
ISBN 0-8223-0943-2
1. Folklore—North Carolina.   2. North
Carolina—Social life and customs.   I. Patter-
son, Daniel W. (Daniel Watkins)   II. Zug,
Charles G. III
GRI10.N8F75   1990
398′.09756—dc 19   89-1212 CIP

For
Guy Benton Johnson
Ralph Steele Boggs
Arthur Palmer Hudson
and
Archie Green
Founders and Sustainers
of
The Curriculum in Folklore

Contents

Of Communities

Acknowledgments

From initial conception to the swaddling of the new manuscript in postal wrapping paper, this book was a long time a-birthing. We shall not tell how many years. And it left us with debts to those who provided midwifery or obstetrics. But we must drop this light metaphor, for we owe serious thanks. We appreciate the financial assistance given us by the University Research Council and the Kenan Fund of the University of North Carolina at Chapel Hill. We are grateful to those who helped us prepare the manuscript: Ingrid Towey, Martha Nelson, Elizabeth Howell, and especially the secretary of the Curriculum in Folklore, Debbie Simmons. The authors of the essays have shown astonishing patience. We are grateful for that, and above all grateful for the stimulation and education they and their fellow students in the Curriculum in Folklore have given us for many a year. It is a pleasure to salute them all.

Last, we gratefully acknowledge our sources for the following essays:

John Forrest, "Why Do Duck Decoys Have Eyes?" *North Carolina Folklore Journal* 31 (Spring–Summer 1983): 23–30. Reprinted by permission of the publisher. Copyright © 1983, the North Carolina Folklore Society.

Charlotte Paige Gutierrez, "The Narrative Style of Marshall Ward, Jack Tale Teller," *North Carolina Folklore Journal* 26 (September 1978): 111–26. Reprinted, with changes, by permission of the publisher. Copyright © 1978, the North Carolina Folklore Society.

Rachel B. Osborn, "The Hugh Dixon Homestead: What to Make of Tradition?" *North Carolina Folklore Journal* 32 (Spring–Summer

1984): 2–17. Reprinted, with changes, by permission of the publisher. Copyright © 1984, the North Carolina Folklore Society.

Brett Sutton, "In the Good Old Way: Primitive Baptist Tradition in an Age of Change," *Southern Exposure* 5 (Summer and Fall 1977): 97–104. Reprinted, with changes, by permission of the publisher. Copyright © 1977, Institute for Southern Studies.

James Wise, "Tugging on Superman's Cape: The Making of a College Legend," *Western Folklore* 36 (July 1977): 227–38. Reprinted by permission of the publisher. Copyright © 1977, California Folklore Society.

Arts in Earnest
North Carolina Folklife

Introduction

In 1979 the police in Charlotte, North Carolina's largest and most cosmopolitan city, investigated the death of a sixty-two-year-old crippled man. In his house they found a mimeographed sheaf of "curses, spells, prayers and charms." The man had been a root doctor and had used this manual in his practice. "TO STOP WITCHCRAFT IN MINUTES," it directed, "say 'Old Tom Walker' under your hat binded by God the Father, God the Son and God the Holy Ghost." Alternatively, "AGAINST ALL WITCHCRAFT WROUND THE HOUSE" you might "Buy 4 cans of lye; punch 9 holes in the bottom of each can; turn the holes toward the ground and bury one can round on 4 corners of your yard. Sprinkle some salt, red pepper and sulpher around your front yard and back doorsteps."[1]

This pamphlet gives a glimpse of folklife that coexists in North Carolina with shopping malls and high-rise office complexes. A journalist recognized that it would have more reader interest than the obligatory cycle of feature articles on folklore that most North Carolina newspapers print each year: the one at New Year on the eating of hog jowls and peas, the springtime piece on the pagan connections of the Easter Bunny, the one in the fall on weather forecasts encoded in the fur of the woolly worm, and those on equinoctial or solstitial rites lurking behind Halloween or Christmas. A story on the root doctor might even appeal to readers more than the perennial local-color pieces on Tarheel traditions: the Hollerin' Contest at Spivey's Corner, the Devil's Tramping Ground and the Brown Mountain Lights, or the ballads and legends of Tom Dula, Nell Cropsey, or Poor Omie Wise. So the journalist sped into print with a feature article headlined "Murder Charge Dismissed Against Woman Under 'Spell.' "[2]

The article, as such pieces generally do, made the most of what was exotic—or even erotic—in the incident. The murderer had gone both to mental-health centers and to the root doctor for relief from symptoms that began in the wake of the breakup of her marriage. She apparently relied chiefly on the root doctor, who "described her problems" and offered the diagnosis that "a man she'd been dating might have put witchcraft in her through intercourse." He himself had sex with her to help her and gave her a "mojo bag for good luck, containing a root, coins, graveyard dirt, flax seed and a little crushed red pepper" and also "something to sprinkle around her house to 'cleanse away the evil spirits.'" She subsequently came to believe that the root doctor himself had also put a spell upon her, and after "a few choice words" with him, shot him to death. The police put her in jail, where she "didn't eat or sleep, repeatedly tore her clothes off," and "lay on the floor with her legs in the air and talked to the ceiling, speaking of Peter who walked with Christ."

The general public believes that in the study of traditional culture folklorists stop their work where the journalist does, with the recording of bizarre or charming old beliefs, customs, songs, and tales. Yet this sensational incident clearly calls for a higher order of seriousness. Two lives were in crisis. The woman had come to the root doctor in a state of distress, but their relationship turned into a grim conflict. He lost his life; she would have to live with the consequences of murder. An obscure woman had become a problem for public institutions, the mental hospital, and the court of law.

The murder itself was an extreme and unusual outcome, but the woman's recourse to a root doctor was not. In North Carolina and most other states as well, seeking help from a root doctor or some other traditional healer is common in the medical history of a sizable portion of the population. The root doctor's pamphlet, moreover, offered remedies for stresses felt within a wide ethnic and economic subculture. It prescribed cures for physical ailments ("to take down swelling in the stomach"); for sexual conflicts ("to draw or force love," "to get rid of or break up love"); for strains within the family (to "aid in rearing children," "to turn a person against alcohol," "to make up after a disagreement," "for the return of husband or wife"); for the neighborhood disputes ("to overcome gossip & slander," "to gain power or con-

trol: if you have an enemy whom you desire that he do you no harm");
and for coping with the larger society (for "keeping and finding jobs
and business," to get "protection against the law," and "to change your
luck"). The anxieties of the woman, the practice of the root doctor,
and the prescriptions in his manual also implied concepts of causality at
odds with the assumptions of mainstream America. The exploration of
folklore, then, is not an antiquarian pursuit; it leads directly into earnest intellectual, social, and human issues.

In this belief we offer the following collection of essays on North
Carolina folklife. None probes an event as sensational as the murder of
a local root doctor, but all of them do reflect the serious concerns of
the contemporary folklorist. They combine with library research the
extended fieldwork that is a primary method of folklore study. The authors of the essays began their research during graduate training in the
Curriculum in Folklore at the University of North Carolina at Chapel
Hill, and this volume is a companion to the recently published *Diversities of Gifts: Field Studies in Southern Religion,* the contributors to
which were also either faculty members or graduates trained in folklore, anthropology, or religious studies at the university.[3]

A glance at the history of folklore studies, and particularly of studies in the southern region, may clarify the nature and goals of the two
volumes. In the English-speaking world, folklore developed as an academic discipline in the mid–nineteenth century. A succession of leading literary scholars at Harvard University gave it prestige in the
United States, and their work stimulated teachers—primarily of language and literature—in state and private universities all over the South
to introduce folk narrative and song into their courses or to propose
new courses devoted to these subjects. At the University of North Carolina the first such course was one on "the science of folklore" offered
by Ralph Steele Boggs within the comparative literature department in
1930. Over the next decade the number of folklore courses increased
sufficiently at the university that in 1940 Boggs was able to get approval
for the establishment of a Curriculum in Folklore, drawing upon the
interests of faculty members like Guy B. Johnson, Arthur Palmer Hudson, Richard Jente, and Jan P. Schinhan. It was the first graduate program in folklore in the United States.[4] Folklore is now taught and
studied at many other colleges and universities in the state—at Duke

University, Davidson College, Warren Wilson College, the University of North Carolina at Wilmington, East Carolina University, North Carolina State University, and Appalachian State University.

The record of North Carolina folklife is, of course, far older than the teaching and study of it. The state is rich in artifacts produced by early traditional cultures—whether Native American, as at a village site like Town Creek; or Afro-American, as in the landscape created by slaves at Somerset Plantation; or Euro-American, as in the abundant surviving log and stone buildings, grave markers, furniture, textiles, pottery, and hand tools.

In the manuscript departments of major libraries in the state we have extensive preservation even of early oral traditions, beliefs, and customs. Family papers may hold, for example, medical lore—prescriptions "To Cure a Cancer," "A Cure for the Dropsy," or "A Cure for the Scald Head."[5] Church minutes reveal beliefs, recording that an eighteenth-century Presbyterian congregation deliberated on an accusation of witchcraft brought by one member against another[6] and that a nineteenth-century Methodist body disciplined a member who played the fiddle "in violation of the feelings of his Brethren."[7] Unpublished memoirs hold song texts, local legends, and informed descriptions of work necessary for survival in the early backwoods—hunting, fishing, farming, weaving, quilting, soap making—and of the social activities that arose to support, or give relief from, the work: quilting parties, logrollings, corn shuckings, and dances.[8]

Eighteenth- and nineteenth-century publications are equally rich in data concerning North Carolina folklife. John Lawson's travel book *A New Voyage to Carolina*, published in 1709, holds celebrated descriptions of Native American life.[9] A century and a half later Harden Taliaferro's *Fisher's River (North Carolina) Scenes and Characters* painted vivid, if comically exaggerated pictures of the life and yarn spinning of backcountry plain whites.[10] Local journalism of that era also dipped into vernacular culture for jokes, comic sketches, and sermon parodies. William Hauser of Forsyth County, editor of two shapenote religious songsters, even published folk melodies he had learned by 1818—the earliest musical record of traditional singing in the state.[11]

As some of the essays in the present book will show, these early artifacts, manuscripts, and printed sources have their uses in contemporary folklore scholarship. But in themselves, the materials are fragmentary and uninterpreted. The initial self-conscious efforts to document folklore in the state are scarcely more revealing.

Perhaps the first specimens of North Carolina folklore ever deliberately "collected" for publication—the texts and tunes of eight spirituals—were included in *Slave Songs of the United States,* issued in 1867. The editors of this book described black singing (chiefly as they observed it in the South Carolina sea islands) but did not develop their own insight that the songs would be "peculiarly interesting in illustrating the feelings, opinions and habits of the slaves." They acknowledged, in fact, that they had "only gleaned upon the surface, and in a very narrow field."[12]

The next significant collection—published a half-century later—was much more hefty: Cecil Sharp's *English Folk Songs from the Southern Appalachians.* Working for forty-six weeks in 1916, 1917, and 1918 in a region where he found "singing was as common and almost as universal as speaking," the English collector took down 1,612 tunes, nearly a third of them in North Carolina.[13] Important as his collection is, Sharp based it on fieldwork along a long and narrow path through a broad region, and his introduction is brief, anecdotal, and impressionistic.

By Sharp's time, and increasingly across the next two decades, other folklore collectors were bestirring themselves in North Carolina. Dramatists in the Carolina Playmakers gathered lore to use in their "folk plays," the most serious being the Pulitzer Prize winner, Paul Green. Others, like I. G. Greer[14] and Bascom Lamar Lunsford,[15] were reared in traditional families; knew songs, tales, and the full range of Appalachian folklife from childhood; collected materials from their acquaintances and kin, and used their repertoires primarily in public performances—or in the case of Lunsford also in the organizing of his pioneering and influential Mountain Dance and Folk Festival. Still others such as Richard Chase[16] and Frank and Anne Warner[17] were outsiders who collected songs and tales on which they drew for phonograph albums and popular books as well as for personal performances. Important field-workers, like R. W. Gordon[18] and John and Alan Lomax,[19] included North Carolina in their sweeping tours on behalf of the Archive of American Folk-Song at the Library of Congress.

Most of the collectors in the state, however, were high-school and college teachers, local historians, and free-lance journalists, persons with ties to the regional folk culture who had become aware in school that academics accorded respect to folklore. Some did fieldwork for a graduate thesis, like Mercedes Steely,[20] others to publish collections, like Louis W. Chappell,[21] and a few to teach folklore courses in universities in the state, like W. Amos "Doc" Abrams and Joseph Clark. Maude Minish Sutton is perhaps representative of the greater number, an intelligent and enthusiastic amateur who collected when and how she could in a life filled with other activities.[22]

The collections of many such persons would have been lost or would have had limited significance but for the zeal and labor of a group of scholars—Frank C. Brown, Newman Ivey White, and Paull F. Baum at Duke University, and colleagues at other schools whose help they enlisted—who gathered the collections and built them into a monument, familiarly known in folklore circles simply as the *Brown Collection*. With the publication of the seven fat volumes of *The Frank C. Brown Collection of North Carolina Folklore* (1952–1961), North Carolina vaulted into the top ranks of state folklore collections. Wayland D. Hand, editor of the last two volumes, proudly declared the *Brown Collection* to be "the most comprehensive general survey of folklore for any single state." In addition, he recognized the broader value of these materials as comparative data for scholars working in other areas of the country. "Several of the individual volumes and parts of the Collection constitute not only basic compilations for North Carolina, but in default of broader surveys, are coming to be standard works of reference."[23]

This is high praise, indeed, but it is rarely remembered that these volumes were over half a century in the making. It is difficult to assign a precise starting date—Frank C. Brown was collecting old ballads like "Lord Thomas and Fair Annet" before the turn of this century—but a fair beginning would be late 1912, when Brown convened a group of enthusiastic North Carolinians to establish a North Carolina Folklore Society and initiate an active program of collecting and publication.[24] Many individuals, both scholars and laymen, joined Brown and over the next several decades experienced the joy of ferreting out old folk songs and tales, customs, and beliefs from all regions of the state. But the publication of these findings was to be long in the coming. In part the delay was understandable: there were many expenses and difficulties in assimilating the work and interests of so many contributors. The major impediment, however, was Brown himself. Though an efficient organizer, he was a decidedly possessive man who regarded the bulk of the collection as his. To make matters worse, he was also a perfectionist, who "clung to his old conviction that the collection should be 'completed' before it was published."[25] And, like most folklorists, he much preferred fieldwork to writing. In a revealing moment, he once wrote to Maude Minish Sutton that "when I try to write an article, . . . I almost invariably lose interest in it before I get my notes copied."[26]

For obvious reasons, then, it was only after Brown's death in the late spring of 1943 that a group of concerned scholars could actually examine the collection, inventory its contents, and assign appropriate editors for the major sections. The quantity of materials that they discovered was staggering. "For the whole collection," recalls Newman I. White, "there are 556 contributors of 29,647 items from all but 14 of North Carolina's 100 counties, and 95 contributors of 1,409 items from 20 other states and Canada. This does not include about 9,000 items contributed anonymously or without indication of locality, a grand total of over 38,000. If all contributions could be clearly localized, there is little doubt that every county in the state would be represented."[27] With numbers like this it is hardly surprising that another eighteen years would pass before the final volumes were in print. In all, the *Brown Collection* is a much "older" work than its dates of publication suggest. Because most of its lore was harvested between the years of 1912 and 1943, it represents an earlier age of scholarship, when folklorists' interests and methods differed very greatly from those of the current era.

Essentially the *Brown Collection* is a collection of texts, texts of games, riddles, tales, songs, beliefs, and so forth. Most of the items are accompanied by a brief statement identifying the contributor, place and date, as, for example,

183. Why are washerwomen great flirts?—Because they wring men's bosoms.
Jessie Hauser, Forsyth County, 1923[28]

Frequently the place or date is absent, and sometimes there is no attribution whatever. If additional commentary is present, it is invariably comparative data, indicating sources in which similar riddles may be found. Totally lacking, then, is any consideration of the context or function of the lore, that is, what it meant to the performer and the audience. By the time the *Brown Collection* was being edited and printed, American folklorists were regularly applying anthropological theories and techniques to fathom the social and cultural meanings of their fieldwork. But such explorations were impossible here, since Brown and his contemporaries pursued an essentially literary approach, one that dictated that the text was central and the context virtually irrelevant.

In part this persistent focus on the text stemmed from an evolutionary bias that remains apparent even in White's "General Introduction." In defining "the nature of folklore," he writes: "It is in fact a group of all the studies necessary to understand a primitive or illiterate society and the multifarious survivals from that society in the midst of the sophisticated culture that succeeded it." White does allow that there is a "considerable body of folklore which still functions actively in sophisticated societies,"[29] but for the most part the *Brown Collection* is concerned with retrieving those "multifarious survivals" from an earlier "primitive or illiterate society." According to such evolutionary logic, there is no need to study the functions or meanings of the lore. Because it emanates from an earlier state of civilization, its original context is now lost. Thus, it remains only to rescue the text from oblivion. This is not to detract from the value of the historical research and comparative notes that accompany many entries in the *Brown Collection*, most particularly the work of Arthur Palmer Hudson on the North Carolina ballads and folk songs. But the primary emphasis throughout is on texts divorced from their living contexts.

Long before the *Brown Collection* reached print, some scholars were not merely "collecting" folklore of states like North Carolina but using it to explore the history and culture of regional, ethnic, and occupational groups. Predictably, one stimulus for this approach came not from literary scholars but from anthropologists, who were active in folklore studies from the early years of the discipline. Two early books came from ethnologist James Mooney's intensive fieldwork with the Cherokees in North Carolina between 1887 and 1890: *The Sacred Formulas of the Cherokee* and *Myths of the Cherokee*.[30] Both works are field collections rather than cultural analyses, but *Myths* does contain a detailed historical essay on the Cherokee, and *Sacred Formulas* an account of Mooney's informants and his negotiations for access to Cherokee lore that reveals nearly as much about Cherokee culture as do the formulas themselves. Since anthropologists had long confined their research in this country to Native American cultures, it fell to regional sociologists to direct attention to the cultural implications of the lore of other groups. The pioneers in this field were Howard W. Odum and Guy B. Johnson at the University of North Carolina.[31] In the mid-1920s Odum had his graduate assistant Johnson help him turn a trunkful of black folk songs he had already collected into a study of the worldview implicit in the song texts. This project resulted in *The Negro and His Songs,* which appeared in 1925 as the first of a series from Odum's newly founded Institute for Research in the Social Sciences, published in collaboration with The University of North Carolina Press. The two men continued their approach with fresh field research in their next book, *Negro Workaday Songs,* the first substantial study of black laborers' songs. Subsequently Johnson did fieldwork on the South Carolina coast for his *Folk Culture on St. Helena Island,* and in North Carolina and West Virginia for his *John Henry: Tracking Down a Negro Legend*—the latter being the first major study of an American ballad, its associated legends, and the context that gave it a powerful appeal for a body of singers.[32] Years would pass before others in the state would give equally serious attention to the cultural matrix of the folklore.

Since the 1960s, however, American folklorists have greatly expanded their understanding and interpretation of folklore by adopting a performance-oriented approach, one that regards folklore as an event or process, not merely a text or an object. This is a much more dynamic and holistic perspective, since it necessitates simultaneous consideration of the performer, the audience, and the immediate context of the event as well as the folklore text. To understand the meaning of the riddle cited above, the folklorist would ask such questions as: What is the riddler's social relationship to the members of the audience? Is the audience male or female, young or old? Is the context formal, as in a school, or informal, such as a playground? To paraphrase Marshall McLuhan, the whole medium becomes the message here, not just the riddle itself. In fact, drawing on communication theory, Dan Ben-Amos has proposed that "folklore is artistic communication in small groups."[33] In like manner, Roger Abrahams sees folklore as "an implement of argument, a tool of persuasion. A piece is enacted by a performer who tries to use it to affect an audience in some way." Thus, folklore is a kind of traditional rhetoric: "It uses arguments and persuasive techniques developed in the past to cope with recurrences of social problem situations."[34]

Such definitions have obvious advantages. First, they shift the emphasis away from merely collecting texts to considering the total communication event and its meanings. Second, they avoid the connotation of folklore as a residual culture, or survivals of old, outmoded traditions. Instead, the performance approach encourages the scholar to focus on healthy, ongoing social and cultural forms, including those in the "sophisticated societies" of North Carolina's cities as well as in the fabled mountains and the Outer Banks.

Although the essays we offer in this book range widely in subject matter, they are all bound by a common thread: extensive field research. Using both historical sources and tape-recorded interviews, the authors have labored hard to move beyond texts or objects to the performers' attitudes and feelings toward their lore. This type of fieldwork can evolve only out of an extended and mutually trusting relationship between folklorist and informant, one that is well illustrated in Cecelia Conway's study of the banjo songs of Dink Roberts. On the surface, Roberts's minimal texts seem mere fragments, fleeting scraps of some half-forgotten songs. But Conway convincingly demonstrates that these elusive banjo pieces are anything but incomplete. They are like the tip of an iceberg—beneath the surface lies a mass of personal and cultural meanings for black singers like Roberts. In fact, the songs are sufficiently widespread that they constitute a distinct genre. In a similar manner, John Porter records the memories of Harry Chepriss, who left his native Greece in 1900 at the tender age of fourteen and eventually settled in Asheville. Over a period of five years, Porter obtained a moving account of one immigrant's hardships in adjusting to a new land and culture. One part of these reminiscences is a full description and text of "The Performance of Panáretos," a very old, pre-Lenten folk drama that had been performed annually in Chepriss's hometown of Karpeníssi at the end of the nineteenth century. The Americanized description of the performance is compelling in itself, but the reasons for his retaining this anachronism are more striking. Contrary to what one might expect, it was the *lack* of community, of contact with fellow

Greeks, that inspired Chepriss to cling to the play. Recalling his youthful role in the drama, explains Porter, "could temporarily provide the illusion that he was back in Greece, secure among family and friends." Thus, Chepriss's vivid memories of the "Panáretos" filled a cultural void and helped him adjust to urban, twentieth-century America.

In addition to discovering unexpected personal and cultural meanings, many of the essays focus on aesthetics, that is, the performer's standards and intentions in creating a song or a tale, a quilt or a decoy. All too often, folk artists are characterized as "naive" or "unselfconscious" or "anonymous," almost as though they were automatons who create without any forethought or self-awareness. Clearly this is not the case; the process of creation is never so random or impersonal. Artists—folk or otherwise—know what they are doing and why. In a very witty response to the seemingly obvious question, "Why Do Duck Decoys Have Eyes?" John Forrest demonstrates that hunting is an aesthetic act for participants on the North Carolina coast, and that the eyes on the wood and canvas birds are not intended to attract the incoming fowl. And by way of passing, he suggests a virgin field of folk art—the cow-manure decoy.

Ordinarily an aesthetic act leads to a finished product, but Kathleen Condon's work with the contemporary wood-carver Clyde Jones of Bynum, Chatham County, suggests another possibility. A self-trained artist who enjoys chainsawing fantastic, brightly colored animals, largely out of tree trunks, branches, and discarded objects, Jones shows little interest in completing (or selling) his now extensive menagerie. To him it is the *process* of creation that matters; thus, he is continually reconstructing, repainting, and moving his "mess," as he calls it. Jones's attitudes strongly resemble those of other self-taught artists at work in North Carolina and elsewhere, and Condon's careful analysis does much to explain their seeming eccentricity and indifference to their work.

Folk traditions usually change very slowly over time. Nowhere is the insulating power of the spoken word better illustrated than in Brett Sutton's sympathetic picture of the Primitive Baptist service. The primary medium for the discovery of spiritual truth is spontaneous expression, supported by all the creative vigor of 150 years of oral tradition. Through private testimony and public sermon and song, the members have maintained "the good old way" with only minimal concessions to modern tastes and values.

More commonly, however, folk traditions evolve as subtle forces gradually create new forms and functions. Always there is an inherent tension between innovation and tradition, between the individual and the community. Thomas Carter explores one important chapter in the evolution of southern music, when the fiddle and the banjo came together to form the seminal string band, a powerful combination that remains central in today's folk and popular music. Himself a skilled fiddler and banjo player, Carter closely delineates the adjustments in repertoire and style that resulted from the union of the essentially melodic fiddle and the rhythmic banjo. The result was a "creative dynamic," "one that reflected not so much the eclipse of the old-time music as it did a type of continuing evolution."

An appropriate sequel to Carter's essay is Kip Lornell's sharply etched portrait of black life and music in rural Cedar Grove and nearby Durham during the early twentieth century. In the countryside blacks worked the land and retained the string-band tradition that they shared with the whites. As they moved into the city, however, they encountered a new set of social and economic conditions over which the blues held sway. In place of the old seasonal dances, the new music was played on the streets, at the tobacco warehouses, and at weekly house parties. It served to help the newcomers adjust to the intensified racism and often bewildering hardships of urban life.

Change is most often dictated by such larger historical and cultural trends, but sometimes a single individual may redirect an old tradition. One case in point is Jack-tale-teller Marshall Ward, who lived all his life in the Beech Mountain region of western North Carolina. Ward acquired his extensive repertoire as a small boy from listening to his father; when he became a teacher, he told the tales every Friday to his fifth-grade class for some thirty years. In a well-documented analysis, Paige Gutierrez explains how Ward altered the content and moral values of the tales for his students and even devised new forms out of other folktales or his reading of a work like *Gulliver's Travels*. In a broader sense, Gutierrez interprets Ward's changes as emblematic of the modernization of this once-isolated region and the replacement of frontier values by a middle-class culture.

If folklorists' methods have changed greatly since the period during which the *Brown Collection* was assembled, so also have their fields of interest. True to his time, Frank Brown was most interested in folk songs, particularly the classic Child ballads that made their way into the New World from the British Isles.[35] Throughout his lifetime he avidly participated in the interstate competition to record the greatest number of these rarities, and largely through his efforts, North Carolina achieved a very high score, possibly second only to that of Maine.[36] Brown's obsession with song is reflected in the final weighting of the *Brown Collection*—four of the seven volumes cover this genre. But much to his credit, two of these volumes contain musical scores, an interest that was shared by few folklorists during his era or even later, and only one of the remaining two is devoted to ballads. Folk song, of course, remains a central interest to folklorists today, though as these essays suggest, contemporary scholars study a far wider range of religious, ethnic, and instrumental music.

The section on the folktale is surprisingly meager in the *Brown Collection*. Like the ballad, tales appealed to the scholars of Brown's era because they were narratives and hence subject to standard literary analysis. Thus it is curious that Brown and his associates collected so few and such a limited range of types. Most of those included are supernatural legends and feature witches, ghosts, and buried treasures. This preference—combined with the final two volumes, *Popular Beliefs and Superstitions*—suggest that the collectors sought out stories that embodied curious superstitions. There is also a scattering of tall tales, animal tales, and jokes, all of which are actively told today. Apparently these had little appeal to early collectors—most likely they were too commonplace and familiar to qualify as "survivals."

Perhaps the most astounding omission is the Jack tale, which today is almost the hallmark of the state's tale-telling tradition. Paige Gutierrez's essay attests to the extraordinary longevity of this genre in the North Carolina mountains. Certainly Brown and his editors must have been aware of the range and vitality of the Jack tale. It had been written up by Isabel Gordon Carter in the *Journal of American Folklore* as early as 1925 and then popularized by Richard Chase in 1943.[37] Understandably missing is the so-called urban legend, recently featured in the writings of Jan Harold Brunvand[38] and locally published in the *North Carolina Folklore Journal*.[39] These are the tales that have the greatest currency at the present time, like the legend of the Duke University football player who single-handedly beats up two carloads of townies. As explained by James Wise, the story embodies three sets of tensions within the university community: town versus gown, white versus black, and athlete versus nonathlete. Like many of the other essays in this collection, what makes Wise's analysis convincing is that he carefully discriminates between the renditions of different types of narrators. The jock, for example, revels in providing the most detailed version of the story, because he uses it to assert his power over ordinary students and counteract the "animal" stereotype that other students often have of him. Stories such as this are found in all areas of modern life, and they frequently embody situations or values about which people feel ambivalent.

From the college campus of a large, urban university, it is a short step to another source of modern bureaucracy, American business. For the early field-workers who created the *Brown Collection*, industrial folklore was never a consideration; with their agrarian, past-oriented view of folklore, it is unlikely that many of them even conceived the possibility of industrial lore. Granted, North Carolina has remained rural longer than most states. "When the entire country reached an urban majority in 1920, North Carolina was still overwhelmingly rural (80.8 percent). By 1970, the state had its largest number and proportion of urban residents ever, yet with 45 percent so classified, it was still well behind the national proportion of 73.5 percent."[40] Industry was thus slow in coming, but over the past century North Carolina has become a predominant force in tobacco, textiles, and furniture.

Folklorists themselves have been equally slow—only in the past decade has the discipline expanded to include industrial as well as preindustrial folklore.[41] However, two of the essays in this volume offer a glimpse of the rewards that await future students of occupational folklore. William Mansfield provides a full historical account of a very familiar figure in this region, the tobacco auctioneer, who for more than a century has entertained audiences and sold tons of the golden leaf with his musical chant. Mansfield documents the traditional learning of this skill and shows how the auctioneer's cries have evolved over time in response to changing market conditions. Then Douglas DeNatale moves right into the factory itself, a textile mill in Bynum, to explore the varied meanings of the workers' pranks. In a discriminating analysis based on extensive interviews, he reveals the tacit codes of conduct that underlie these seemingly subversive activities. In fact, the pranks—and DeNatale documents enough of them to supply several mills—

serve to assert the identity of the mill community to outsiders and to reinforce the need for cooperation and mutual responsibility throughout the production process. The pranks are anything but trivial. Perhaps in the near future, similar studies of expressive behavior will be carried out in North Carolina's newest industry, the high-technology laboratories of the Research Triangle Park.

Without question the most exciting branch of folklore study since the publication of the *Brown Collection* has been that of material culture. Since the appearance of Henry Glassie's *Pattern in the Material Folk Culture of the Eastern United States* in 1968,[42] a wide-ranging essay on folk architecture, crafts, arts, food ways, clothing, tools, and technology, American folklorists have begun to collect and analyze objects as well as the more familiar verbal artifacts. European scholars have always done this; now the term "folklife" has come into frequent use in the United States, perhaps derived from the Swedish *folkliv* or the German *Volkskunde*. The rationale for this new interest is obvious enough. Material objects are not just mechanical responses to the environment or mere solutions for survival. No less than songs or tales, they are the products of human intelligence and thus call for similar interpretation and understanding.[43]

Since the 1970s there has been an explosion of study of material culture in North Carolina. In architecture the Division of Archives and History, Department of Cultural Resources, has undertaken a statewide survey that has already produced numerous publications on specific cities and counties.[44] In addition, Doug Swaim has edited a volume of essays on vernacular architecture entitled *Carolina Dwelling: Toward Preservation of Place: In Celebration of the North Carolina Vernacular Landscape*.[45]

Rachel Osborn's close study of a Quaker family's homestead in Snow Camp, Alamance County, well illustrates the potential cultural insights embedded in architectural forms. When Hugh Dixon built his new farmhouse in 1866 he naturally drew on local, traditional ideas about where and what a house should be. At the same time, however, he devised a somewhat idiosyncratic floor plan, incorporated balloon framing and numerous manufactured components, and even added a few touches of popular styling in the Greek Revival, Gothic, and Italianate modes. Thus, his home demonstrates the dynamic nature of folk housing, the ever-present tension between tradition and innovation. It also suggests the organic quality of traditional architecture. When Hugh Dixon designed his house, he ensured that it responded to his immediate needs. It contained space for numerous inhabitants (his five children, hired help, teachers from the local Quaker school), an office area for his businesses, and even a granary in the attic. Osborn concludes by proposing that Dixon's home embodies his Quaker heritage, in that it reflects the ideals of simplicity and plainness, yet also an interest in education and industrial enterprises.

Together with architecture, pottery has been given much attention by North Carolina scholars—hardly surprising, as no other state today possesses so many indigenous potteries with roots running directly back into the folk tradition. Some of the old families at work today, such as the Cravens and the Coles, can trace their craft lineage straight back into the eighteenth century. Two lengthy, detailed studies—one by John Bivins on the Moravians[46] and the other by Charles G. Zug III on the larger folk tradition[47]—are now available, and numerous exhibitions have further stirred public interest. In 1980 the Mint Museum of Charlotte displayed alkaline-glazed stoneware in an exhibition entitled *Potters of the Catawba Valley, North Carolina*,[48] and the next year the Ackland Art Museum at the University of North Carolina at Chapel Hill followed suit with a more comprehensive survey, *The Traditional Pottery of North Carolina.*[49]

Two other institutions that have spearheaded studies in furniture, textiles, ceramics, metalwares, and the arts are Old Salem and the associated Museum of Early Southern Decorative Arts (MESDA) in Winston-Salem. The former oversees the town of Old Salem, which has evolved, in part, into a living history museum.[50] The latter maintains a superb collection of furnished period rooms from Southern homes, publishes the *Journal of Early Southern Decorative Arts*, and carries on extensive educational and research activities.

Altogether, six of the essays in this volume fall under the general heading of material culture: one on architecture, two on quilts, two on decoys, and one on art. Both quilt making and quilt collecting have long been popular in North Carolina; in recent years there have been two major exhibitions of quilts and numerous local ones. From November 1974 through January 1975 the North Carolina Museum of History in Raleigh displayed *Artistry in Quilts* by mounting 120 examples spanning two centuries.[51] Exactly four years later the Ackland Art Museum organized *North Carolina Country Quilts: Regional Variations*, which contrasted representative groups of quilts from regions of the state settled by the English, Germans, and Scotch-Irish.[52] Laurel Horton was one of the organizers of that exhibition; here she explores the preferences in quilt making among two early ethnic groups in North Carolina, the Scotch-Irish and the Germans, both of whom settled in Rowan County in the eighteenth century. Her close investigation of historical sources, notably early newspaper advertisements, reveals that quilt makers could purchase a surprisingly wide range of materials during the first half of the nineteenth century, even in this backcountry setting. Since the Scotch-Irish were actively engaged in politics and commerce, they tended to adopt the very latest patterns and types of fabric. The Germans, on the other hand, insulated by their language and self-sufficient farming practices, tended to retain old designs and produce their own materials and dyes. However, by the second half of the nineteenth century, acculturation was beginning to blur these ethnic distinctions.

Quilts serve a variety of functions: on the utilitarian level they keep people warm; on another level they provide opportunities—in quilting bees or frolics—for social interaction. But as Mary Anne McDonald explains in her essay, they may also embody very deep personal feelings. The use of funeral ribbons as the raw materials for quilts may seem a lugubrious practice to some, but these materials fit neatly into the Afro-American tradition. They possess the bright colors preferred by many black quilters, and their form lends itself to the strip construction many of the quilt makers prefer. Although there is a common tradition here and the three women McDonald studies are friends, they evince different attitudes toward their creations. For one, the funeral-ribbon quilt has no particular symbolic value; it is attractive because of its shiny materials. But for the other two, these unusual quilts commemorate kin or friends whose loss meant much. McDonald's analysis reiterates the importance of going beyond the object to its maker and underscores how much has been lost in the past by the failure to do so.

Decoys have also played a major role in North Carolina life, though only along the upper two thirds of the coast, from, roughly, the Virginia border to Bogue Sound in the south. To complement John Forrest's essay on the aesthetics of hunting, Stephen Matchak provides a full history of the decoy from its introduction into the region in the middle of the nineteenth century to the present day. At the core of Matchak's chronicle is a fine portrait of John W. Austin of Corolla, a decoy carver who worked as a market hunter and sportsman's guide, and shot fowl for his own table. Despite the passage of the Migratory Bird Treaty Act in 1918 and the decline of the gun clubs during the depression, many decoy makers remain at work today. However, the old utilitarian tradition has evolved into an art; today most decoys sit at rest on collectors' mantels rather than ride in great rigs out on the marshes and sounds.

A smiliar evolution has occurred in many of the old crafts. As tastes and needs change and modern producers like Henredon Furniture or Pine State Dairy dominate the markets, there is little demand for a handmade slat-back chair or a salt-glazed stoneware churn. Like the decoy makers, the North Carolina potters have shifted over from jugs and jars to artware, but other traditional craftsmen have simply vanished. Thus, one new field of interest for contemporary folklorists will be the so-called self-taught or outsider artist, individuals like Clyde Jones of Bynum, who has filled his and others' yards with his imaginative chainsawed animals.

Two similar figures were recently featured during early 1986 in an exhibition of Five North Carolina Folk Artists at the Ackland Art Museum in Chapel Hill.[53] One, Edgar Alexander McKillop (1897–1950) of Balfour, Henderson County, was a mill worker and jack-of-all-trades who carved an enormous assortment of walnut animals and men that inhabited his modest mill house with him and his family. The other was Minnie Smith Reinhardt (1898–1986), a farmwife who lived in southern Catawba County all of her life and painted scenes of rural life— "memory paintings," as they are sometimes called—very much in the manner of the famed Grandma Moses. Like Clyde Jones, McKillop and Reinhardt are not strictly *folk* artists—they did not learn to chainsaw, carve, or paint from a "master" in their neighborhood; they largely taught themselves. In short, they did not work out of an already existing, informally transmitted, folk tradition. But they sprang from a traditional community, and they created aesthetic objects that have given pleasure to their friends and neighbors. Although they hang in a sort of cultural limbo between folk and academic art, they clearly deserve the folklorist's interest. As Kathleen Condon's essay suggests, their work and attitudes may tease and frustrate, but they will also enlarge our understanding of the kinds of creative acts with which people fulfill themselves and communicate with others.

In exploring wood carvers or quilters, string-band music or congregational song, Jack tales or urban legends, the contemporary folklorist uses tools of documentation, study, and dissemination that were not part of the working gear of many folklorists of Frank C. Brown's generation: sound recordings, still photography, film, and videotape. The anthropologist Jesse Walter Fewkes had attempted field recordings in 1890 with Passamaquoddy Indians in Maine, and other anthropologists continued to record Native Americans throughout the early decades of this century.[54] In England the classical pianist and folk-music enthusiast and arranger Percy Grainger recorded wax cylinders with "genuine Peasant singers" between 1906 and 1908, and even prevailed upon His Master's Voice to release a few discs of authentic traditional singing.[55]

Field use of the technology of sound recording came late to North Carolina, however. Frank C. Brown had an Ediphone cylinder recording machine by 1915,[56] and R. W. Gordon recorded some cylinders in Asheville in 1925. By the mid 1920s commercial recording companies had begun (innocent of any folkloric intent) to record traditional musicians—including bluesmen from Durham, fiddlers and banjo players from the Blue Ridge Mountains, gospel and country singers from the Charlotte area—for marketing to newly discovered ethnic and regional consumers.[57] But even to the end of the 1920s, field collecting in the state was being done mostly with pencil and notepad, subject to the vagaries of ear and memory and the musical illiteracy of the collector. This was how Cecil Sharp and Maude Minish Sutton worked. Guy Johnson carried an Ediphone on his St. Helena Island trip, but it failed immediately.[58] The field instrument at that time was unreliable, hard to transport, and able to record only short pieces at close range. With instrument or without, early field-workers could accurately document a song text or a riddle, but not a long, spoken narrative like a Jack tale or a complex musical performance or a full religious service or the spontaneous give-and-take of a house party. This would not be possible until tape recorders became available shortly after World War II.

Moreover, dissemination of field recordings for pleasure listening, classroom use, and study did not begin until the 1940s, when the Library of Congress first issued 78-rpm discs from the Lomax field trips.

The long-playing album, introduced by Columbia Records in 1948, greatly encouraged other pioneers in the field, notably Folkways Records, which released extraordinary field recordings, most of them taped and edited by dedicated nonacademic "folk-music revival" collectors and performers such as Ralph Rinzler, Mike Seeger, and John Cohen. By the 1970s small record companies—County Records, Folk-Legacy, Arhoolie, Flyright, Trix, Rounder, and dozens of others—had followed the lead of Folkways, though each with a smaller and more specialized catalogue.

North Carolina was a beneficiary of this development. Many of its major folk performers became widely known outside their own circles through these recordings: the tale teller Ray Hicks, the ballad singers Frank Proffitt and Dillard Chandler, the fiddler Tommy Jarrell, the guitarists Blind Gary Davis, Elizabeth Cotten, and Doc Watson, and such surviving bluesmen as Sonny Terry, Willie Trice, and Guitar Shorty.[59] Such recordings continue to appear in modest numbers. Three contributors to this book—Tom Carter, Kip Lornell, and Brett Sutton—have edited important albums from their fieldwork, and their album notes help set standards for documentation and analysis. Sutton's album *Primitive Baptist Hymns of the Blue Ridge,* for example, won praise in the *Journal of American Folklore* from a reviewer who called it "a model ethnography of religious folklife expression."[60]

The early commercial recordings of bluesmen, gospel singers, string-band musicians, and others were in the meantime "discovered" by folk-music enthusiasts in the early 1950s and then by academics. From this discovery has come a stream of "reissues" in long-play format, at first minimally documented, but increasingly accompanied by substantial album booklets that incorporate both library and field research. And this has further led to new field recordings of singers located in the search for artists issued on early 78-rpm discs. Among the notable albums illustrating these developments are Archie Green's *Babies in the Mill,* featuring the Dixon family, textile workers from Rockingham,[61] and a series of blues albums edited and produced by Bruce Bastin.[62] Research has also produced studies of early recorded performers and songs, such as Bastin's *Red River Blues* and Norm Cohen's *Long Steel Rail.*[63] A major repository of these recordings is the Southern Folklife Collection at the university in Chapel Hill.

Photography is a much older technology than sound recording, but because early folklorists were preoccupied with musical and verbal texts they made little use of this tool for fieldwork. The Brown Collection files, for instance, hold only a scattering of snapshots of informants. Library collections, however, have early photographs full of valuable information about North Carolina houses and barns, farmsteads and factories, corn shuckings and river baptisms, dress and food ways, singing schools and musical instruments. These photographs are not the work of professional folklorists. Many of the more valuable are not even the work of professional art photographers like Doris Ulmann, who passed through the state, but of little-known amateur or journeymen photographers like Bayard Wootten,[64] who shot many local-color scenes, especially in the Appalachians, and of social-reform photographers like Lewis W. Hine, who photographed child laborers in textile mills between 1908 and 1916.[65]

The beginnings of a more systematic visual documentation of North Carolina folklife are found in the Farm Security Administration photographs of the late 1930s and in photographic projects sponsored by Howard Odum at about the same time.[66] The latter collection provides, for example, a fairly comprehensive visual record of tobacco production in the northern Piedmont from planting to auction. But highly intensive photodocumentation did not come until the mid-1970s, when several institutions simultaneously began focused photographic projects: the North Carolina Division of Archives and History starting a county-by-county survey of buildings; the Museum of Early Southern Decorative Arts the photographing of architecture, furniture, and craft objects surviving from before 1820; and faculty members and students in the Curriculum in Folklore photographic research with such artifacts as pottery, grave markers,[67] wildfowl decoys, and quilts. The authors of three papers in this book—Horton, McDonald, and Matchak— pioneered in this work.

The project of Horton and her coworkers Joyce Joines Newman and Mary Ann Medlin has had a spreading influence on quilt studies in other states and particularly on the major statewide survey being carried out by the North Carolina Quilt Project. Headed by Ruth Roberson of Durham, this grass-roots, nonprofit organization is largely made up of intelligent amateurs with a serious interest in both making and studying quilts. Already they have documented and photographed more than ten thousand quilts in North Carolina. Two products of their work were a major exhibition at the North Carolina Museum of History in 1988 and a well-illustrated book, *North Carolina Quilts*.[68]

The medium used in all these projects has been still photography, as the most appropriate for material-culture objects. But for documentation and dissemination of events and performances and the personal and social worlds within which they take place, film and videotape are obviously superior. The latter promises to be an inexpensive medium in which to compile research footage. Mike Seeger, for one, has already used it to record archival footage of Appalachian dance, and Wayne Martin and Nancy Kalow are currently engaged in similar documentation of technical features of traditional fiddling in North Carolina.[69] Until now, the constantly changing technology of videotape has made 16-mm film, though expensive, the primary format, but the history of its use for folkloric documentation in this state is short. John Cohen's *The End of an Old Song*—undertaken in 1967 to record the powerful traditional singing of Dillard Chandler and his neighbors in Madison County—was the first important folklore documentary about North Carolina.[70] Subsequently, a few other films have been shot here as commercial ventures from outside the state—most notably *Welcome to Spivey's Corner, N.C.* (on the hollering contest and its Coharie Indian champion hollerer, Leonard Emanuel) and *The Angel that Stands by Me* (on the black artist Minnie Evans and her visionary paintings.)[71]

Two institutions outside North Carolina—Appalshop, Inc. and East Tennessee State University—have also explored several film subjects in the Appalachian region of North Carolina, including a film by each on tale teller Ray Hicks.[72] Within North Carolina, as one of his many admirable documentation projects, George Holt of the Folklife Section of the North Carolina Arts Council collaborated with the Smithsonian Institution on *Free Show Tonite*, using surviving veteran performers to recreate a traveling medicine show.[73] The University of North Carolina Curriculum in Folklore has collaborated with independent filmmaker Tom Davenport on an American Traditional Culture Series, which includes three documentaries with footage shot in North Carolina: *Born for Hard Luck* on the black medicine-show musician Arthur "Peg Leg Sam" Jackson, *Being a Joines: A Life in the Brushy Mountains* on the Appalachian tale teller John E. Joines and his wife Blanche, and *A Singing Stream: A Black Family Chronicle*, filmed with the Golden Echoes gospel quartet and the Landis family of Granville County.[74]

Several of the contributors to his book were among the students who participated in one or another of these film projects, and Cecelia Conway has been a moving spirit in two other films related to research for her essay on banjo songs. The first, *Dink: Pre-Blues Musician*, was a student project supported by a tiny grant from the North Carolina Bicentennial Commission, but holds highly important footage of traditional Piedmont black banjo playing. The other film, *Sprout Wings and Fly*—a prize-winning documentary on which Conway collaborated with Alice Gerrard and filmmaker Les Blank—features the respected fiddler Tommy Jarrell of Mount Airy, a leading tradition bearer.[75]

What does all this busy filming, photographing, sound recording, interviewing, observing, and writing amount to? Certainly not yet to a beautifully recreated holograph of North Carolina folklife. Folklorists, for all their dedication, still struggle to shed their intellectual and academic biases and the racial, class, and gender assumptions of their place and time. They struggle too to master new technological and conceptual tools not available to earlier scholars. At present their research into the regional culture is far from complete. Nevertheless the studies that follow do more than the earlier work to enrich our understanding of little-noticed cultures of the state. But the promise of such studies lies less in an understanding of a past we can recover only in part than in our usefulness to a present we observe—awakened by prior folkloric concerns—with more than common attentiveness.

The folklife of the old North Carolina disappears. Tobacco barns sag and rot beneath mounds of trumpet vines. Past them the highway crews lay sand-white bands of concrete that roll over successive hilltops between the towns of the Triangle and the Triad. The towns themselves soon follow after the roads, spreading and meshing with one another. Service to tourists replaces the family farm. Developers turn the textile mill into a shopping mall. Rock videos resound on the commercial airwaves, while the Center for Public Broadcasting wafts out British comedies and glossy National Geographic "specials" on the costumes of ptarmigans. An enterprising Texan suddenly beams down a giant emerald skyscraper onto a piney hilltop in Durham.

But all these changes give rise to new tensions and new folklife. The corridors of the skyscraper rustle with acidic jokes bred by the tedium and jockeying for power in corporate America. Outside, resentful neighbors pass a rumor that the building has a tilt and will have to be torn down. At a nearby college campus a gathering of young Lumbees encircles a drum, chanting powwow songs learned in the Great Plains. In Raleigh, a few miles downhill from the capitol building, a new gospel choir of black and white "inmates" in a "women's correctional facility" sing in call-and-response their discovery of God's love. In nearby counties Mexican-born workers tend dairy cattle and on weekends dance to the music of the Fuerza Quatro at a baile. Scattered through the piedmont, pockets of Hmong and Montagnard refugees displaced from highland villages of Vietnam or Laos struggle to make room for themselves in a world of alien ways. Meanwhile sheriffs in Wilkes and Mecklenburg counties report calls from parents terrified by rumors of cults that plan to kidnap a hundred blond boys. And a journalist in North Carolina's largest and most cosmopolitan city hears of a shooting and speeds into print with a news story headlined "Murder Charge Dismissed Against Woman Under 'Spell.'"

We see an outline forming for more earnest future folklife studies: explorations of negotiations that little-noticed people from four different continents are carrying on here with the state's varied terrains, with changing economies and social balances, with each other, with the arts and ideas of their own forebears, and with the common crises of human life.

Of the Past

1. The North Carolina Wildfowl Decoy Tradition

Stephen Matchak

Wildfowl-decoy carving has been a folk tradition since the middle of the nineteenth century, and many hands have contributed to it. In the antique collectors' scheme of things, however, North Carolina decoys fare poorly; William Mackey describes the regional decoys as "solid, crude, roughly finished and poorly painted."[1] But hunters design decoys not for collectors, but as tools to lure passing birds within range of their guns. The decoys have specific functions within the busy lives of men like John W. Austin of Corolla, North Carolina.[2]

Austin was born in Hatteras, North Carolina, in 1891 and moved to Corolla when his father became the lighthouse keeper. As a boy, Austin watched his father and older brothers make decoys. He also helped paint their decoys and accompanied them in hunting. While in the field, he watched and handled birds, slowly building a storehouse of practical knowledge. Austin told me that when he was fourteen he decided to hunt for himself and consequently had to carve his own decoys. He started by copying his father's decoys and remembers that his first few tries produced funny-looking results—birds that rode awkwardly in the water and failed to resemble the intended species. After a while, he "got pretty good at it" and through the years, refined his craftsmanship and expanded his repertoire.

Austin made decoys for use in three different hunting situations in successive phases of his life. As a young man, like many good shots, he worked as a market hunter, shipping his daily kill on steamboats to northern markets. In effect, he was a small businessman, having invested in a sailboat, large decoy rig, and armaments to harvest nature's bounty. When he returned from the First World War, however, Austin found that his occupation had been outlawed by the Migratory

Figure 1.1. John W. Austin (1891–1981), decoy carver from Corolla, N.C. (courtesy of Norris Austin).

Bird Treaty Act of 1918. He turned to the Lighthouse Club for employment and worked as a guide for "sports" who desired to shoot gamebirds, and during the slack season he made decoys for the sport market.

Austin guided until the Great Depression brought declining economic fortunes, changed leisure activities, and closed many hunting clubs. He then become the postmaster in Corolla and continued to fish and hunt in accord with the seasons. Even in his retirement, he continued to carve decoys and to hunt for pleasure and for the table. Looking back on his world, Austin observed that nature "was all there was here, you know, for people to live on for a livelihood. The natives come in, and our forefathers run the Indians out—and all they had was hunting raccoons, possums, and ducks. And they had plenty of oysters, clams, and fish, and they didn't have to worry about anything, except something to wrap up in. And, there was plenty of game, you know, all the time."

Crude or elegant, bird decoys have serious uses in lives like John Austin's, and the North Carolina decoys were shaped by an even longer and more complex history than his. They exhibit a diversity of forms arising out of the complexities of the hunt itself and out of an ever-changing local ecology and economy.

When the earliest colonists settled North Carolina, they had no need for decoys. An eighteenth-century traveler through this region, John Brickell, saw a flock of swans so large it appeared like "Land covered with Snow. About Christmas they are frequently so fat, that some of them are scarce able to fly."[3] John Lawson, North Carolina's colonial natural historian, comments on the variety of local bird species and notes that redhead ducks were difficult to shoot: "They are very good Meat, but hard to kill, because hard to come near."[4] However, hunters had little trouble finding easy prey within musket range. Instead of using decoys, Brickell records, hunters "frequently set Fire to these Savannas and Marshes, and as soon as the Grass is burnt off, these Fowl will come in great Flocks to eat the Roots, by which means they shoot vast Numbers of them."[5]

Before 1700, colonial settlers streamed south from coastal Virginia, drove out the local Indians, planted crops, and harvested an ever-growing amount of wildlife. David Stick emphasizes that these colonists had several occupations: "Each of them was the same time a farmer, a fisherman, a hunter, and a wrecker."[6] These folk built crofting communities along the banks in which they provided for virtually all their needs and exported their surpluses to Virginia's markets. A local historian, H. B. Ansell (1832–1920), describes the region during this era as a rustic paradise, with "fish, oysters, wild turkeys, pigeons, ducks, geese and other birds in abundance to replenish the tables of the new-comers with all necessaries except bread; and soon the corn and sweet potato patches made that want less."[7]

Ansell also records the hunting methods of the 1830s through the 1850s as part of his social history of Knotts Island. Realizing that "it has ever been in evidence in all time that the young enjoy nothing more than tales told of the far past," he writes of the "details of the events, incidents and traditional stories," from his youth.[8] In these recollections, he includes material about his boyhood adventures, old-fashioned hunting styles, and the transition from muskets to breech-loading weapons.

In his boyhood, Ansell and his cronies stole birds' eggs and hunted fowl, which they later sold for toys and candy. Boys "would hunt for birds' nests, and rob the innocent creatures of their eggs; the poor, chattering mother and mate, bewailing the destruction of their off-spring in embryo, would be ruthlessly clubbed away. . . . Every boy had his myrtle 'birding club,' cross-bow and arrows, his springs for rabbits, his traps for birds, in every briery branch and fence-lock. By this means hundreds of strings of dead birds, even sparrows, were shipped to market by the boys, whence were obtained ginger-cakes, tops and chords, and other trinkets."⁹

In their hunting, these boys unself-consciously imitated their fathers, who hunted bigger game with muskets for food and for cash.

In the days of these old fowlers and from time immemorial the mode of duck-shooting was not as now. The ducks were shot sitting and at the rise. The crawling practice was then in vogue. Go into the marsh with noiseless care; look over the coves, creeks and ponds; see if any of the feathered tribe had ventured near enough to shore for a shot; if so, down on hands and knees, often in the mud and water; crawl to the water's edge; peep through the marginal marsh or galls; see where the ducks were thickest; Ready-aim-go bang. Fuss and feathers, what a scramble and chatter: There might be three or four or a score of ducks left dead and crippled. In went the hunter attending to cripples first, often chasing a wing-brake a great distance. He would then gather up his trophy and return to shore wet, at least, from waist down. When there were two gunners together, the procedure was the same except when ready to shoot, they would aim in the right and left wings of the thickest bunches—a bunch each, if more than one, and fire away at the word of command—Ready-aim-fire. Sometimes one would shoot at the sitting, the other at the rise or flirt.¹⁰

The accuracy and type of weaponry influenced hunting strategy greatly. In Ansell's youth, local hunters used

English and French muskets; these were as large as the modern gun No. 8 I recond [reckon], and were of the flint & steel, cock & pan make. These guns often missed fire, especially in damp weather. The steel being damp the flint would fail to knock fire in the pan; even if it did, the powder in the pan might be moist or corroded about the touch-hole, then it would be a miss-fire—"a flash in the pan" as it was called. If this should happen when a good shoot of ducks were in the front, there would likely be some big cuss-words uttered or mumbled against gunlock and powder. To make sure the next time, the dry part of the woolen coattail or the under part of the sleeve was applied to that pan till it glittered; the flint was ragged with the Jack-knife; the touch-hole opened; dry powder put into the pan, with dry tow thereon, and all clamped down; then, with the gun lock part of the gun under his coat tail, the hunter was off for better luck.[11]

To increase the odds of bagging wildfowl, local hunters frequently used other methods as well.

The marsh being interspersed with coves, ponds, creeks, etc, where, if permitted, ducks frequented at nights, to feed and rest. The mode of hunting this way: go on the East side of cove, creek, or pond, before night; build a blind so that the reflection of the departing sun glaze a path West; lie down and await the coming. Whir, down flat, pish-shu-u. If near dark the sun's glazed way was watched and if the duck or ducks swam across this glazed way—go bang. This went on from Sundown till dark. A chance shot might kill after dark. In this way, the people seldom went home without a mess of ducks.[12]

In those days and until the 1920s, people would "raise wild geese from cripples, would tie them out for decoys, and in a strong westerly wind, when the tide was full, often killed a hundred in one day on the margin of the beach or on some conspicuous shoal. They also tied out for decoys, tame ducks along the margin of islands and marsh and often done well. This was before wood decoys came along."[13] Another mode of hunting dating from this era is firelighting. To firelight, hunters went out at night and blinded game with lantern light, which immobilized them. In 1822 the North Carolina legislature declared firelighting "not [to] be lawful for any person whatsoever, to hunt with fire after fowl, on any of the waters of the county of Currituck."[14] If caught and prosecuted an offender faced a twenty-dollar fine. However, law officials never enforced the law, and hunters frequently firelighted throughout the nineteenth and early twentieth centuries.

In these ways, local fowlers shot more than enough game for their tables and shipped their surplus to Norfolk markets. Ansell recorded the pre–Civil War prices as one dollar for a pair of canvasback ducks, seventy-five cents for a pair of redhead, and twenty-five to fifty cents for the "common ducks." Even though they sold for less, hunters usually hunted common marsh ducks; it did not pay for a fowler to gun for canvasback and "wade often to the armpits after them, when there were plenty of the common [ducks] to be had with less trouble."[15] Freighters—small sailboats holding a cartload or two of goods—carried game north through the Dismal Swamp Canal, or teams of horses dragged heavily laden carts through mud and mire to market. Ansell counted thirty freighters that regularly sailed from Knotts Island carrying a cargo of mixed produce—fish, vegetables, meat, and fowl. On a good run, the round trip took thirty-six hours, and the transportation charge was a third of the load.[16] Before the 1850s the prices were low, the transport charges high, the game abundant, and the wildfowl decoy never floated in local waters.

In the 1850s, however, this fowling tradition slowly began to change. One catalyst was the introduction of the breech-loading shotgun to Knotts Island. Young Wilson Cooper bought the first of these new guns seen on the island and amused local crowds by shooting hats thrown into the air. After destroying many hats, he started to shoot "ducks on the wing, and soon took them down as easily as he ragged old hats. This mode was a great innovation on the duck-killing of that day; indeed, there were protests against introducing this radical departure from the old method, mainly on account of waste of ammunition."[17] But the younger generation ignored their elders' protests and followed Cooper's lead.

Cooper and his partner, young Timothy Bowen, also took the lead in using wood decoys and in market hunting. "At first they tied live decoys beside marshy islands and points or on shoals; after being deprived of the marsh by owners, they resorted to wooden decoys and bush-blind placed in deeper waters."[18] Although Ansell fails to describe the introduction of the decoy, others do. A traveling preacher, Richard Randolph Michaux, judges that "the men of wealth and leisure, who came to the North Carolina coast to shoot game, do not practice the methods employed by the natives."[19] Instead, northern sportsmen set rigs of live and wooden decoys before their blinds. Soon market hunters—spurred, no doubt, by the opening of the Albemarle and Chesapeake Canal and by the beginning of rail service from Norfolk, both in 1859—began to use decoys. Edmund Ruffin, another chronicler, watched gunners tie a line of live decoys on either side of the blinds and set a rig of wood decoys between them. When a hunter prepared to fire, his live decoys would "speedily swim apart on either side, as far as their confining lines permit, from the central space, which is swept by deadly shot." This proved so effective that in "some cases, the wild fowls continue to come so fast, that the gunners do not leave their blinds until near sunset, when they go to pick up and save all the dead birds that have not floated off." One businessman, Edgar Burroughs, even hired thirty gunners who in one winter spent four tons of shot, one ton of gunpowder, and forty-six thousand percussion caps.[20]

The hunters of the mid-nineteenth century carved sturdy decoys that still typify the regional tradition. John Austin's craft offers a sharp focus on many aspects of this folk tradition. In the slack time between corn harvest and the arrival of migrating waterfowl, Austin worked on his rig of wildfowl decoys, preparing it for each upcoming hunting season. He made new decoys, repaired old ones, and usually repainted his entire rig. Decoy making began with the selection of thick juniper planks. Using a hatchet, Austin roughed out the decoy body, starting at the decoy's breast, and methodically shaped the form toward its tail. He never needed a pattern: years of experience taught him the size, shape, and expressions of each species. Holding the decoy body firmly between his knees, Austin then trimmed and smoothed the form with a spokeshave and finished the body with sandpaper. Sitting under a shade tree, Austin enjoyed passing leisure hours chatting with friends and whittling decoy heads. These heads, also of juniper, took hours to carve to catch faithfully a bird's expression. After he accumulated a pile of decoy bodies and a batch of heads, Austin nailed the pieces together with three eight- or ten-penny nails. He once estimated that working flat out he could carve three decoys a day. But he never did. Decoy making was a gradual process of accumulation—in his heyday Austin owned and used several decoy rigs totaling hundreds of decoys.

Each fall Austin or his children repainted the entire rig. Abuse from the hunting season and neglect during the remainder of the year always wore off a coat of paint. No one cared much about the quality of the paint job. All that mattered was that the right colors were on

Figure 1.2. Two duck decoys by John W. Austin. Redhead, of juniper wood (top), *and widgeon, with wooden head and base, body of canvas over wire* (bottom) (*photo by Charles G. Zug III*).

the proper locations. After all, "if a bird was close enough to tell the difference, it was close enough to shoot."

At this time, Austin rigged the decoys for the water. He screwed a one-pound lead keel to the decoy's underside to steady it in open water and nailed a long anchor line to the decoy's prow. Usually Austin bought both the keel and anchor from a foundry in Elizabeth City. The decoys now became part of a hunting rig and were ready for the hunt.

Most other decoy carvers also preferred red juniper, which sold for about twenty cents per decoy in six-inch-thick planks during the years just before the First World War. At the same time, carvers in the Hatteras area commonly bought their lumber as fence posts for fifty cents each—posts were four feet long and typically yielded three or four decoy bodies. A few found cheaper but far more arduous ways of acquiring timber. In the summer, when the water was low, they poled skiffs into freshwater swamps that lumber companies had already logged, and they pulled the juniper stumps left behind. These were floated home and dried before carving. Others let the sea supply their wood. Fred Waterfield remembers that one year his father salvaged a redwood mast and turned it into over two hundred decoys. Along with driftwood, men in the Hatteras and Ocracoke communities used abandoned cypress telephone poles—especially for the larger brant and geese bodies. Cypress, in fact, was a distant second to juniper in popularity, and many carvers used cypress knees for decoy heads mounted on juniper bodies. During the First World War, balsa wood and cork drifted ashore inside life preservers. Local carvers experimented with these woods, praised them for their lightness, but preferred the harder woods. Today little wood drifts ashore, and the supply of juniper is dwindling. Many now buy juniper boards and glue them into the proper thickness.

Decoy carvers have shaped the wood with a variety of tools. Charlie Waterfield used the fewest: a hatchet, a cheap pocketknife, and in the days before sandpaper, pieces of broken glass. Most men, like John Austin, work with spokeshaves, wood rasps, drawknives, and sandpaper. To some extent, power tools have replaced these hand tools. Band saws and disk sanders ease the tedium of handwork. Despite the obvious advantages, however, most carvers still prefer to work with time-honored hand tools. Throughout, experience has guided their hands; patterns have rarely been used.

Virtually all the regional decoys have solid bodies carved from a single block of wood. Only two men ever tried to make hollow-body decoys. One split the decoy body, gouged out a large cavity, and glued the halves together. The other sandwiched three boards together after cutting out the middle piece's center. Both experiments leaked so badly and rode so poorly in the water that they were never repeated.

Decoy heads, in contrast, have either been whittled or made from suggestively shaped roots. Unlike realistically carved heads, root heads present abstract impressions of wildfowl heads. To make one, a carver finds an apt branch or root and trims it. The root's main stem becomes the neck and a small offshoot suggests the bird's bill. These root-head decoys are common throughout the Hatteras-Ocracoke area, primarily for brant and shorebirds, but are relatively rare farther north around Currituck Sound. But whittled heads are common throughout the entire region, and whittling them became a leisure activity. Men passed the time and shared each other's company while occupying their hands carving. Each locality had its own gathering place; a general store, a barber shop, or a few large shade trees. After a carver had made both bodies and heads, he joined them together either with several nails or a wooden dowel. Most used the simpler method of hammering two or three large nails through the head and into the body. A few drilled a starter hole to prevent splitting, but most did not bother. Irving Fulcher, one of the few to use dowels, drills half-inch holes into both pieces and glues a dowel inside. Some carvers caulk the joint between the body and head with a paste of beeswax and white lead to prevent water from rusting the nails and to prepare the decoys for finishing.

. Wildfowl shy from shiny objects, so carvers sometimes rasp their decoys to leave a rough surface and always coat them with flat paint. To deaden the colors, they often add kerosene or lampblack. One old-timer recalls that in addition to dulling colors, some would rub soot from stove pipes on shorebird decoys to texture them. As a general rule, carvers paint boldly using a simple pattern and ignore naturalistic detail. They feel that a detailed finish is a waste of time and consider repainting decoys a child's summer chore. Mitchell Fulcher, an exception to this rule, takes care to finish his decoys artistically. He uses a twenty-two caliber shell to mark the decoy's eyes and a well-chewed snuff stick to stipple the bird's back to produce a feathered effect. Fulcher first paints the entire decoy white; then he uses a darker color for the second coat, which he stipples while wet.

After finishing a decoy, carvers rig it to float or to stand on the shore. Local men use a variety of materials to weight and balance decoys. Some cast sheet-lead anchors and keels in wood or sand molds, others flatten lead conduit into rough shapes, and a few adapt discarded automobile parts. Most, however, nail or screw commercially produced keels to the decoy's underside and tie an anchor line to a brad driven in the decoy's front. Compared to the floating decoys, the standing decoy, locally known as a "stick-up," is much easier to rig. A carver drills a hole into the underside of the decoy and fits a stick or a piece of wire into the hole.

Shorebird decoys are often constructed using special methods. Because the shorebird is small, a carver normally whittles the entire decoy from one block of wood, compressing the three steps—shaping the body, whittling the head, and joining the two—into one step. Since the shorebird's bill is delicate and hard to copy in wood, carvers usually hammer a long nail into the decoy's head to suggest a bill.

A third type of decoy is the two-dimensional silhouette made from juniper boards. Carvers trace the bird's outline on the board, saw it out, and paint it with flat colors. This type of decoy is lighter, easier to carry, and quicker to make. In the market-hunting era, carvers made silhouettes of shorebirds and egrets but stopped when shooting them became illegal. Recently hunters have revived this type of decoy for geese. They saw the outline from a half-inch sheet of marine plywood and nail it to a wooden stake. There is always the exception: one old-timer recalls that as a boy, he cut shorebird silhouettes from cardboard.

By these means, decoy carvers craft a wide repertoire of bird forms. The repertoire and number of decoys largely depends on hunting techniques and purposes. Some hunt only for themselves and use either a few wooden decoys or non-decoy strategies. Others work as sports guides or market hunters and need decoys daily. These activities have been commercially important as seasonal jobs in many coastal communities.

Sports guiding is a seasonal job that requires decoys and has spread decoys along the North Carolina coast. Before the Civil War sport shooting thrived around Back Bay and northern Currituck Sound; during it, business halted—Southern patriots even burned one club on Currituck Sound. After the war, wealthy Northern sportsmen returned in increasing numbers. Social hunting and membership in gun clubs grew in popularity throughout the later nineteenth century and lasted until the Great Depression. Mike Wade, a guide and caretaker for the Swan Island Club, told me of his club, which began in 1872. While sailing from Boston to Florida, seven sportsmen ran aground on Swan Island. Instead of continuing, they enjoyed the local wildfowling and subsequently built a clubhouse on Swan Island. Each year the members elected one of their number president to oversee the club's operation. As the years passed, older members left their memberships to younger men along with their guns and decoys.

Decoys were a necessity. No rich businessman intended to spend his holiday slinking around in a marsh hoping to spy a few birds. Instead sportsmen sat in relative comfort within a blind and waited for the birds. Decoys lured the birds to the hunters, who happily fired away before the guide retrieved the kill. To aid them, sportsmen often bought Northern factory decoys and also used local products. Wade remembers that the Swan Island Club kept many decoys: "At one time, must have been twelve, fifteen thousand decoys—all factory decoys—and some never used. In summertime, some of those old fellows go through a sports shop, and he'd see these new ducks and say they'd look good and send down two dozen of them. Ship down to Swan Island. Well the company send them down to here. And they'd get down here and chances were the old guides didn't like them. They were too heavy or too small or they didn't look right. And there were hundreds and hundreds of ducks over there that were never tied out— never used."[21]

Club members also bought decoys from local men who tailored their work specifically to local conditions. During the summer, carvers might make seventy-five or one hundred decoys to sell in the fall. Many of the guides, who chose the decoys, preferred local decoys far above any import. Buying local products funneled the sport's money into the local economy.

Guides certainly worked for their pay. Their job demanded long hours, physical endurance, and detailed knowledge of wildfowl. Shortly before the season, after the snakes had left the marsh and before the hunters arrived, guides built or repaired the shore blinds on property owned by the club. These blinds could be either a boxlike structure camouflaged with brush or a naturally dense clump of marsh undergrowth. On the morning of the hunt, the guide selected his blind according to weather conditions and set the decoy rig. Guides rigged two dozen decoys to resemble a small raft of fowl. Wade found that a balanced rig showing several bird species and, in the old days, live decoys, presented a realistic setting. Like blind selection, the actual placing of the decoys depended on weather conditions. The repertoire, however, emphasized either marsh ducks or geese, which usually feed on shoreline vegetation. Once deceived, wildfowl landed to join the decoys; the hunters fired just when a bird dropped speed and braked before landing in the water. The guides then either sent a dog to retrieve the kill or waded out to get it themselves. After spending a long day instructing and serving the sport, the guide packed up the whole rig and often cleaned guns well into the night.

Because guiding was essentially a service occupation, market hunters enjoyed far more prestige in the community. The market hunter was a self-employed man who shot game and shipped it north to urban markets. Swelling populations and an appetite for game made for an

insatiable demand for fresh game. Like the lot of sports guides, however, the lot of market hunters involved hard work, stamina, and
knowledge of wildfowl. As a business, market hunting necessitated a
large sailboat, a battery box, a huge decoy rig, and a team of several
people.

The day began before dawn, when the hunters set sail to the feeding grounds. They anchored the battery box and tied out over three
hundred decoys, mostly canvasback, to its lee. The decoys formed a
rough triangle with the battery box as the apex, and hunters always left
a convenient hole for passing fowl to land in near the blind. A market
hunter, like Austin, shot from sunup to sundown while his partner
collected the kill as it floated with the current. At dusk both men
gathered the decoys, loaded the battery box across the sailboat's beam,
and headed home. Their work, however, was far from done; they
packed the game in barrels of ice and shipped it north on the nightly
steamboat to Norfolk. Prices, of course, varied during the season and
over the years. Toward the end of the market-hunting era, however,
canvasback duck sold for five dollars a pair, marsh ducks for a few
dollars a pair, and ruddy duck for a dollar. Immediately after supper,
Austin cleaned his gun and loaded hundreds of brass gun shells before
retiring by midnight.

On very good days, a market hunter could shoot more than five
hundred ducks and gross over a thousand dollars. The vagaries of
weather, the luck of the season, and the local customs, however,
severely restricted actual income. Around Knotts Island it was customary to shoot only on Monday, Wednesday, and Friday. Tuesday,
Thursday, and the weekend were "lay days" that gave the game a rest.
Hunters felt that continuous gunning scared the game and proved
counterproductive. Expenses were also considerable. Austin had to pay
for the sailboat, battery box, decoys, and munitions. He also paid his
partner a third of the gross. But Austin made enough money during
the good years to offset the bad ones.

To men like Austin, decoys were simply tools in a complex and
risky business. Most of his decoys resembled canvasbacks because these
birds rafted together by the hundreds and brought the highest price at
market.

Austin and other hunters used both oversized and natural-sized
decoys to attract the maximum number of birds. As the story goes,

Figure 1.3. A market hunter from Currituck Sound displays a day's work, ca. 1910 (courtesy of the North Carolina Museum of Natural History and Ken Taylor).

one year when hunting was poor in the Hatteras and Ocracoke areas, hunters, desperate for game, sailed north with their goose and brant decoys. Having neither the money nor the inclination to carve new decoys, they repainted their decoys as canvasbacks. To everyone's surprise, these decoys worked better than the regular models. According to local reasoning, flying game saw the larger birds from farther away and came to them more quickly. However, the oversized decoys never worked for shore-blind gunners. Along the shore, the birds shied away from the giant decoys seen against the perspective of marsh vegetation. One of the region's few professional carvers, Ned Burgess, specialized in oversized decoys sold to market hunters.

The canny hunters of the Hatteras and Ocracoke areas also deserve credit for another innovation. They purposely fashioned the brant decoy into a more abstract shape by narrowing the decoy's breast and flaring the bird's tail. This forced the decoy's white tail high into the air. The brant seemed to be attracted to the white under the tail and thus was more easily decoyed to the hunters.

Though the decoy had proved its worth, decoy carving spread

south very slowly, reaching Bogue Sound in 1908. And some hunters continued to use other hunting methods. Illegal firelighting continued. One hunter, Captain Ballance, was said to firelight every possible night and kill four barrels of game a night. Other game, such as shorebirds, egrets, or birds shot by plume hunters, were hunted without decoys. And other means were always available, even for ducks and geese. The fishermen in Bogue Sound often set gill nets in the feeding grounds. The birds became entangled in the nets, struggled, and drowned. By the next morning, the game was bloated but still edible. In winter, when the sound froze over, ducks came to lumps of turf turned out on the ice or to holes of open water cut by waiting gunners.

Along the northern North Carolina coast duck hunting predominated; to the south, geese and brants held sway. There are two reasons for this pattern: the wildfowl distribution and the transportation network. The fresh waters of Currituck Sound attracted more diving ducks than elsewhere. But brant and geese favored the saltwater marshes near Cape Hatteras and Ocracoke. Although many kinds of ducks and geese wintered along the Core Banks, virtually no brant migrated that far south. But during the summer egrets, herons, and terns bred there. Not surprisingly, the transportation system matched the natural distribution of game: quick, daily steamboat service characterized the north, where market hunters had to ship their kill nightly; the south had only weekly freighter service because the plume hunters, who gunned in desolate areas, skinned their kill, and shipped these skins north in bulk. Thus they did not need daily service. With better transportation, market hunting could have developed along the Core and Outer Banks, but the hunters lacked the best resource—an uncountable number of diving ducks.

Modernization also affected the decoy tradition. When watermen began switching from sailboats to powerboats, they needed lighter decoys. A rig of solid decoys was just too heavy for a small powerboat to tote around. An unknown carver invented an alternative, the framed decoy, near Duck, North Carolina, sometime in 1917. His invention spread immediately through the entire region.

John Austin saw this decoy when he returned from World War I and learned how to make it. First, he saws the decoy's base into an elongated oval from a one-and-one-half-inch juniper board. Then he whittles the head and neck from the same piece of juniper stock and

Figure 1.4. Mannie Haywood of Kill Devil Hills, Dare County, N.C., painting a rig of canvas geese, ca. 1950 (courtesy of Ken Taylor).

nails it to the front of the base as a stem post. Galvanized wire driven into the base's perimeter forms a series of ribs, which suggests the contours of the fowl's body. Austin then stretches a sheet of eight-ounce duck canvas over the frame and tacks it tightly around the bottom edge. Finally, he paints the decoy as he always has and attaches the customary anchor line.

Other carvers vary in their choices of material, construction, and appurtenances for the framed decoy. Some prefer marine plywood to juniper, copper wire to steel, and bed ticking to canvas. A few men always fit a wooden backbone into the frame to strengthen the top, but most do not. Recently a couple of carvers have started to stuff the frame with styrofoam to make it unsinkable and almost gunshot-proof. The range and repertoire of these decoys is more limited than that of the earlier types of decoy. Most of the framed decoys are for brant and geese and are popular in the Hatteras and Ocracoke areas. Farther north in Currituck Sound, framed decoys are less frequent and represent a broad variety of ducks.

As commercial hunting and sport guiding developed, wildfowl decreased. Ansell finds that only 25 percent of the former fowl population remained in the early twentieth century. Moreover a growing number of hunters—where there were "one hundred hunters then, there are one thousand now"—overshot the game.[22] If one hunter missed, there were fifty other battery boxes "to hammer the life" out of any venturesome flock. One plume hunter told Gilbert Pearson that "there ain't one striker or gull in a hundred to what there used to be. We've got 'em about all cleaned out." Pearson also visited storage houses filled with game awaiting shipment—one shipper sent over a thousand birds to market at a time.[23]

In response to the mounting slaughter and inevitable extinction of wildfowl, the Audubon Society and other conservation groups battled to pass and enforce strict game laws. Their efforts on the local level were often thwarted by officials who turned a blind eye to hunters or failed to enforce the laws. On the national level, however, intense lobbying helped pass two laws—the Migratory Bird Act of 1913 and the Migratory Bird Treaty Act of 1918—that effectively ended plume and market hunting respectively. Subsequent laws outlawed the use of live decoys, forbade the battery box, and set bag limits on daily hunting. Although tales abound about hunters who continued to break game laws, the laws of 1913 and 1918 effectively stopped the commercial killing of wildfowl.

With the sharp decline in hunting, regional decoy carving has gradually evolved into an art form. The first decoy exhibition was staged in Bellport, Long Island, in 1923 by Joel Barber, an avid decoy collector and enthusiast. The show succeeded in attracting the attention of antique buffs and collectors of Americana. Soon other decoy exhibitions featuring regional, antique, and decorative decoys flourished. To supply these shows and expand their private holdings, decoy collectors combed the coastal areas, purchasing old decoys from local hunters, who often saw little use or value in them. These collectors, however, judged decoys by their own aesthetic standards. According to one, Quintina Colio, the decoy's original purpose of luring wildfowl "has receded, and new values have emerged."[24] Adele Earnest defines these values as the decoy's ability to "catch the bird in body and spirit. If it does, we may truly call it art."[25]

Collectors tend to view North Carolina decoys as extremely primitive and aesthetically inferior. They recognize the shorebird's nail bill and the local invention of the framed decoy as distinctive to the state but regard the framed decoy as manifesting "the same crudeness and lack of finished workmanship as the all-wooden models."[26] Collectors attribute the crudeness of the regional style to the vast numbers of migrating fowl: "It is axiomatic that the more ducks in any given area, the less need for decoys. The second decoy axiom is that the less need for decoys, the cruder they usually are."[27]

While "crudeness" appears to be the norm, collectors find the work of four North Carolina carvers—Lee Dudley (1861–1942), Lem Dudley (1861–1932), John Williams (1857–1937), and Ned Burgess (1863–1956)—to be exceptions. Mackey describes the Dudley decoys as having "smallish, competently carved but on the whole very ordinary bodies" and "the most beautifully conceived and splendidly carved heads ever placed on duck decoys."[28] In the same tenor Adele Earnest praises the Dudley ruddy duck as the "best of their kind, and everything a ruddy duck should be—gay, fat, and saucy."[29] While they prize any Dudley decoy, collectors fancy John Williams's swan and ruddy decoys for their grace and realism. Mackey lauds Williams as a true artist whose decoys enrich American folk art.[30] Out of the hundreds of local men who carved decoys, the collectors pick only a few and, by and large, ignore the rest. Recently, however, authors such as Neal Conoley have taken a broader perspective on regional decoys and helped the general public see the diversity and beauty of this traditional handicraft.[31]

The collectors' standards often contradict local values and sentiments. For example, the collectors prize the work of the Dudley brothers. The Dudleys were farmers who learned decoy carving from their father, Robert, and faithfully replicated his styling. They hunted from shore blinds and consequently carved relatively few decoys and mostly for themselves. Other hunters thought that their decoy bodies were a bit small and usually bought decoys from others. The Dudleys themselves never paid much attention to their decoys either. One year, for instance, they piled their decoys in the barnyard and allowed their herd of cows to crush the rig into splinters. Before the next hunting season, they had to carve a brand new rig. Local hunters generally preferred the work of Ned Burgess of Coinjock, North Carolina. Burgess, one of the region's few professional decoy carvers, produced thousands of decoys over his lifetime. Most of his decoys were oversized canvas-

Figure 1.5. Decorative balsa wood egret carved by Curtis Waterfield about 1974–75, painted by his son (photo by Stephen Matchak).

backs, especially designed for market hunters. The decoy bodies were big and the heads crude. Burgess continued to carve even after his vision had deteriorated severely. Local hunters preferred Burgess's decoys for one simple reason: they attracted game better than those of other carvers.

In the last thirty years, however, collectors, not success in hunting, have had the primary impact on local decoy-carving traditions. Collectors have taught the general public to appreciate realistic decoys as art and have introduced their aesthetic into local communities. Decoy carvers never really assimilated the artistic decoy until outsiders created the new demand. In the last twenty to thirty years, Carolina's beaches have attracted an astounding number of tourists. Many of them want authentic local souvenirs to recall their trips and decorate their homes. Aware of local history and artistic decoys, tourists have become the major market for local decoys. Old decoy carvers and young artists have further developed the decoy-carving tradition to satisfy the new market.

Carvers now create a wide variety of artistic decoys made in a number of media. Lem Scarborough began carving in his retirement by shaping styrofoam from broken surfboards into shorebird sculptures. Others, like Curtis Waterfield, strive to create realistic decoys and even burn the feathering into balsa-wood decoys. Still others turn out miniature decoys, jewelry, and wildfowl windmills. Some products are colorfully painted, others are stained. Local work ranges from suggestively shaped forms to highly detailed pieces. Perhaps Curtis Waterfield best sets the measure of local success and demonstrates the transition from tool to art. The Smithsonian Institution invited him and his son to participate in the Bicentennial festivities in Washington as folk artists. During his residence there, Curtis carved a large bald eagle as a piece of American folk art.

Today some North Carolinians carve decoys as their fathers did; others seize the new opportunities and create works of art. Sometimes the same carver will produce both working and decorative decoys for different markets. The decoy originally possessed little monetary value and even less aesthetic appeal. The history of its construction recalls how isolated craftspeople used what resources they had to produce satisfactory and replaceable tools for obtaining their daily needs. The construction of modern decoys, on the other hand, embodies new attitudes toward the environment and charts the path from our abuse of natural resources to our appreciation of them. Wildfowl sculpture now catches only the waterfowl's expression and spirit, not the living bird.

2. "I Never Could Play Alone": The Emergence of the New River Valley String Band, 1875–1915

Thomas Carter

Musical Notation and Analysis by Thomas Sauber

"You can find Joe Caudill's place up in the Vox Community along the state line. Go west from here until you get to state road 1414, then head north. You can ask up there for the house." These words from the man at the store in Ennice, North Carolina, led me on a cold rainy day in November of 1972 to Joe Caudill's farm. I had heard about Joe from local musicians during the previous summer's fieldwork, and now I wanted to find him, talk to him about his days of playing music, and see if he could still fiddle the old tunes.

Like many others before me, I had been drawn to the New River section of the Blue Ridge (figure 2.1) by an abiding interest in the local banjo-fiddle string-band music, a music that had achieved a degree of national exposure in the early 1960s due to the release of several commercial records. Produced from field recordings by Eric Davidson and Paul Newman, these albums focused on Grayson and Carroll counties in Virginia and represented the first attempt to describe carefully the music of the string band and to trace its historical development over several generations.[1] Subsequent fieldwork expanded the regional boundaries of string-band music; particularly important was the discovery in the late 1960s of musicians in Surry County, North Carolina, and Patrick County, Virginia, by folklorist Alan Jabbour.[2] My own fieldwork was directed toward locating previously unrecorded fiddlers—getting, that is, the music down on tape before it disappeared. Beyond a general understanding that it was old and therefore important, I had not thought much about the music or what it might mean. My travels eventually led me over into Alleghany County, North Carolina, and to Joe Caudill's farm. Winter was closing in, but the stove was warm and

Joe willing to visit. As I set up the tape machine, I was eager to hear Joe's fiddling, and I did not realize at the time that I was in fact starting a longer project—one that would end over a decade later in an attempt to tell the story of Joe's music.

Joe Caudill (figure 2.2) was born in 1885 at a point not far from where the New River flows across the Alleghany-Grayson county line.[3] Eighty-seven years old when I met him, Joe had spent most of his life farming and running a sawmill. His father Sidney had been a fiddler, but Joe received most of his musical instruction from his older brother Huston, or Hus for short, who had himself learned from Sidney. Joe started to fiddle at the age of fifteen, about 1900, and in the next decade and a half became a dance fiddler of considerable local reputation, often being called, along with Hus, who accompanied him on banjo, to travel great distances to perform. For a time the two brothers contemplated making their living by playing music, but soon the responsibilities of farming and raising families turned their attention

Figure 2.1 The New River Valley region (map by Thomas Carter).

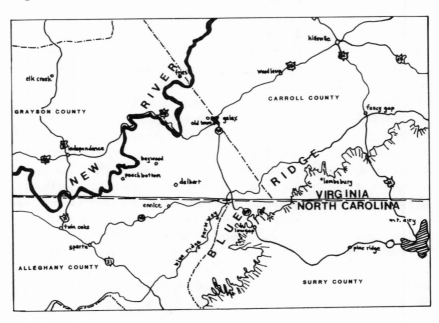

Figure 2.2. Joe Caudill at his home near En-nice, N.C., spring 1972 (photo by Thomas Carter).

away from a life tied to traveling and being on the road. So in the years just before America entered the First World War, Joe set aside his music; he had, as he often reminded me, "something else to do." Joe did not start to fiddle again until the mid-1960s, when along with his banjo-playing sister, Bertie, he began playing the old tunes again at parties and local festivals.

From all outward appearances Joe Caudill had the qualities I was looking for in an old-time fiddler. First, he had learned to play in the traditional manner by listening to and watching his older brother; and second, his active playing occurred in the days before such outside influences as the radio and phonograph brought new musical styles into the area. Here, it seemed, was an ideal opportunity to see and hear the "old original" music. As Joe set his fiddle against his chest and began to play, I was indeed rewarded with what I had come to know as the old-time string-band music of the New River Valley. His repertoire, characterized by a binary, "A" and "B" strain tune performed in a repetitive AABB pattern, was small but generally typical of local fiddlers and included fine versions of popular dance tunes like "Sally Ann," "Western Country," and "Pretty Little Gal," tunes making up the basic stock of the dance band.[4] Joe's tunes included the following:

Tunes in the Key of D
1. Black-Eyed Susie
2. Cindy
3. County Jail
4. Down the Road
5. Fortune
6. Geese on the Millpond
7. Holliding
8. Johnny's Gone to the War
9. Johnson Boys
10. Mississippi Sawyers
11. Molly Put the Kettle On
12. New River Train
13. Sally Ann
14. Sugar Hill
15. Walking in the Parlor
16. Western Country

Tunes in the Key of A
1. Cluck Old Hen
2. Cripple Creek
3. John Henry
4. Pretty Little Gal
5. Sourwood Mountain

Tunes in the Key of G
1. Cacklin' Hen
2. Did You Ever See the Devil, Uncle Joe?
3. Old Dad
4. Piney Woods Gal
5. Round Town Gals
6. Sally Goodin'
7. Waves on the Ocean
8. West Virginia Farewell

Also typical of string-band fiddlers was Joe's style. He seldom varied his performance, repeating the same set melody over and over; his tunes were sparse and unornamented; he preferred the pentatonic over the diatonic scale; he tuned his fiddle either in the EADG or EAEA tuning to achieve a full sound with dronelike qualities; and his music had the expected heavily accented rhythm.[5] The key to the rhythm lay in the bowing, and careful listening revealed later on that he used two basic techniques common in fiddling of the area (figure 2.3). First is the use of mid-bow accents or stresses (>) to emphasize certain notes with an upward (weaker) rather than a downward (stronger) bow stroke. Second is the use of bowing slurs where there is more than one note played per bow stroke (⌢). These bowing patterns contributed directly to the strong pulsating rhythm and subtle syncopation of the music. Since the string-band music was meant to be played with a banjo accompaniment, it is not surprising that Joe was quick to point out that playing without a banjo made him uncomfortable. "I never could play alone," he repeatedly interjected.[6]

Joe was a fiddler of considerable talent, yet his music presented problems for me. What I knew of the string band's history had come

Figure 2.3. Typical string-band bowing pattern showing mid-bow accents (>) and bow slurs (⌢). Joe Caudill's "Geese on the Millpond."

from Davidson and Newman's record notes, which maintained that the band dated back to the years soon after the Civil War when the banjo became popular in the area. It was a music that, according to their 1960s informants, had "always" been in the area.[7] When pressed by my questions about his own playing, however, Joe Caudill had a consistent response. The "old-time" music of the area, Joe said, was the kind played by his father and others of the preceding generation. While he said that he did know several of the "old" pieces, pieces that he had from his father, these he played only occasionally and then principally as solo pieces. For the most part Joe claimed that as he was learning he heard and picked up tunes that the old fiddlers did not play, tunes like "Down the Road" ("Ida Red"), "Sally Ann," "Holliding" ("Step-Back, Cindy"), and "County Jail" ("Fall on my Knees"). It was a music that his father did not care for, as this segment of Joe's comment reveals:

> These new tunes, they wasn't in style when he was playing. Tunes we play now, back in his day, he didn't play 'em. He played tunes like "Pineywoods," "Waves on the Ocean," "Billy in the Low-ground," them old tunes like that. Now the tunes that I play begin to come in long about the time he was quitting. The old-time fiddlers, my daddy and on back there, they play them tunes, but after I learnt, we got to playing the tunes which I play. My daddy said when me and my brother, he picked the banjo, when we was to play he'd say, "Why don't you play these old tunes like 'Forked Deer' and 'Cricket on the Hearth'?" Why he says, "there ain't no music at yours." My father was with our tunes like we are with this rock and roll stuff. Now I wouldn't go out to the road to hear all of that.[8]

Joe's recollection of his father's response to his own playing was echoed by his brother Hus. Two years older than Joe, Hus had learned to fiddle from Sidney in the late 1890s. When asked about one popular local tune, "Sally Ann," a tune considered by many the archetypal string-band tune, Hus pointed out that this was not one of his father's tunes:

> *Caudill:* No, he couldn't play that.
> *Carter:* Why not?
> *Caudill:* He never did know it. They [such tunes] come in after he learned. It's like this rock and roll coming in now, I can't play that. That's the way he was. He said that wasn't no tune.[9]

Hus explained that "Sally Ann" had "come in" to the area with one of his uncles, Fate Caudill, who picked the tune on the banjo, though it is not clear where he learned it, only that it was from outside the area. Oddly, here was one of the principal tunes of the band fiddlers' repertoire that was not considered, at least by these two musicians, "old." Furthermore, by drawing a distinction between their own playing and the "old" way of their father, Joe and Hus were suggesting that a change had occurred in the music during the late nineteenth century— at some point between the time when Sid Caudill had learned, probably in the 1870s and 1880s, and when his boys were learning in the early 1900s.

The Caudill interviews proved intriguing, for they disputed the existing thinking on how and when the string band developed. Were these men simply wrong? They were, after all, in their late eighties when I met them. On the other hand, both Joe and Hus were strong and active despite their years, and both had been right on many other verifiable points. Rather than old, could the band actually be a fairly recent phenomenon? The idea was compelling, and I set out to find an answer, to write, that is, a history—this history—of the New River Valley string band. The task presented many obstacles, not the least of which was overcoming an enduring perception of tradition as an unchanging and relatively static phenomenon.

Folk music, like other aspects of folklore, is often defined according to its mode of transmission. That is, folk music is music that is learned traditionally by listening and watching older musicians in the community, rather than by reading from popular tune books or copying phonograph recordings. As tunes pass through several generations, variation of course occurs, but only of a minor nature. Any significant change—for instance, the alteration of the tune itself—is considered suspect, leading to the contamination and ultimate demise of the tradition.[10] While folklorists do not think this way today, in the early 1970s this basically antiquarian approach to folk music was very much the practice, particularly among younger folklorists (like myself) drawn to the field by certain nostalgic and romantic impulses of the 1960s. It is not surprising that much of my initial work with Joe Caudill and other New River Valley musicians involved rethinking the concept of tradition itself, for clearly I was confronting a music that was both folk *and* dynamic. A year of fieldwork along the Blue Ridge convinced me that the change described by the Caudills was in fact real, and in the notes to an album of recordings in 1975, I noted that "traditions don't always endure unchanged waiting to be inundated by the forces of modernization; rather, they are constantly in a state of internal adaptation and movement."[11] Yet what forces were at work to make people in a conservative, tradition-bound community like this do things differently? What indeed was the rationale for change? I found the answer to these questions, much to my surprise, in area that I had once thought foreign to folklore, and this was the realm of creativity.

If one thing may be said to characterize folklore scholarship during the past decade, it would be the recognition of the dynamic nature of tradition. Folk things, whether they be stories, fiddle tunes, or houses, are not unreflectingly transported through time by the simple act of copying and repeating older forms. Rather, folk performance constitutes a process whereby customary and traditionally acquired knowledge is constantly being reinterpreted in specific performance situations or contexts that bring the folk performer into direct contact with the tastes, values, and norms of his or her group or community. As older traditional ways are exposed to new and innovative ideas, several outcomes may be expected. There can be the retention of the old, or the wholesale adoption of the new, or, as is often the case, the synthesis of old and new concepts and the creation of new if nonetheless familiar forms.[12] The gradual emergence of the string band in the New River Valley between 1870 and 1900 may best be understood in terms of this later dynamic, for musicians here drew heavily upon the existing fiddle tradition to fashion a new music, one that reflected not so much the eclipse of the old-time music as it did a type of continuing evolution. This essay, then, represents an attempt to describe the musical change that occurred in the New River Valley during the turn-of-the-century period, specifically in terms of the creative dynamic that lay behind it.

The New River Valley, composed of sections of Ashe, Alleghany, and Surry counties in North Carolina and Grayson and Carroll counties in Virginia, was occupied during the late eighteenth century by settlers moving east across the piedmont and south down the valley of Virginia.[13] These settlers were mostly descendants of English and Scotch-Irish immigrants moving west to find cheap land and better opportunity. In what one early visitor called an "ocean of mountains," they found the river bottoms and adjoining creek hollows well suited to their homesteading needs. A landscape of small, isolated, and self-sufficient farms emerged. It was not a homogeneous landscape, but one that clearly reflected the diverse cultural traditions of the newcomers. Music at this time was intensely local; and though the basic style was firmly established in British tradition, several generations of living in the New World had already effected important changes. A good example of the early folk music in the valley is found in the playing of Emmett Lundy of Delhart, in Grayson County. Although recorded in 1941 by Alan and Elizabeth Lomax for the Library of Congress, Emmett Lundy's fiddling is nevertheless linked to the early nineteenth century by an association with Green Leonard, a prominent Grayson County fiddler.

Emmett Lundy was born in 1864, the son of Churchwell and Caroline Ward Lundy (figure 2.4).[14] The Lundys had emigrated from England during the seventeenth century, living in Pennsylvania and New Jersey before Emmett's great-grandfather, John Lundy, moved to Grayson County in 1787. During Emmett's childhood, life in the mountain country around his home was largely traditional—methods of farming, preparing food, building houses, and playing music were based on customary practice.[15] Lundy quickly became absorbed in the music that he heard at neighborhood dances and work gatherings and as a teenager during the late 1870s and early 1880s learned to play the fiddle himself.

The young Lundy's main influence was an old fiddler named Green Leonard who lived at Old Town, just a few miles north of the Lundy farm.[16] Leonard was born in 1810 in Grayson County and was a man about sixty-five years old when Lundy met him. As he was a

Figure 2.4. Emmett Lundy, ca. 1890 (courtesy of Kelly Lundy).

musician of considerable local reputation who learned to play at least as early as the 1830s, it seems safe to assume that Leonard's style and repertoire fairly represent pre–Civil War Grayson County fiddling. Emmett Lundy's student relationship with Leonard is explained in an interview conducted by Elizabeth Lomax:

> *Lomax:* Who did you learn to fiddle from as a boy?
> *Lundy:* Green Leonard.
> *Lomax:* Would you tell me something about him?
> *Lundy:* Well, he was practically an old mountain boomer here. He liked his dram and he enjoyed his fiddling and was said to be the best fiddler there was in the mountains here. 'Bout all I could speak of him.
> *Lomax:* Did he teach you most of the old pieces that you know, would you say?
> *Lundy:* No, he didn't teach them to me, but I catched them from him. And in his last days he told me that I was the only one that had tracked him down, and he wanted to learn me some old pieces before he died—didn't want them to be buried—and live after he was gone. But I never did get to learn them all.[17]

Lundy learned most of his music from Green Leonard during the years between 1880 and 1895, when the old fiddler died. Family members and other local musicians strongly assert that Lundy's music changed little during his lifetime, so the 1941 Lomax recordings are an important source for understanding the early fiddling of the area.

Though it may be said that Emmett Lundy's playing displays certain British influences—for instance, his use of bowed triplets (bouncing the bow to produce a quick triad of thirty-second notes), left-hand embellishment (particularly trills), a highly developed melody, and a preference for the classical EADG tuning (beginning with the first string) and the four major keys, G, C, D, and A—closer inspection of his style reveals a decidedly "Southern" quality to his music. First, the best part of his repertoire consists of thoroughly American reels such as "Forky Deer," "Sheep Shell Corn," and "Western Country."[18] Second, the syncopated rhythm associated with later string-band fiddlers is already in evidence, though not as strongly emphasized. Evidence that Lundy's playing no longer represented an unadulterated British tradition is seen in his playing of "Belles of Lexington," a hornpipe more commonly known in England and Ireland as "Kitty's Wedding."[19]

Lundy's version of "Belles of Lexington," compared here to "Kitty's Wedding" (figure 2.5) reveals not only significant melodic deviation from the British tune, but also stylistic traits such as the use of mid-bow accents and bowing slurs, which we have already seen in the playing of Joe Caudill—traits that appear to be uniquely Southern and that produce the subtle syncopation found in fiddling through the southern United States. A recent paper by the folklorist Alan Jabbour is useful in understanding the character of early fiddling in the valley.

Jabbour suggests that by the late eighteenth century fiddling in the southern United States had clearly departed from British models and had acquired a distinctly New World identity in both style and repertoire.[20] Southern fiddlers employed distinctive syncopated rhythms in their playing. This syncopated type of bowing differed from both the older traditions in Scotland, Ireland, and England, *and* that found in the northern United States. Jabbour attributes this distinctive regional fiddle style to the cultural influence of black musicians in the South, which had by the nineteenth century become deeply ingrained in the Southern fiddling tradition. The extent to which Afro-American concepts had penetrated Anglo-American culture in the nineteenth century is illustrated by Emmett Lundy's music, for the syncopated bowing Jabbour associates with black fiddlers is evident even in tunes like "Highlander's Farewell," a tune having distinct Old World connections (figure 2.6).[21]

Such evidence supports Jabbour's estimation of black influences on white fiddling in the antebellum period, and such music as that of Green Leonard can no longer be said to be of pure British stock. Rather, it is part of a wider tradition of Southern music shaped, as Jabbour notes, by the "prominent participation" of blacks.

Betraying the unique blend of old and new world, white and black influences, Emmett Lundy's music serves as an important index to the early music of the New River Valley: it is technically sophisticated, it is characterized by complex melodies, it is in many ways an individualized art (witness, for example, Green Leonard's reluctance to share his tunes with the young Lundy), and while it is linked formally to the British Isles, in terms of the tunes themselves and the style of playing them, it is already in the process of becoming generally American, and

Belles of Lexington

Kitty's Wedding

Figure 2.5. Comparison of Emmett Lundy's "Belles of Lexington" (AAFS 4938 A4) with the Irish "Kitty's Wedding" (from O'Neill's The Dance Music of Ireland).

Figure 2.6. Southern bowing features—the mid-bow accent and the bow slur—in Emmett Lundy's "Highlander's Farewell" (AAFS 4939 A5).

more specifically, Virginian. Yet, Emmett Lundy's music was not, at least in the 1880s, string-band music. For one thing, the basic fiddle-tune repertoire was significantly larger and more varied than the condensed, dance-tune repertoire of the string band. Lundy's repertoire contained the following pieces:[22]

Tunes in D
 1. Arkansas Traveler
 2. Belles of Lexington
 3. Black-Eyed Susie
 4. Bonaparte's Retreat
 5. Chapel Hill March
 6. Cleveland's March
 7. Drunken Hiccups
 8. Ducks on the Millpond
 9. Durang's Hornpipe
 10. Fisher's Hornpipe
 11. Forked Deer
 12. Fortune
 13. Jackson's March
 14. Julie Ann Johnson
 15. Kingdom Come
 16. Mississippi Sawyer
 17. Molly Hare
 18. Molly Put the Kettle On
 19. Natchez Under the Hill
 20. Johnny's Gone to the War
 21. Richmond Cotillion
 22. Soldier's Joy

Tunes in A
 1. Big-Eyed Rabbit
 2. Breaking Up Christmas
 3. Cacklin' Hen
 4. Cluck Old Hen
 5. George Booker
 6. Highlander's Farewell
 7. John Henry
 8. June Apple
 9. Old Joe Clark
 10. Pretty Little Gal
 11. Shady Grove
 12. Sheep Shell Corn
 13. Sourwood Mountain
 14. Train on the Island

Tunes in G
 1. Cumberland Gap
 2. Evening Star Waltz
 3. Fisher's Hornpipe
 4. Flatwoods
 5. Flying Cloud
 6. Hop Light Ladies

Also, the driving rhythm associated with the string band was not yet fully in place. The change from an individualized fiddle tradition to an ensemble string-band music occurred within the lifetime of the following generation, men like Luther Davis, Joe Caudill, and Tommy Jarrell, who were born in the 1880s and 1890s and learned their music during the turn-of-the-century period. Comparing these younger fiddlers' playing of a tune like "Ducks on the Millpond" with that of Emmett Lundy is instructive, for it illuminates the nature of stylistic change.

Emmett Lundy's rendition of "Ducks on the Millpond" (figure 2.7) is typical of his playing in general.[23] The melody is full and intricate (see in particular measures 9 and 10) and there are bowed triplets (measures 3 and 5). Also there is a third strain—a variant of the second—that lends both rhythmic and melodic diversity to the tune, qualities that are conspicuously absent from the playing of younger fiddlers in the area, like Luther Davis.

Luther Davis was born in 1888 in the Delhart community of Grayson County. He played the banjo first, but when he was about fifteen he started learning the fiddle by watching older musicians in the area, men such as Isom and Fielden Rector, Sidney Caudill, and Emmett Lundy.[24] Comparing Luther's version of "Ducks on the Millpond" (figure 2.8) with Lundy's, the first thing we notice is the absence of bowed triplets. The melody is altered somewhat and simplified slightly, but much of Lundy's bowing is retained (note measures 1, 2, 4, 5, 8, 10, 12). Perhaps the most significant difference between the two versions is in the way Davis uses bowing slurs in the repeated sections of the tune. While duplicating Lundy's bowing in measure 3, in measure 7 Davis rhythmically "fills in" the passage, using a two-note slur with a mid-bow accent on an upward bow. Similarly, Davis uses

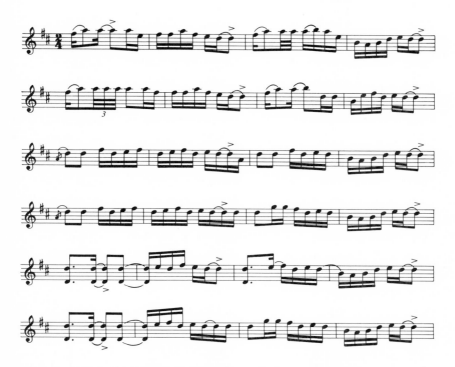

Figure 2.7. Emmett Lundy's "Ducks on the Millpond" (AAFS 4945 A3).

single bow strokes to go from measure 9 to 10, as did Lundy, but employs an upward slur going from measure 13 to measure 14. And again, Davis uses Lundy's bowing in measures 10 through 12, while using a three-note upward slur in measure 14 and again to cross the bar line between measure 15 and 16. Although Luther Davis must be considered a "transitional" fiddler, one who stylistically participated in the older fiddle music and the new string-band tradition, such changes in his basic approach to the tune helped emphasize the rhythmic qualities of the music at the expense of melody, a pattern that becomes increasingly evident in other fiddlers of Luther's generation.

Joe Caudill grew up not far from Luther Davis, yet knew this tune by the name "Geese on the Millpond." There are also differences between his rendition of the tune and that of Lundy and Davis (figure 2.9).[25] Absent from Caudill's playing are not only bowed triplets but

Figure 2.8. Luther Davis's "Ducks on the Millpond" (recorded at Delhart by Tom Carter and Blanton Owen, 8 February 1974).

also many of the bowing slurs and accents used by both Lundy and Davis (see measures 2, 4, 6, and 8). The melody too is greatly simplified. Only in measures 1 and 3 do the melody and bowing coincide with Lundy's. Caudill's straightforward version is oriented, more than either Lundy's or Davis's, to the strong beats of the measure, often accentuating them by sliding into notes with the left hand (measures 2, 5, 6, and 7) or by using a long, downward bow to anticipate the downbeat (measure 2). Such techniques impart to the tune a feeling more "forward" (the tune is literally pushed forward by the anticipation of the downbeat) and regular.

One final example of "Ducks on the Millpond" is found in the playing of Tommy Jarrell of Mount Airy, Surry County, North Carolina (figure 2.10). Tommy Jarrell was born in 1900 and learned to fiddle from older fiddlers in the vicinity of his home in Low Gap, also in Surry County. His main influence was his father Ben Jarrell. "Any time he'd take his fiddle out I'd take a strong interest in it. I'd pay close attention to how he'd use his bow arm and I'd watch just exactly how he'd note. I was young, about thirteen, and it would sink in back then."[26] Tommy Jarrell's version, called "Ducks on the Pond," is similar to Joe Caudill's in its basic orientation (though not quite

Figure 2.9. Joe Caudill's "Geese on the Millpond" (recorded by Tom Carter, 21 January 1973).

so pronounced as Joe's) to the strong beats of the measure. Like Joe, Tommy uses long downward bows to anticipate the down beat (measures 2 and 6) and uses (though not as frequently as Caudill) left-hand slides (measures 10 and 14). Melodically, however, Jarrell's tune is considerably more developed than Caudill's, though not so highly complex as Lundy's. Jarrell uses three-note upward slurs more frequently than the other fiddlers both within the measure (measures 2, 3, 6, 7, 8) and across bar lines (measures 4, 8, and 10). His use of an upward slur to cross the bar line into measure 14 duplicates that of Davis, and while not using it as often as Lundy, Jarrell does employ mid-bow accents in the same manner and position as Lundy (measures 1, 4, and 16). Jarrell's playing of "Ducks on the Pond" might thus be characterized as having a somewhat simplified melody with a stronger rhythmic emphasis while retaining the older, syncopated bowing patterns.

Through the playing of these fiddlers, then, it is possible to see certain similarities among musicians in the New River Valley area. The "Ducks on the Millpond" tune itself is recognizable in all the versions, and the basic Southwide syncopated bowing pattern is present. Yet there are also important if subtle differences to be noted. During the later years of the nineteenth century, the trend was toward an overall simplification of the melody and an emphasis on rhythm. This later aspect of the music is achieved not so much by the heavy articulation of the downbeat as it is by the increasingly "forward" feeling of the bowing. The evenness of bowing associated with Emmett Lundy gives way to an increasingly rhythmic ("dotted") tune structure in the following generation (figure 2.11).

The stylistic change outlined here is the one involved in the move

Figure 2.10. Tommy Jarrell's "Ducks on the Pond" (Mountain 302).

from a fiddle to an ensemble musical tradition—from a melodically complex to a more rhythmically sophisticated fiddle music. Older tunes like "Ducks on the Millpond"—tunes that were flexible enough to accommodate such modifications—remained an integral part of the emerging string-band music; those that for one reason or another could not accommodate modifications were discarded.[27] As we have seen, this change was not the simple replacing of an older British music with a newer American form. The imported British tradition had by the late eighteenth century already been transformed in the South by its contact with African blacks. The stylistic move toward the string band was then not such a radical one, but one that involved, first of all, the gradual exaggeration of certain rhythmic tendencies in the music, and second (actually the result of the first), the melding of various local styles into a larger (in the sense of being more widely known) regional music. The catalyst for this synthesis was the five-string banjo, for not only did it become the "other" instrument in the string band, but it also brought something to the music that excited the musicians, a certain quality that compensated for what it did not do very well, and that is play melody. Discovering what the banjo did for the music lies at the heart of understanding the essence of the string-band tradition.

The circumstances surrounding the arrival of the banjo in the Southern mountains is the subject of some debate. It is generally recognized that the instrument itself and the downstroking style in which it is played here are Afro-American in origin. Robert Winans has de-

Figure 2.11. Late nineteenth-century bowing patterns.

scribed in several places the link between Southern white banjo styles and the antebellum minstrelsy tradition. Winans suggests that the banjo moved into the mountain South with the traveling troupes of minstrel performers during the mid–nineteenth century.[28] Cecelia Conway, on the other hand, specifically records the development of the downstroking style among blacks and suggests that the "various tunings and complex playing techniques, of downstroking in particular, were transmitted largely intact from Afro-Americans living in the Piedmont South in the early nineteenth century to twentieth-century Piedmont blacks and mountain whites."[29] For the purposes of this discussion, the question of whether the banjo arrived in the New River Valley via the minstrel stage or through direct contact with Piedmont blacks is not relevant. What is important is that the five-string banjo and the downstroking style of playing it were Afro-American in origin and that they were known in the area at least by the time of the Civil War (figure 2.12).[30] It seems likely that the string band did not develop overnight, but rather grew slowly, gaining momentum in the 1870s and 1880s before reaching fruition by around 1900, when the banjo-fiddle combination eventually came to be seen as a musical whole. As the string band emerged, the banjo played a leading role in defining the structure of the new music in three areas, rhythm, melody, and key.

Early banjo playing in the New River Valley area is similar to that found through most of the upland South. It involves a basic downward rapping motion across the strings with the right hand while noting the strings on the fingerboard with the left.[31] In this downstroking style, called locally "clawhammer" playing because of the similarity of the right, or striking hand to the claw of a hammer, the nail of the index finger of the rapping hand strikes down on one of the four lower

Figure 2.12. Houston Gaylean and unidentified banjo player, ca. 1880, Fisher's Peak area, Surry County, N.C. (courtesy of Barry Poss).

Figure 2.13. Basic banjo figures. The tablature below the music illustrates the actions of the right hand (I = index finger, T = thumb) and five lines of the scale correspond to the five strings of the banjo, beginning with the first string at the top.

strings while the thumb continually catches and sounds the short fifth string, which acts as a drone. The basic downstroking motion, one melody note followed by a rhythmic brush and fifth-string drone, is shown here in figure 2.13 at A; the brush stroke may be eliminated, as shown at B; or, in yet another variation of pattern, the thumb may be brought down to catch the second or more rarely the third string to increase the melodic capabilities of the motion, as shown at C. This "drop-thumb" or "double-noting" technique is characteristic of downstroke playing but in actual performance is used rather sparingly. The downward movement of the right hand acquires a momentum of its own and has the tendency both to accent the downstroke and to lend a certain syncopation to the music. Rhythmically, the banjo stroke closely approximates that found in the fiddle in the string-band style (figure 2.14).

Underscoring the rhythmic nature of the new ensemble music, the banjo and the way it was played also had an effect on the melody. While the right hand in the downstroking style serves to pick out the melody and to add a percussive sound, the banjo player's left hand is reserved for noting the strings. Because most rural banjos were fretless in the nineteenth century, noting was confined to the area below the fifth-string peg and the melodic range of the instrument was limited to just more than one octave. Thus, the more the banjo was viewed as a full participant in the music, the more the tunes had to be simplified and flattened out. Comparing Emmett Lundy's playing of "Forked Deer" with the banjo version of Sidna Myers, a fine banjoist from

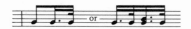

Figure 2.14. Basic rhythmic pattern in the clawhammer style.

Grayson County, it is possible to see the lack of fit between the two instruments; the banjo cannot fully duplicate the intricate melody of the fiddle (figure 2.15).[32] In this way the banjo directly influenced the types of tunes that could become ensemble pieces; older fiddle tunes either had to be simplified to correspond to the banjo melody or dropped altogether. The way in which the banjo was tuned also had a limiting effect on the string band.

In the downstroking style, different banjo tunings are employed for each of the primary fiddle keys, A (aEAC♯E), G (gDGBD), D (aDADE), and C (gCGCD).[33] The use of such open tunings has been documented in Afro-American tradition, and it seems likely that the idea for retuning the banjo to the principal tones in a key, if not the specific tunings themselves, was transmitted from blacks to mountain whites along with the downstroking style itself.[34] Such retuning made tunes easier to note out on the instrument and produced a sympathetic droning of the nonmelody strings that served to accentuate the rhythmic qualities of the style. It also made it harder for banjo players to switch from key to key. To change from the key of D to the key of A, they had to retune only two strings: aDADE (D) to aEAC♯E (A). The move to G, however, required dropping the A tuning one full step to gDGBD, or using one of several tunings, gDGDE or gEADE, which required chording with the left hand, a technique that was difficult on the unfretted early banjos. Compounding the banjo player's difficulties was the fact that G fiddle tunes quite often exhibited considerable melodic range, making them difficult to follow on an instrument with a single-octave capability (figure 2.16). Complicated G tunes, or similarly difficult pieces in the other keys, lay outside the technical capabilities of the banjo, and few of these pieces have been recorded by New River Valley banjoists. Davidson and Newman note that "we

Forked Deer (Lundy)

Forkey Deer (Myers)

Figure 2.15. Comparison of Emmett Lundy's "Forked Deer" with the banjo version of Sidna Myers.

have often heard clawhammer banjo players complain of not being able to follow the 'funny lick' of fiddlers playing these tunes."[35]

As the band idea became popular the process of synthesis was initially one of contraction. As the musical core of the string-band tradition was formed, many of the older fiddle tunes in the region had to be dropped—they simply would not fit the banjo style. It is interesting to note that about 20 percent of Emmett Lundy's tunes failed to make the transition to Joe Caudill's generation, and these tunes are invariably the ones with greatest melodic content and range.[36] Once the band concept was established, however, there came a period of expansion when new tunes were added to the repertoire. The expansive nature of the string-band music spilled over into the realm of style too, for the possible combinations of fiddle and banjo parts were seemingly endless. What was at first glance a more simplified musical form was, in fact, fully as complex and sophisticated as the older fiddle music it replaced, only in this case individual achievement was traded for that of the ensemble. What the string band sacrificed in the way of melody, it made up for in the complex interaction of the two instruments.

Waves on the Ocean

Figure 2.16. Joe Caudill's "Waves on the Ocean." This complicated old fiddle tune in the key of G is rarely found in the New River Valley and not at all among local banjoists.

The string-band ensemble fascinated musicians in the New River Valley during the late nineteenth century. Certainly, two instruments were louder than one, and the driving rhythm of the band was an ideal accompaniment for dancing. It was perhaps more important, however, that the new music allowed considerable personal interaction between musicians, a relationship that stimulated truly extraordinary performances.

The fiddle-banjo music of the string band has often been characterized as an essentially monophonic sound, a symmetrical performance by two instruments.[37] Such is not in fact the case, for while the two instruments do share much common ground, they rarely achieve a note-for-note balance. In the string band there exists a subtle asymmetry—a lack of synchrony—that provides the musical spark, the tension, that underlies and makes the fiddle-banjo partnership work both aesthetically and intellectually.

The New River Valley string band reached its apogee in the Round Peak section of Surry County and in two of this area's most able performers, fiddler Tommy Jarrell and banjoist Fred Cockerham, may be seen its true power. Even a casual hearing of Tommy and Fred's "Old Bunch of Keys" reveals the excitement of performance (figure 2.17).[38] The two musicians render the melody simultaneously. Upon closer analysis, however, it becomes apparent that rather than playing the same melody note for note, the banjo and fiddle play melodies that are, more often than not, slightly divergent. Scrutiny of the transcription of the tune, with the melodies superimposed on the same staff, reveals that although the two instruments occasionally play in perfect unison (measure 6), they more often play at close harmonic intervals (measures 1, 3, and 4). Even more significant are the instances in which a particular note is first played by one instrument and then immediately sounded one-sixteenth note later by the other—one instrument, in effect, anticipating the other and setting up an internal tension that tends to drive the music forward. Both the banjo (measures 2 and 3) and the fiddle (measures 1 and 3) assume the role of anticipator, but the fiddle especially uses this technique to advantage by first sounding a note that is then played by the banjo in unison as it is being repeated or sustained by the fiddle (measures 4, 5, 6, and 7). A further refinement or variation of this technique finds the fiddle anticipating the banjo (while playing at an interval with it), then playing the same note in unison

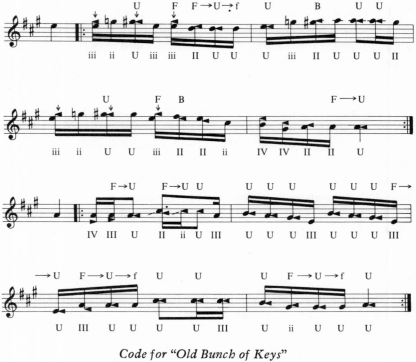

Code for "Old Bunch of Keys"

•–fiddle
–banjo
F–fiddle plays note before banjo
B–banjo plays note before fiddle
U–note played by both instruments at the same time
F→U–fiddle plays note first, followed by unison
F→U→f–fiddle first, then together, fiddle alone
ii, iii, etc.–minor second, third, etc.
II, III, etc.–major second, third, etc.

Banjo transcription does not reflect fifth-string drone or brush strokes. Many notes played on the fiddle have no corresponding note on the banjo. Intervals, in those instances, are determined by taking into account the sustaining quality of the preceding note played on the banjo. Intervals in which the banjo plays microtones (↓) are approximations.

Figure 2.17. "Old Bunch of Keys," Tommy Jarrell, fiddle; Fred Cockerham, five-string banjo (Down to the Cider Mill, County 713 [1968]).

with the banjo, and finally, repeating the note again alone over the sustain of the previous banjo note. The result of this highly innovative and complex musical interaction is a music with a strong rhythmic effect, as the same note is played in rapid succession first by the fiddle, then the banjo, and finally, again by the fiddle.

In the music of the Round Peak musicians and those of the New River Valley generally, we find instead of perfect unison, often discordant harmonies (such as minor thirds and even seconds) scattered here and there, and instead of rhythmic symmetry—the mashing down on the downbeat—we discover a dynamic rhythmic counterpoint, all of which results in the generation of a subtle tension that is "felt" more than heard and that gives the string band much of its power, both aesthetically and intellectually. If the string band delivers less tune, there is more drive; and if the string band is less individually complex, it is socially more powerful, for it involves the presence and participation of two or more musicians. String-band music is an intensely social music intended for dancing and for people to play together, not alone.[39] The band music comes into its own only in actual performance, for here the individual virtuosity of the old fiddle music is transformed into the group virtuosity of the band, and ultimately, into the expression of a regional folk-music style. It is no wonder that Joe Caudill disliked playing alone.

What conclusions, then, may be drawn from this analysis of stylistic change in New River Valley folk music? Beyond underscoring (once more) the creative nature of folk performance, the emergence of the string band during the late nineteenth century reflects the more general history of the region.

In a study of the architecture of the New River Valley, Davyd Foard Hood discovers that the late 1800s—the period when the string band developed—was a period of change in the domestic architecture of the area. Hood finds that the "group of buildings whose appearance predominates in the New River Valley were either built or remodeled in the years between 1885 and 1915."[40] Hood attributes this surge in local building to increased economic prosperity in the area as residents became increasingly capable of producing surplus crops and quality livestock for sale both locally and outside the area. The completion of the Norfolk and Western railroad line to Marion, Virginia, in 1887 also served to stimulate the local economy by connecting the valley to markets in the Piedmont and tidewater areas. Hood describes a society in the throes of change. Valley residents found their horizons expanding, their expectations increasing. The extreme isolation of the area was breaking down, both internally and externally. People knew more about the folks in the next community and their next-door neighbors. New, more uptown buildings, usually nice white I-houses, symbolized this change, as perhaps did the new music, for string music became popular in various localized forms over a wide area of the mountains. The full historical implications of the changes in the architecture and fiddling in the valley during the turn-of-the-century period lie outside the scope and capabilities of this study, but certainly, coincidental or not, they point to a period of cultural transition that has not received the attention it deserves. Music, like I-houses perhaps, helped people here forge a new identity, one encompassing the land beyond their homes, one bringing them a step closer to the larger American scene.

3. The Hugh Dixon Homestead: What to Make of Tradition?

Rachel B. Osborn

In 1866 a small, unpretentious farmhouse was built in the Quaker community of Snow Camp, Alamance County, North Carolina. Given the context of rural life in the Piedmont, it is not surprising that the moderately prosperous Hugh Dixon should choose to build a new structure for his growing family on land that had belonged to his family for over a generation. Nor, at first glance, does the house exhibit any startling deviations from the vernacular housing traditions of the area. Sitting atop a shaded knoll, the white clapboard house is bordered on the north by the meandering Cane Creek and flanked by weathered wooden outbuildings. From the gently sagging front porch, one looks across a plowed field to the quiet country road running parallel to the farmhouse. Inside as well as outside the dwelling, we find evidence of the traditional rural lifeways that have continued here for 122 years.

Yet a closer look at the house and community of which it is part reveals that innovation as well as tradition is a significant cultural value here. From its founding in 1752 until the late nineteenth century, Snow Camp was a manufacturing center as well as an agricultural hamlet of small subsistence farms. Simon Dixon's gristmill, the first built on Cane Creek, operated from the middle of the eighteenth century to the middle of the twentieth. In 1830 Joseph Dixon—Simon Dixon's grandson, and Hugh Dixon's father—established one of the first foundries for casting iron in North Carolina. These and other manufacturing concerns, including textile factories, rose and fell during the nineteenth century. In 1880 the decision not to build a new railroad through Snow Camp spelled the eventual demise of all of them.

Thus, in 1866 Snow Camp was not the quiet backwater it appears today. It was a place where rural folkways were being challenged by

Figure 3.1. Hugh Dixon House, Snow Camp, N.C., 1989 (photo by Charles G. Zug III).

manufacturing innovations; it was the time when a transition from folk culture to popular culture was taking place here and throughout the United States. Hugh Dixon's house, unpretentious as it is, faithfully reflects the dynamic interplay between continuity and change that was occurring in his community.

Like any other human-made artifact, the house is, in James Deetz's words, "the *direct* expression of changing values, images, perceptions and ways of life as well as of certain constancies."[1] It is the concrete realization of an abstract idea, the product of the builder/owner's choice among the variables of ideology, technology, function, and style that his culture offers him. In examining the house, we are investigating the psyche of the builder/owner, the local traditions of his community, and the widespread attributes of the cultural area in which the artifact is found. To study adequately the material object and the human beings who produced it, we must consider not only the structure of the dwelling, but the needs of the maker and the values of the culture. As Henry Glassie points out: "It will be necessary to know not only what an object is and what its history and distribution are, but also what its

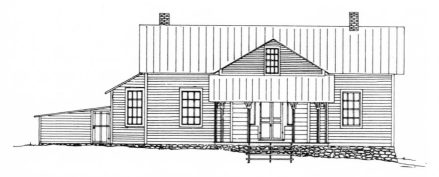

Figure 3.2. Line drawing of the Hugh Dixon house (Roger Manley).

role in the culture of the producer and user is, and what mental intricacies surround, support, and are reflected in its existence."[2]

The focus of this essay is the form, construction, and use of the Hugh Dixon house through time. I will describe the house as conceived and as realized by the builder, and as experienced and altered by successive occupants and owners. I will view the homestead from within the matrix of folk traditions in the area, yet consider the precise folk nature of the house to be somewhat problematic. When traditional and innovative techniques intertwine, as they do in this house, how are we to classify and explain the resultant artifact? What meanings are to be found in the structure and function of such a house?

At the outset of this process, we need to understand the mind of the builder and the kinds of influences Hugh Dixon experienced while he was growing up in the Snow Camp community. From contemporary as well as more recent Quaker documents, we fortunately can get a fairly clear picture of Hugh Dixon and the religious traditions surrounding him. From Carl Lounsbury's *Alamance County Architectural Heritage,* published in 1980, we gain a companion insight into the processes of time as reflected in Snow Camp's built environment.

In 1825 Hugh Woody Dixon was the first child born to Joseph and Mary Woody Dixon, who lived in a farmhouse close to the Cane Creek Friends Meeting. This area, then the northern border of Chatham County, became part of Alamance County later that century. Like other farmers in this section of the county, the Dixons would have engaged primarily in the cultivation of wheat and other grains. The soil was not suited for tobacco, which in any event would have required more personnel than the nonslaveholding Friends could have supplied. Cotton and other crops were grown principally for family use. Thus "at no time did a plantation economy and society emerge as the predominant feature of the region's culture. It was always a landscape filled with small farmsteads cultivated by individual families."[3]

Though participating in the subsistence-farm traditions of the region, the Dixons also displayed mechanical genius and a flair for business enterprise. In 1830 Joseph Dixon started his Snow Camp Foundry, which operated until 1875. The 1840 census shows one member of the household engaged in the "learned professions and engineers," and one involved in "manufacture and trades"—this latter most likely Hugh Dixon, age fifteen.[4]

Dedicated Quakers, family members also displayed elements of conservatism and innovation in their religious lives. Adhering to the Quaker doctrines of simplicity, pacificism, and Spirit-led worship, the Dixons clung to the "moderation and plainness in gesture, speech, apparel and furniture of house" strictly required of Meeting members.[5] Yet the Dixons also valued higher education at a time when many Friends found it mere "creaturely activity." Hugh Dixon was sent to the New Garden (Friends) Boarding School in Greensboro in 1838 and spent the winters of 1842 through 1844 teaching there. In 1841 a miraculous recovery from a grave illness led him to his lifelong involvement in Christian causes and Quaker organizations. In 1855, however, he deliberately violated the Quaker discipline by marrying a non-Friend, Flora Adaline Murchison. Far from apologizing for his misdeed, he boldly chose to criticize the discipline instead. "Hugh W. Dixon," notes one biographer, "combined the family traditions of zealous piety, a broad interest in community affairs, and moderate prosperity, with a streak of stubborn independence."[6]

From 1844 until 1857 Hugh Dixon lived in Snow Camp and worked as a partner in the Snow Camp Foundry, except for the years between 1853 and 1855, when he was involved in building the Graham and Gulf Plank Road. As the vice-president of the company that built the road, he did the survey work and operated the sawmill that produced the planks for the toll road. By 1850 Hugh Dixon had a hundred-acre farm valued at $500.[7] Its moderate size and output, compared to other farms in the area, indicate that farming was not his prime concern at this juncture.

The new industrial enterprises in which Hugh Dixon was closely involved helped to alter the local building traditions that had developed during the previous hundred years. Carl Lounsbury states that from Alamance County's initial period of settlement until the end of the Civil War, log construction was the most prevalent building technique. What is found in the county is "the confluence and interplay of these two regional building traditions—the Pennsylvania penchant for log and stone compared to the Tidewater reliance upon hewn frame construction; house types with centrally-located chimneys compared to house types with gable-end chimneys; principal rafter roofs compared to common rafter roofs. . . . From origins in cultural diversity, there arose in the eighteenth century a homegrown vernacular way of building."[8]

Although the hall-parlor form was the most popular type of antebellum house in Alamance County, a minor type was the three-room plan, found only in the southern section and most notably Snow Camp. Whether or not William Penn exhorted his fellow Quakers to use this so-called Quaker plan, it seems clear that the Pennsylvania Quakers who founded Snow Camp brought this house type with them. Possibly, too, the unadorned bicameral style of Quaker meetinghouses in Pennsylvania—replicated in the plan of the Cane Creek Meeting as it progressed beyond the log stage—influenced the dwelling styles and structures of Snow Camp Friends as well. Lounsbury notes: "A major change in the traditional house types occurred in the country in the last two decades before the Civil War, with the appearance of the central passageway. . . . By the 1850's most of the larger new farmhouses incorporated this new development in their design."[9]

All these architectural elements were destined to have their effects upon the post–Civil War Hugh Dixon house, even as its entrepreneurial builder moved beyond his formative folk traditions. We might also speculate that the vernacular architecture that Dixon saw during his stay in Guilford County also influenced his building concepts, but no concrete evidence to support this possibility has been found.[10]

In 1858 Hugh and Adaline Dixon moved from Snow Camp ten miles down the Plank Road to Ore Hill in Chatham County, just east of what is now Mount Vernon Springs. It is likely that his work on the Plank Road had brought Hugh Dixon into contact with an area of greater economic opportunity than Snow Camp. At any rate, "by industry and economy he in a few years surrounded himself with a comfortable living, bought land, about seven hundred acres, and two mill sites, erected two grist mills and a steam saw mill, and was interested in a small way in the Chatham Ore Hill Company."[11] The records do not state whether he built himself a house at this site, but it seems reasonable to suppose so.

From Hugh Dixon's entries in his 1858 sawmill ledger, we can begin to assess the impact that this kind of early manufacturing had on the building traditions in the area. Items such as logs for sills and posts, shingles, rafters, joists, ceiling and flooring, screws, six-penny nails, locks, handmade bricks and doors could be produced at Dixon's mill.[12] In Chatham and Alamance counties, as elsewhere in the country, manufactured goods began to nudge aside folk methods of production. The mid–nineteenth century also saw the advent of the steam-powered saw (Hugh Dixon owned one) and the increased popularity of balloon framing. At this point, building methods and materials began to shift away from vernacular traditions toward something more akin to popular styles. Hugh Dixon was intimately involved in this transition.

Dixon continued his milling and dairy farming as a resident in the Ore Hill area until 1866. Along with other Quaker men, he avoided combat in the Civil War by paying a $500 fine levied against pacifists. Despite his abolitionist, Whiggish views and the economic decline of the area during the war, Dixon appears to have prospered during this period. Then in the depressed aftermath of the war, Dixon was given an opportunity he appeared to value more than the pursuit of economic advantage in Ore Hill. In 1866 the philanthropic Baltimore Association of Friends offered to assist the Cane Creek Meeting in starting a Quaker school in Snow Camp. Hugh Dixon promptly moved back to his home community to help set up the school and to give his children the precious experience of a Quaker education.

Dixon's choice of the hilly, wooded terrain southwest of the Simon Dixon gristmill for his new homesite was made in accord with a number of strong rural traditions. Moving onto a section of land originally acquired by one's forebears was—and is—common practice, not just in the Cane Creek Valley. Amos Rapoport points out that "in this

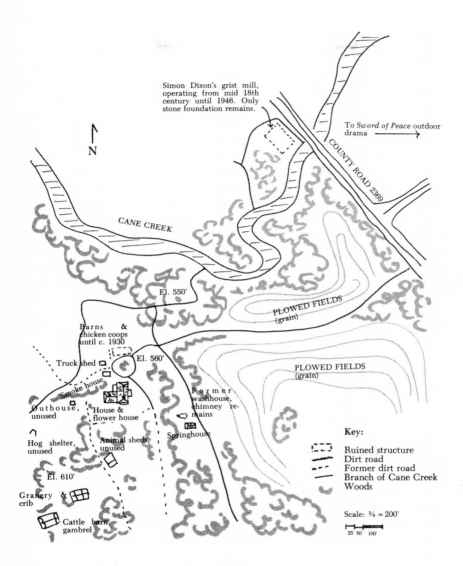

Simon Dixon's grist mill, operating from mid 18th century until 1946. Only stone foundation remains.

To *Sword of Peace* outdoor drama →

N

COUNTY ROAD 2369

CANE CREEK

El. 550'

PLOWED FIELDS (grain)

Barns & chicken coops until c. 1930

Truck shed   El. 560'

Smoke house

Outhouse, unused

House & flower house

Former washhouse, chimney remains

PLOWED FIELDS (grain)

Springhouse

Hog shelter, unused

Animal sheds, unused

El. 610'

Granery & crib

Cattle barn, gambrel

Key:

- - -   Ruined structure
——   Dirt road
- - -   Former dirt road
——   Branch of Cane Creek
         Woods

Scale: ¾ = 200'

25' 50'   100'

Figure 3.3. Site diagram of the Hugh Dixon homestead.

choice, access to food or water, exposure to wind, defensive potential, the sparing of land for agriculture, and transportation all play a role."[13] The knoll on which Dixon built his house was well watered by a spring; the thicket on the hill behind the house protected it from the summer heat and winter winds. The homestead's due-east orientation afforded an excellent view of its cultivated fields and a close watch on the road running before them. Economy of site is evident in both the agricultural locus and the awareness of human traffic beyond the farm. Like other post–Civil War rural builders, Hugh Dixon incorporated older and recent folk practices in constructing his environment.

Dixon may have cultivated this site as his farm in 1850 before he moved to Ore Hill. The layout of the farm and the presence of a stone springhouse suggest occupancy prior to 1866.[14] Internal evidence indicates that the original structure, probably log constructed, was all but invisibly incorporated into the ell of the current house. Such an adaptation would conform to the general Southern pattern of transforming first structures into summer kitchens and then into kitchen/dining ells for new houses. The rectangular dimensions of the original building can be traced along existing walls of the ell as they align with two dysfunctional framing members: a small exposed section of hewn beam in the kitchen and a post in a bedroom off the dining room. The unity of this area is suggested by the uniform ceiling height, wooden-plank paneling, and common square-cut nails. North of the original floor line, the ceiling is lower, the floor sags, and beaded paneling covers both walls and ceiling. A double stone fireplace once stood in the center of this structure. When the present owner, Sarah Kimball, and her family moved to the Dixon house in 1931, they "had a fireplace there until we built the flue. I can't remember what year we built that. But you talk about a mess! The fireplace, both of them, was big, of course, and they [were] put together with clay. We tore it down in the summertime, and you'd go all through the house and write your name on everything there was because all that dust. We rolled the rocks out and made us a back porch."[15]

The house that Hugh Dixon built in front of this structure in 1866 was a reinterpretation of that area's folk-housing traditions, suited to his needs and purposes. Carl Lounsbury believes the plan of this house is unique to Snow Camp and probably Alamance County. In part an idiosyncratic structure, the Dixon house nevertheless shares enough features with vernacular buildings in the area to demonstrate both the fixity and fluidity of folk traditions.

Initially Dixon's floor plan appears to be a variant of the one-story Georgian-plan house type.[16] Four rooms built around two internal double fireplaces are symmetrically arranged along a central passageway. Chronologically as well as structurally, this form makes sense; 1866 was a time when concerns with symmetry and formal balance strongly influenced the shape of vernacular buildings. Yet a good look shows that the room placements, fireplaces, and wall piercings are not symmetrical. The structure is also just one-and-a-half stories high. Perhaps because of this, there is a gable roof instead of the hipped or pyramid roof often found in one-story Georgian-plan houses. The house has a moderate-sized porch typical of that plan, and an ell appendage common to many vernacular house types.

Clearly the Quaker plan favored in Snow Camp and Guilford County and other single-pile central-hallway houses in the area powerfully affected the shape of Dixon's house. There were numerous close examples by which he could have been influenced.[17] We see aspects reminiscent of the Quaker plan in the stone foundations of the house, its (11.5-feet square) front hallway that directly accesses the two northern rooms, and the boxed stairway tucked away from view in the rear hallway. Boxed stairways, which go back to medieval times, are, of course, found in cabins and hall-parlor houses as well. Lounsbury notes that in Alamance "only a handful of houses featured [the] double pile plan. At first the plan was limited to one story houses. . . . [There are] only two two-story double pile houses in the county."[18] So Dixon's inspiration for his one-and-a-half story, double-pile design must have come from elsewhere than his home area.

In attempting to classify the curious amalgam of structural styles that is the Hugh Dixon house, we can conclude only that it is an unusual conflation of the Quaker plan with a central-hallway Georgian-plan type, complete with unique structural details. This fusion of rural traditions with more urbane innovations resulted from the aspirations and intentions of the builder in constructing a dwelling suited to his particular needs. It was a house meant to reflect at once the well-being of the successful dairy farmer, the humble simplicity of the plain Friend, and the forward-looking attitude of the technological innovator.

The home had to provide space for a family of five children, domestic help and hired help, and the Quaker boarders who taught at the Sylvan School just up the road. The house also had to supply office space for Hugh Dixon to carry out the concerns of his gristmill and other business enterprises. In addition, since there was then no granary on the farm, storage space for grain had to be found in the attic. Hugh Dixon's house design both bespeaks and fulfills these various needs.

In function as well as structure, this dwelling stands on a threshold between folk and popular culture. As characteristic of older folk houses, it provides both for intimacy and the flexible use of interior space. Yet it favors the symmetry of plan and the specialization of function that typifies the popular styles of a later period. Its growth through time was first organic, then frontally symmetric with prosperity, and finally organic again. It is as though the economic decline that began in the latter part of the nineteenth century in Snow Camp occasioned a reversion to earlier folk custom in this house form.

The front of the 1866 house constituted the formal and public section. The first two rooms on either side of the entrance hall, served, respectively, as parlor and living room; the two rooms behind them were bedrooms for family and guests. The large front hallway provided Hugh Dixon's office space, in which his secretary and bookcase still stand and where a number of his books and ledgers can still be seen. In this section of the house, the needs of traders, business associates, guests, and older family members were attended to.

The small rear hallway, which contained the boxed stair leading to the attic, opened onto the back section of the dwelling—the ell and the yard. It led to the hearth and to the outdoors: toward privacy, informality, and the agricultural side of the Dixons' life. Grain could be brought virtually directly from the fields into the attic and stored in its unpaneled southern section. The more finished northern section of the attic was partitioned into two paneled rooms where the hired help and perhaps boarders slept. The ell appendage reserved the function of "hearth": the preparation and consumption of food in a closely personal and relaxed setting.

As one moved from the front of the house to the back, then, one traveled from public toward private space, from formality toward informality; from business and entertainment functions toward familial and agricultural pursuits. Henry Glassie might claim that this division of function, along with the dwelling's tripartite and bilaterally symmetrical form, evinces a desire for control over the environment and human events. But the plan is not so much contrived as sensible. It provides well for the flow of weather outside and the movement of people inside the house. The balanced placement of doors, windows, and fireplaces, for example, gives the house an orderly aspect. More important, this arrangement efficiently regulates the temperature inside the dwelling: aligned wall piercings cool better, and internal double fireplaces heat better. Here the Hugh Dixon house is a product of the symbiotic folk relationship with nature, even as it makes an innovative cultural statement in form.

The competence of the builder, as he waded in the "template pool" and drew out the design that met his needs, was certainly adequate to the purpose. But the performance of the house, its concrete realization into wood, brick, and stone, is a bit less accomplished. In its materials and manner of construction, the Dixon house exhibits a curious range of attributes. Gaps show in the sheathing over the sturdy frame construction; a somewhat unaesthetic plainness is touched up with various Greek Revival, Gothic, and Italianate details; and the trimly purposeful lines of the 1866 house are marred by uncertain additions, such as cellar stairs that lead nowhere. Generally the house is somewhat crudely constructed. Perhaps the builder's haste to leave Ore Hill and construct his new house in Snow Camp in less than a year may have had something to do with this. Or perhaps for innovator Hugh Dixon, the conception of an idea was more important than its precise rendering into form.

The essential structure of the house, however, is sound. The two-foot-thick fieldstone base—four feet high in the northern section—forms the foundation of the thirty-seven-by-twenty-five-foot house. At the ground level, hand-hewn sills and summer beams support the balloon-frame structure and the circular-sawed floor joists and floorboards of the first floor. In the attic, the main studs are pegged into both the sills and the secondary plate. The ridge board, rafters, and collar beams are also circular sawed, and the rafters are pegged into the collar beams. Throughout the 1866 section of the house, square-cut eight-penny nails are the most common, but round nails are also found. The frame is sheathed internally by nine-inch-wide, horizontal-matched pine boarding; the flooring is nine- to eleven-inch-wide unfinished oak boarding.

Outside, six-inch clapboards are placed against corner boards. Most likely the present tin roof replaced an earlier shingled one.

The two fireplaces typify the combination of popular, folk, and crude elements that characterize the finishing details of the house. Formed of the fieldstone bases and brick chimneys common to the vernacular tradition here, the fireplaces were evidently meant to conform to Georgian-inspired ideas of formal balance. In this attempt they do not completely succeed. The northern fireplace, which appears to have been built first, rises from a massive four-by-six-foot plastered stone base in the cellar and emerges from the roof right on the ridge line. By contrast, the southern fireplace appears to have been an afterthought. It is supported simply by a few stones laid over packed earth in the undug portion of the cellar. Standing shorter than its counterpart, this fireplace is placed much closer to the outside wall and emerges behind the ridgepole. Chimney bricks in both are handmade, but differ in color and sharpness from one chimney to the other, further indicating two distinct construction dates. The emphasis given the earlier fireplace lends further support to the conclusion that an initial Quaker-plan style was extended to the south by a Georgian-plan overlay.

Other plain/stylish contrasts are found in the internal decoration of the house. Hugh Dixon had no mantlepieces built; the fireplaces are simply plastered over. Walls and ceilings were given a common coat of whitewash throughout. In contrast are decorative touches like the deep green paint that enhances the woodwork, window frames, and door stiles in both rear bedrooms. The pale turquoise paint on the panels of both bedroom doors and the built-in wardrobe in the northwest bedroom also appears to be original. This wardrobe, built of pine or cedar panels with black walnut stiles and rails with wood-buttoned closings, was a useful and attractive item. A second one was built in the southwest bedroom with a later addition to the house. One of the area's skilled furniture makers was perhaps responsible for these well-crafted items.

Decorative elements on the outside of the house show Dixon's continued concern with simplicity as well as with stylishness. On the threshold, Greek Revival two-panel double doors are framed by sidelights. Here the wide pine sheathing used internally is brought to the outside, emphasizing the transition area linking porch and front hallway. The six-over-six sash windows are also in Greek Revival style. The influence of the Gothic Revival is seen in the gable addition, the curved brackets between the porch posts, and in the "Chinese" latticework on both the front and side porches. These decorations were machine made, as were the Italianate brackets beneath the eaves. The range of interests indicated by Hugh Dixon's library suggests that he may have been influenced by some popular literature of the era, like *Rural Architecture* or *Farm Buildings*. Still, the lack of ostentation in these decorations shows Dixon's adherence to the ideal of Quaker plainness.

Later nineteenth-century additions and alterations to the house continue the pattern of stylish ideas and indifferent construction. Necessitated by the increased number of people in the house, the quality of the first, circa 1883 expansion was tempered by the economic stagnation of the farm and the area. In 1880 there were eight people living in the house. It seems likely that among them were Dixon's oldest daughter Mary and her husband Zeno Dixon, who from 1882 to 1886 tried—and failed—to revive the flagging Sylvan School. They may have overseen the additions to the house and the ell that took place sometime in Hugh Dixon's early sixties.[19]

The addition to the south side of the house meant a more spacious parlor and bedroom, with internal fireplaces; the dining area in the expanded ell now had two bedrooms leading into it. The unique skylight in the dining room brought more light into the area darkened by this addition. The style consciousness of the six-paneled glass and wooden doors in this room echo that of the two-paneled doors found in the 1866 section of the house. Yet the new bedrooms in the ell have low, sagging ceilings and walls made of inexpensive vertical-beaded boarding. One has a plain batten door that leads into the kitchen. The pass-through pantry and cupboard between the kitchen and dining room was a clever idea, useful in storing and serving food for large numbers of people. But its low-quality construction repeats the pattern set elsewhere: form does not quite live up to concept.

The even-later addition of a flower house to the new southern section destroyed the initial attempted symmetry of Dixon's house. Since this structure is placed to the side, rather than hidden at the rear of the house, it displaces frontal formality. Here the house style reverts back to older, more organic and less symmetric folk-building traditions. It reflects the economic and social decline of the family and of the community.

After Hugh Dixon died in 1901, his house was rented out to various families. Some of them were connected to the public Sylvan School that replaced the private one; others were farmers. Sarah Kimball's parents—Quakers and farmers—moved to the house in 1931 and bought it in the next decade. During that time, outbuildings typical of the upland South were constructed, exhibiting both vernacular and popular-style features. For reasons of ecology as well as style, the barn was relocated from its original creek-side site in front of the house to the hill behind it. Sarah Kimball remembers hauling bags of corn down to the old Simon Dixon gristmill until 1946, when the structure was bought and torn down.

The Kimballs' traditional usage of house, outbuildings, and land shows the influence of the previous use of the Dixon property while demonstrating the continued rural folk patterns of the Piedmont and the changes wrought by modernization. The homestead still shapes and is shaped by the values, economics, and lifestyle of those using it.

Though we have described the Hugh Dixon house in its physical and cultural settings, there remains the problem of the degree to which it can be considered a folk structure. Its site placement, design, and use show a symbiotic relationship between nature, human life, and the creative use of new concepts and techniques. With the expansion and decline of the dwelling over time, we see a flow of function from section to section: from the original cabin to the public part of the new house, then—in recent years—back to the original hearth area. The multiple uses of space that characterize folk dwellings have in this house been conditioned by popular culture's more rigid division of function. But folk culture is always flexible enough to allow for variations upon a theme. Hugh Dixon's eclectic combination of crude construction methods and various popular styles, both conditioned by the requirements of his folk traditions, was characteristic of vernacular housing as it developed in the last third of the nineteenth century.

As a "fossilized idea," this house speaks of a culture that is past, yet one that gives clear shape to the present. Standing upon the threshold between the popular culture of this century and the agrarian folklife of the last, the Hugh Dixon house makes an innovative statement about traditional patterns. It does so in a manner that will not be repeated, but that can be understood.

4. Economic and Cultural Influences on German and Scotch-Irish Quilts in Antebellum Rowan County, North Carolina

Laurel Horton

In 1976 while surveying old quilts in Rowan County, North Carolina, I was struck by the contrasts shown by two particular examples. One was constructed in a "central medallion" style, that is, having a large central motif surrounded by smaller motifs and concentric borders. The fabrics were floral-printed chintzes in soft hues. This one seemed typical of descriptions of fine Southern quilts. The second consisted of repeated blocks of a tulip pattern cut from solid-color fabrics and appliquéd, or laid and sewn, upon a background of a small figured print. The large flower blocks, separated by sashing strips and surrounded by a scalloped border, created a bold visual effect. Both of these strikingly different quilts originated in Rowan County, the first about 1845, the second about 1852. I was puzzled that such visually diverse quilts could emanate from the same area in the same period and undertook to uncover an explanation (figures 4.1 and 4.2).

The study of American quilts has developed from early publications of a general nature to recent more thorough works. This more thorough scholarship has led to a revision of basic assumptions about the role of quilts in American life. Earlier writers stressed the cohesiveness and universality of American quilt making; they based their general statements about regional variations within the tradition on observations of available quilts with little attempt to define a representative sample or to examine the quilts in context.

Recently scholars have begun to undertake a more systematic investigation of American quilts.[1] This has required a closer focus on smaller groups of quilts and an examination of the historical or social contexts in which they were made. The result is the emergence of a

Figure 4.1 (above). Pieced and appliqué quilt, "Floral Central Medallion,"
Scotch-Irish, made by Jane Locke Young Graham, ca. 1845. Figure 4.2 (be-
low). Appliqué quilt, "Tulip," German, made by Annie Lingle Trexler, ca.
1852.

complex composite portrait of American quilt-making traditions that replaces an appealing but simplistic view.

A number of factors can influence quilt making in a particular area. These include the circumstances of early settlement, the economic and agricultural conditions, the location of the area relative to markets and cultural centers, the availability and cost of local or imported fabric, the cultural traditions of early and subsequent immigrants, and especially their inherited or acquired notions of what quilts should be or how they should look.

Rowan County provides an excellent laboratory for investigating the influence of geography and settlement patterns on quilts. The county is located in the Piedmont, roughly in the center of North Carolina. It was part of the "backcountry," the vast inland area that remained unsettled long after the Carolina coast had developed an established society.[2] The Piedmont was settled not as an extension of coastal communities, but by waves of German and Scotch-Irish migrants from Pennsylvania. Moreover, because Rowan is the parent county for the northwest corner of the state, public records dating back to early settlement provide documentary support in one location.

The majority of the original settlers in the North Carolina Piedmont, including both Germans and Scotch-Irish, migrated from southeastern Pennsylvania in the mid-eighteenth century.[3] The availability of cheap land made the area especially attractive at that time; consequently, the population grew rapidly. Rowan County was formed in 1753, then including that part of the state north and west of its present borders. The county seat of Salisbury was laid out in 1755, and although it did not grow as large or as rapidly as cities located on waterways, it became and remained for years an important center for commerce and politics for the western part of the state. The Old Wagon Road, the area's major trade route, connected Salisbury with Philadelphia to the north and Charleston to the south. The latter city, the largest in the colonial South, became increasingly important as the port through which Rowan's agricultural products were exchanged for imported goods.

The original settlers were primarily involved in agriculture, although farmers were often tradesmen or craftsmen as well. Many of the early families had been people of means, and once established in their new homes, they became even more affluent. The gradual development of Rowan County from an area of frontier settlements to one of flourishing communities was accompanied by changes in textile technology and transportation. These changes expanded the range and lowered the cost of available goods and directly influenced quilt making in the area.

The earliest bed covers in use in Rowan County had accompanied the incoming settlers in their wagon loads of household possessions. These were primarily woven coverlets and blankets. After establishing their new homes, the settlers met their needs for additional cover probably by weaving or buying blankets.[4] As these families converted their frontier settlements into rural communities, the women could turn their attention to creating objects of beauty and personal meaning, which included making quilts. Quilt makers in Rowan in the first half of the nineteenth century had several options for selecting fabrics for their quilts.

Home production supplied backcountry households with everyday clothing and household textiles from the earliest settlement until well into the nineteenth century. *The Western Carolinian,* Salisbury's biweekly newspaper, carried advertisements that indicate some of the services available locally to those who produced cloth at home. On 19 September 1820 Azariah Merrell of Abbotts Creek in Davidson County offered to card wool into rolls for ten cents per pound, using a newly developed machine.[5] In 1823 a subscriber announced that he would perform "blue dyeing," using indigo, for 62 ½ cents per pound for the first quality and 30 cents per pound for the second quality.[6] On 26 June 1827, Shelby Parker offered for sale "a quantity of flax and cotton spinning wheels,"[7] but the demand for these declined over the next two decades as cotton mills increased production.

The first cotton mill south of the Potomac was built in 1815 near Lincolnton, North Carolina, about forty miles southwest of Salisbury. This mill and others that soon followed produced yarn only. These yarns were both exported to northern weaving mills and sold locally to home weavers eager to eliminate the tedious and time-consuming tasks of carding and spinning from their production processes. By 1840 there were twenty-five mills in North Carolina producing coarser grades of plain cloth, such as osnaburgs, "nigger cloth," and sheeting, in addition to yarn. On 3 June 1842, the Salisbury Factory announced, "This establishment is now in complete operation. The Company are manufactur-

ing Cotton Yarn, Sheeting, Shirting, and Osnaburg, of a superior quality."⁸ The products of these local factories were all plain, undyed
fabrics until the 1850s, when E. M. Holt's mill on Alamance Creek began the manufacture of the state's first factory-dyed cloth, a coarse
gingham that became known as "Alamance plaid."

Though these local factory products filled the needs for plain
household textile and everyday clothing, Rowan County residents also
had access to fine imported fabrics. Alongside advertisements for local
yarn and spinning wheels appear those of Philadelphia and Charleston
merchants offering a variety of goods from European and American
factories. On 18 July 1820 an article in the *Western Carolinian* described the product of a Philadelphia factory: "We have at this moment before us a piece of jaconet muslin, of a fabrick so perfect in
every particular, that we may safely assert it to be equal in every respect to any thing of the kind produced in any part of the world. . . .
This piece is the first experiment made at the factory of Messrs. Thorp
and Slidell, of this neighborhood, yet it will bear inspection and comparison with any foreign production of the same number of yarn."⁹
On 10 December 1822, D. Parish of Charleston proclaimed the arrival
"from Liverpool and New York of 450 packages Dry Goods, com-
prising the most extensive assortment they have ever offered."¹⁰ By
the 1830s and 1840s a number of dry goods stores were in business in
Salisbury itself, offering a wide assortment of fabrics. The 22 April
1843 issue of the *Carolina Watchman* carried an advertisement for the
store of Jenkins and Biles, which offered "New spring and summer
goods: . . . English and French cloths and cassemeres, satinets, Kentucky jeans and Gentlemen's summer cloths, nankeen and cotton cassi-
meres, French, English, and American prints, painted and figured
French muslins and lawns, satin striped and Paris figured Balsoriens
(new article)" among other imported and domestic fabrics, many with
names unfamiliar today.¹¹

Given this extensive and increasing variety of materials available
to them, quilt makers could exercise a number of options in selecting
fabrics for their quilts. Some of these options were influenced by the
prevailing aesthetic tradition of the community. That is, each community had an unvoiced definition of what a quilt should be. The
Scotch-Irish and German communities within Rowan County developed different cultural and economic patterns that influenced the

aesthetic traditions within each community. In turn, the different community aesthetics of the Scotch-Irish and Germans contributed to the different ways individuals within these groups designed their quilts.

The Scotch-Irish, drawn to the Piedmont from Pennsylvania by the availability of cheap land, formed "Irish" settlements primarily in the northwestern section of present-day Rowan County. The historian James G. Leyburn asserts that the Scotch-Irish believed "in self-reliance, improving their condition in life, thrift and hard work, and the taking of calculated risks."[12] Although described as "industrious and thrifty,"[13] they did not share the conservative agricultural practices of their German neighbors. An earlier writer, Henry J. Ford, described the Scotch-Irish in Pennsylvania as "not succeeding so well as the frugal and industrious Germans," to whom they sold their lands in order to take up new ground to the south.[14] Until the nineteenth century both the Germans and the Scotch-Irish were dependent upon subsistence agriculture. As the cotton industry developed in the South, however, Rowan farmers found themselves on the fringe of the cotton-growing area, and many of them, primarily of Scotch-Irish descent, began to switch from diversified agriculture to cash crops.

The civic, cultural, and business leaders in Salisbury itself were also generally of Scotch-Irish descent. Names such as McCorkle, Steele, Locke, and Macay predominate in the records of the area until well into the nineteenth century. This local trend supports Ford's assertion that the Scotch-Irish, whether in Ulster, Pennsylvania, or elsewhere, were heavily concerned with manufacturing and commerce. He argues that it is no accident that the industrial revolution took place in those areas occupied by the Scotch-Irish.[15]

Throughout the nineteenth century Scotch-Irish merchants in Salisbury depended upon Charleston and its tributary markets.[16] Having fewer cultural barriers than the Germans, they established profitable commercial ties and were exposed to a variety of exotic and attractive goods. Charleston was the model for the fashion conscious, even those in the backcountry. Their styles, amusements, and aspirations followed those of the Charleston gentry.

Generally quilts made within Scotch-Irish communities during this period conform to quilt-making styles elsewhere in the country. In the Rowan Museum collection are two quilts, both dated circa 1840–1850, that represent late adaptations of the chintz appliqué style. These

Figure 4.3 Appliqué quilt, "Bird of Paradise," Scotch-Irish tradition, made by Sarah E. Kincaid, ca. 1848.

chintz quilts were made by cutting individual motifs, such as birds and flowers, from floral printed fabric and sewing them in new arrangements onto plain fabric. This style was immensely popular in England and in America, particularly in the coastal areas, during the eighteenth and early nineteenth centuries. Both of these Rowan examples share the usual "framed center" or "medallion" arrangement, having a large central element surrounded by smaller figures and multiple borders. The first—reportedly made by Sarah E. Kincaid (1835–1882), who lived near Woodleaf and was buried at Franklin Presbyterian Church in northwestern Rowan County—is called "Bird of Paradise" (figure 4.3), and is based upon the "tree of life" motif, which dates from the

Figure 4.4. Pieced quilt, "Star," Scotch-Irish, made by Alice Smith Slater, ca. 1830.

earliest years of cotton printing in India and England. The appliquéd birds and flowers in the center of this quilt are typical of "arborescent" prints, a group of polychrome wood-block-printed chintzes manufactured in England and France about 1775 to 1790.[17]

The second quilt (figure 4.1)—made by Jane Locke Young, who married Andrew Graham in 1845 (these family names were associated with the predominantly Presbyterian "Irish" settlement west of Salisbury)[18]—is a highly simplified version of the framed-center style. The central panel is a single printed block identical to one reproduced by Florence M. Montgomery, identified as English and dated about 1815.[19] This panel and the ten surrounding bouquets appear to have been printed specifically for use in quilts.

A third quilt (figure 4.4)—made by Alice Smith (1807–1867), who was married in 1826 at her father's home in the "Jersey" settlement north of Salisbury, to Fielding Slater, sheriff of Rowan County from 1828 until his death about 1836—features a variation of the popular eight-pointed star pattern, pieced in red, green, and yellow calico prints. Patsy and Myron Orlofsky point out that many quilts dating from the 1830s through the 1850s throughout the country are made primarily from calicos in these colors.[20] The quilts made by Rowan County women of Scotch-Irish descent represent a local interpretation of quilt-making trends popular throughout the eastern United States during the first half of the nineteenth century.

A different heritage shaped the work of German quilters. The Germans, whether in Pennsylvania or North Carolina, were exemplary farmers. Richard H. Shryock describes their approach to agriculture, saying, "Having lived on small holdings in Germany, they had learned to preserve the best soils, to tend and improve livestock, and to vary and cultivate their crops. Perhaps most important of all, they were accustomed to and expected the hardest kind of labor."[21] The success of the German farms was noted by Colonial Governor Dobbs during his 1775 tour of the western settlements: "An industrious people, they raise horses cows and hogs with a few sheep, they raise Indian Corn, wheat, barley, rye and oats make good butter and tolerable cheese, and they have gone into indigo with good success, which they sell at Charles Town. . . . They sow flax for their own use and cotton, and what Hemp they have sown is tall and good."[22] The tendency to produce all or nearly all of what they needed distinguished the German farmers from their English-speaking neighbors. Although a few Germans lived in Salisbury and were merchants and tradesmen, the majority worked as farmers and lived in the surrounding rural areas.

The persistence of the German language in these areas into the mid-nineteenth century prevented its speakers from taking an active role in political, cultural, or business activities. English was the language of commerce, and those Germans who lived in town or had frequent business transactions outside their home communities adopted the language earlier than farmers with few outside contacts. The shift to English occurred gradually, and a bilingual period characterized the first half of the nineteenth century.

To a large extent, the Germans retained their cultural heritage as a deliberate choice. They continued to obtain pastors, teachers, and books from Germany.[23] Religion played a vital role in maintaining the separateness of German communities. Churches of the two characteristic denominations, the German Reformed (now United Church of Christ) and Lutheran, were central to the lives of rural German families. One minister strongly admonished his congregation not to mix German blood with English,[24] a term that included the Scotch-Irish as speakers of the English language. Such extremist views contributed less to the small number of intermarriages than such barriers as language, religion, and proximity. By the end of the nineteenth century, the German language had virtually disappeared, intermarriage was no longer an issue, and German communities had become distinguishable only by church affiliations and by the preponderance of German surnames.

Whereas the quilts made in the Scotch-Irish settlements of Rowan reflect the use of printed fabrics imported from Europe or northern states, those made in nearby German communities contain primarily solid-color fabrics, whether purchased as such or dyed at home with purchased dyes. Two quilts entirely from solid colors were made about 1860 in the Ludwig family, possibly by Julia A. Ludwig (1847–1929), or by an older woman in her family (Julia A. Ludwig married William B. Klutts, and both were members of Union Lutheran Church; their families owned land in the Dutch Second Creek area of southeastern Rowan County). The "Princess Feather" (figure 4.5) was a popular appliqué pattern during the early nineteenth century, and this example displays the usual arrangement of four large star-and-plume motifs in the four quarters of the top. The maker resolved the lack of a central focus inherent in this arrangement by placing an additional star figure in the center, and she filled in empty spaces with additional bird-shaped figures formed from the same diamond elements. The red and green dyes were not of high quality and have faded to dull shades of red-brown and blue-green. The second quilt (figure 4.6) is also of red and green fabric. Here the better-quality "turkey red" dye, made from madder, is still bright, but the unstable green has faded to a dull khaki. The overall design is a variation of the "Rob Peter to Pay Paul" pattern family, called "Hearts and Gizzards."

Another quilt from Dutch Second Creek is an appliqué variation of a tulip pattern (figure 4.2), made according to family tradition by

Figure 4.5. Appliqué quilt, "Princess Feather," German, made in the Ludwig family, ca. 1850.

Annie Lingle (1831–1907), perhaps around the time of her marriage to John A. Trexler in 1852. The Trexlers lived in Providence township in southeastern Rowan County and attended St. Peter's Lutheran Church. This design is related to other stylized floral patterns but may represent an individual or local interpretation. The flowers were cut from red, green, and orange solid fabric. Though the red and green have faded to shades of brown, the orange, derived from antimony, survives. In an unusual reversal, the maker selected solid fabric for her flowers and a print for the background. Although she had an abundance of the black-and-white figured dress goods, she obviously made a deliberate choice

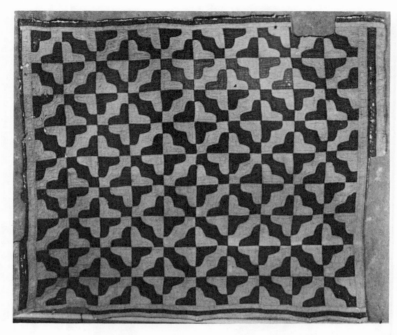

Figure 4.6. Pieced quilt, "Heart and Gizzards," German, made in the Ludwig family, ca. 1850.

to highlight the solid colors and relegate the more expensive print to the background.

Though quilts made in Scotch-Irish communities reflect a very widespread quilt-making tradition, those made in the German communities represent a more conservative one. Even in an era when fabrics were readily available in great abundance and variety, well-to-do German quilt makers continued to make quilts using solid colors and plain fabrics reminiscent of home-dyed and home-woven fabrics. Practicality had influenced the aesthetic choices of these quilt makers, and the community tradition seems to have been stronger than the appeal of newer styles and colors.

Mid-nineteenth-century events, of both local and national significance, had a profound effect upon the economy of Rowan County and upon its quilt-making traditions. The completion in 1856 of the long-awaited railroad link connecting Salisbury to Charlotte and Raleigh, thence to Charleston and Richmond, facilitated the exchange of local products for imported goods. A few years later, the Civil War disrupted the economic and social development of the area and inflated the prices of yarn and cloth.[25] Additionally, two products of industrialization within the textile industry had a dramatic and irrevocable impact upon quilt making. The sewing machine, patented in 1846 and mass marketed beginning in 1856, drastically changed both commercial and home sewing.[26] The development of synthetic aniline dyes, also beginning in 1856, provided a different range of colors available to fabric printers and dyers.[27]

All of the quilts selected for this study date from the period before the influence of these important events. They were made from fabrics produced locally or brought in by wagon, they are entirely hand sewn, and the colors in them come from vegetable and mineral dyes, such as indigo, madder, and antimony. This period also corresponds to the era before the general assimilation of the German and Scotch-Irish communities.

The two quilts with which I began my investigation reflect two quilt-making traditions that existed side by side in Rowan County. The framed-center quilt owned by the Rowan Museum represents the Scotch-Irish tradition, and the tulip quilt made by Annie Lingle Trexler is characteristic of quilts made in the German community.

The dichotomy expressed in these two groups of quilts is also evident in other quilts of the period and extends to a lesser degree to those made in the area later in the century. Within each group there appears to be a relationship between the general approach to agriculture and economics and the aesthetics of quilt makers. Heavy reliance upon home-dyed fabrics made on their self-sufficient homesteads in the early days led the Germans to a preference for solid colors and plain fabrics, even later when prints were available and affordable. Quilts from Scotch-Irish communities reflect the aspirations of English-speaking backcountry dwellers to coastal culture as soon as they could afford the accoutrements. If a small sample of quilts such as this from one area yields the discovery of two parallel and recognizable trends, the implication is clear: careful study will uncover further culturally significant variations in regional American quilt design.

5. The Development of the Bright-Leaf Tobacco Auctioneer's Chant

Bill Mansfield

The chant of the tobacco auctioneer is the best-known folk expression of the tobacco industry. It has been used as a gimmick to sell cigarettes for the American Tobacco Company; it has found its way into country-and-western music; and the R. J. Reynolds Tobacco Company has even sponsored a National Tobacco Auctioneering Championship. Although it has been exploited, however, auction chanting has not suffered the fate of folk crafts found in the artificial context of folklife museums or handicraft guilds, which often preserve a traditional skill, but in such an insulated environment that the development or evolution of the skill is arrested. In such an environment, likely as not, those who maintain the skill are people far removed from the culture that generated it. Taken out of the course of everyday life, the skill retains little significance except as a relic of the past. Auctioneering, by contrast, is a folk craft still thriving in the mainstream of society.

There is no doubt that tobacco auctioneering is a traditional skill. Like story telling, folk singing, making home remedies, or learning any craft by example or imitation, auctioneering is learned outside the bounds of school or instruction manual.[1] Auction schools do exist around the country, but these institutions train students to get licenses to sell real estate, equipment, livestock, and other merchandise that requires certification. Since tobacco auctioneers need no certification, tobacco auctioneering has retained its oral tradition. Auctioneering schools have not even had courses in tobacco auctioneering until recently. In 1976 the Mendenhall School of Auctioneering, in High Point, North Carolina, began offering a course in tobacco auctioneering, but this class has had little impact on the traditional transmission of tobacco auctioneering skills. Indeed, the instructor for this class, a traditionally

Figure 5.1. Tobacco auction in Durham, N.C., 1939 (Howard W. Odum Sub-Regional Photographic Study, courtesy of the Southern Historical Collection, University of North Carolina at Chapel Hill).

"trained" auctioneer himself, feels that the old-fashioned method of learning is superior to classroom instruction.

All of the auctioneers interviewed for this project learned tobacco auctioneering from their families and communities, as did others about whom articles have been written.[2] Stewart Cutts, an auctioneer from Oxford, North Carolina, learned from his uncle and father, who were auctioneers. Cutts has passed the techniques along to his son Michael. Louis Love, of Danville, Virginia, learned the chant while working as a clerk in a tobacco warehouse. Herman Crawford was exposed to the auctioneer's chant while attending tobacco sales with his father, who was a buyer. Leon Tarter, an auctioneer from Bowling Green, Kentucky, also attended tobacco auctions with his father, who was a tobacco farmer.[3]

These men all learned by imitation and tell similar stories about mastering their art. Joe Currin of Angier, North Carolina, tells how his uncle learned to auction tobacco: "He'd go with Granddaddy to market to sell his tobacco. Well, he got to mocking somebody [an auctioneer] and he just practiced the chant. . . . He'd be out working and anything that came by, he would sell it. And those working with him would do the bidding. If a train come by, he'd sell it. If a crow flew over, he'd sell that too." Many aspiring auctioneers also practice the chants incessantly. Leon Tarter says, "Some people practice learning how to sing to pass the time. Well, I'd auction to pass the time."[4] Dave Mitchell, owner of Mitchell Warehouse, in Oxford, North Carolina, adds that: "What most of them would do was go out and . . . they'd sell trees up and down the road or barns or houses or something. And, you know, they'd practice and practice and then the warehouse man would let a young auctioneer come in and sell some. You know, where he didn't feel like it was hurting the customers. . . . And there always was a gentlemanly code, to let a young auctioneer sell some tobacco and the buyers would help him the very best they could, to get him started. You know, 'cause there was never any formal school for auctioneering." Once he had mastered the chant the young auctioneer would go from warehouse to warehouse auditioning. If he showed any promise and there was an opening, he filled the vacancy.

Like the method by which an auctioneer acquires his skill, the way in which he maintains it is traditional. Just as the traditional basket maker uses his knowledge of materials and construction techniques to provide his community with containers of various kinds, so the tobacco auctioneer uses his skill (the ability to cry the bid, as well as his knowledge of tobacco) to serve his community. He sells tobacco for the farmers and warehousemen to the company buyers, serving the community from which he came. It is no coincidence that all the auctioneers interviewed for this project are descended from tobacco farmers, buyers, warehousemen, or auctioneers. As Louis Love observes, tobacco auctioneering is a "family business."

This tie to the founding community is crucial, for a tradition has little significance outside of its proper context. A young urbanite can learn to quilt from a folk master in the traditional manner of imitation, but she can hardly be considered "folk" if she takes this skill back to the city and makes quilts for a craft shop. Tobacco auctioneering remains a folk craft both in the way it is maintained and in the way it serves the "folk." Tobacco auctioneering is a living folk art, not an anachronism.

The world of contemporary auctioneering shows great variety. Auctions differ a great deal in tone, from the sedate and genteel art auction to the rough-and-tumble livestock auction. Auctions also vary structurally. In one form of auction, "candle auctions," a candle is used to time the bidding; when the candle burns past a certain point the biddings close.[5] Another form, the "Dutch auction," is based on descending bids. The Dutch system opens with a high price and descends until someone bids. The English system, the most common type of auction, is the opposite of the Dutch system. With the English system, the bidding rises from a low opening price to a high closing bid.[6] The tobacco auction is based on the English system.

The tobacco auction and the auctioneers' chants are distinctive in several ways from other types of auctions. The most striking difference is the incredible speed at which tobacco auctions are conducted. The present rate is 400 to 600 sales per hour. The average auctioneer "knocks out" a pile of tobacco every six to ten seconds. The livestock auctioneer, the next fastest type of auctioneer, averages only fifty sales per hour.[7]

The high rate of sales in the tobacco auction is facilitated by the way sales are conducted. The auctioneer works in a team with two other men, the warehouse operator, or starter, and the ticket marker. The piles of tobacco are arranged in rows on the warehouse floor. When the sale begins, the warehouse operator, auctioneer, and ticket marker assemble on one side of the piles of tobacco, the buyers on the other side of the row. The warehouse operator begins each sale by calling out a starting price for each pile of tobacco. The auctioneer then cries the bid to the buyers. As each pile is sold, the ticket marker records the purchaser's name and purchase price on a tag, which is placed on the pile of tobacco. The sale is over in a matter of seconds, and the procession moves on to the next pile of tobacco.[8] The warehouse operator speeds the sale by providing the opening price. According to Louis Love, this spares the auctioneer from having to "beg for a bid." The skill of the buyers also quickens the pace. These men are professionals who are trained to understand the seemingly unintelligible chant of the auctioneer. Finally, the government-support price expedites the sale. If no buyer makes a bid for the pile of tobacco, the auctioneer sells it to the government-sponsored cooperative for a minimum guaranteed price. This eliminates a need for descending bidding, as in the Dutch-auction style.

The main difference between a tobacco auctioneer's chant and other auction chants is its speed. The chant of the tobacco auctioneer is geared to the fast pace of the market in which he sells. The singing chant enables the auctioneer to speak rapidly and with enough volume for extended periods of time without tiring his voice. Some auctioneers alter the pronunciation of words to permit rapid enunciation: one becomes "mun," two becomes "doo," three becomes "ree," and so on. Auctioneers may also repeat the last number of the bid. For example, the auctioneer will cry: "Fifty-three, three! Fifty-four, four, four!" and so on. Because of its great speed, the tobacco auctioneer's chant includes less "filler" than the chants of other auctioneers. Auctioneers use filler words or phrases to cover the gaps between bids and maintain the rhythm of the chant. There are two types of filler: words or phrases designed to advance the bid; words or phrases that are nothing more than noisemakers to keep the rhythm going.[9]

Auctioneers in nearly all markets cry the bid in a chanting voice. The chanting gives the auction a rhythm that enables the buyers to intelligently advance the bid. The chanting also causes the sales to build up an excitement or momentum that encourages competition and results in a higher selling price, and holds the attention of the buyers. But no auctioneer chants with the speed of the tobacco auctioneer. H. L. "Speed" Riggs, an auctioneer from Goldsboro, North Carolina, normally chants 460 words per minute. An informal conversation progresses at a rate of 70 to 90 words per minute. Speaking fast enough to accommodate a tobacco sale requires a specialist.[10]

The fast-paced, incomprehensible, musical chant of the tobacco auctioneer is easily distinguishable from other styles of auctioneering. However, tobacco auctioneering has not always been so distinctive. The development of the unique tobacco-auctioneering style is tied to the development of the loose-leaf tobacco market.

From the seventeenth to the eighteenth centuries, Virginia was the leading tobacco market, and all subsequent marketing systems came from that state. Early tobacco marketing systems reflected the aristocratic world of the tobacco planter. Sales took place in tobacco-inspection warehouses established by the Virginia state government. Samples of tobacco were removed from the hogsheads and assigned a number. The auctioneer, sitting at one end of a long table, would read the number of the sample and pass it to buyers lining each side of the table. The buyers would examine the leaf and make their bids.[11] The men selling their tobacco were planters, the backbone of the aristocracy. The buyers were gentlemen of great responsibility and wealth. The auctioneers were also tobacco inspectors and appointed by the governor of Virginia; no doubt they maintained a proper decorum. Though detailed accounts of these sales have not been found, it seems safe to speculate that these auctions were sedate affairs, a gentlemen's game.

This system of sales survived until 1891, when it was replaced by the "Danville system," one that had been developing for thirty years and proved more suited to "common" farmers. Because of its location, Danville, Virginia, was the leading tobacco market in the nation. The city was in the heart of the bright-leaf tobacco region and had easy access to the outside world by rail and water. There were already several plug-tobacco manufacturing firms in the town, and by 1860 loose-leaf tobacco warehousing began.

Rather than packing their tobacco in hogsheads (which was expensive and required a large enough crop to fill a hogshead), the farmers had previously loaded their tobacco in their wagons, driven into town, and sold to company buyers, who flocked around the wagons and made offers for the tobacco. This system was unsatisfactory for a number of reasons. With buyers competing among themselves and arguing with the farmers, the sales consumed a considerable amount of time. Conducted in the streets, the sales were hindered by inclement weather.[12] By 1860 Thomas D. Neal, seeking to remedy this situation, had opened Neal's Warehouse. His warehouse offered a place where farmers and buyers could convene at regular times and be protected from the elements. As an added advantage, the tobacco was graded and weighed by an impartial third party, the warehouse operator, ensuring a fair deal to both farmer and buyer.[13]

Neal's warehouse operation closed during the Civil War but reopened after the end of hostilities and thrived in the tobacco boom that followed the war. Neal's operation soon had several imitators, and the competition to attract the farmer's business became fearsome. Driving past a warehouse, a tobacco farmer would be "pelted by shouts from the door men urging him to drive in."[14] By 1870 there were six warehouses in Danville alone. These establishments competed among themselves, with the old-style market in Lynchburg, and with warehouse markets as far away as Henderson and Reidsville, North Carolina.[15]

Warehouse operators developed a number of tactics to attract the farmer. Along with promising "top-dollar" prices, they advertised "comfortable accommodations for the farmer and his team" (in the days of mules and wagons, a trip to market was an overnight journey).[16] When the federal government imposed a tax on tobacco, one warehouse operator offered to provide the farmer with a record of the sales for tax purposes. One operator tried to improve business by sending his patrons to Grover Cleveland's inauguration.[17] It was in this atmosphere of competition that a new distinctive style of auctioneering began.

By all accounts the man who established the distinctive tobacco auctioneering style that persists today was Chiswell Dabney Langhorne. He began auctioneering in Danville in 1873. His style of crying a bid electrified the town. Large crowds gathered at the warehouse for the sheer entertainment of the auction. Langhorne's auctioneering not only drew large crowds and kept the buyers on the alert, it also brought higher prices.[18] The effect of Langhorne's auctioneering style was not lost on the warehouse operators. A spectacular auctioneer attracted the farmer as easily as "comfortable accommodations" for man and beast and cost less than paying for an excursion to Washington, D.C. Warehouse operators began to use auctioneers as drawing cards.

C. D. Langhorne's "gobble-gobble" auctioneering set the style for tobacco auctioneers. Some question whether it can be established that he originated the tobacco auctioneer's chant, but history has yet to contradict this assertion. Descriptions of auctions prior to Langhorne's appearance make no mention of the musical incomprehensibility that marks the tobacco auctioneer's chant today.[19] An account of a livestock auction, written shortly after Langhorne's debut, fails to mention any peculiarities. However, all reports on tobacco auctions printed after 1879 make special mention of the unique style of auctioneering tobacco. This evidence points to the tobacco-auctioneering style as having originated with Langhorne.[20]

Langhorne's auction style was carried to other tobacco markets. After Garland E. Webb learned his chant from Langhorne, he established Farmers' Warehouse in Durham and then, in 1886, moved to Winston and set the pattern for selling tobacco in that area. Webb also helped start several auction houses in the coastal plains area of North Carolina.[21] John C. Neal, another Danville auctioneer influenced by Langhorne, also spread the Langhorne style of auctioneering. "So great is his reputation in his line [auctioneering], that several North Carolina towns have procured his services at the opening of their warehouses to the public."[22]

As the demand increased, tobacco was cultivated in other areas of the country. The Danville system of auction sales followed the expansion of the tobacco industry, and the unique, lively auctioneering style that began in Danville took hold in these new areas. Tobacco is currently sold by auction in Maryland, Florida, Georgia, South Carolina, North Carolina, Virginia, Tennessee, Kentucky, West Virginia, Ohio, Missouri, Indiana, and Zimbabwe.[23] The influence of Danville and the surrounding bright-leaf tobacco region is felt even in these outlying areas. Because the tobacco-marketing seasons are structured in such a fashion that it is possible for auctioneers to travel from market to market, men from the bright-leaf area of Virginia and North Carolina constitute the majority of the tobacco auctioneers.

The auctioneer's spectacular chant has, however, changed and simplified over the years since Langhorne developed it in the latter half of the nineteenth century. One influence was a contraction in the sales time allotted to the various tobacco markets, which occurred around the time of the First World War. For example, the markets in the bright-leaf area of North Carolina and Virginia once held auctions from October to mid-March for eight hours a day, five days a week. The selling season is now from mid-July to November. Furthermore, as the season contracted, the volume of tobacco increased. The auctioneer has to speed up to keep pace. The selling rate jumped from seventy-five piles an hour in 1873, to 400 piles an hour in 1913.[24]

A change in bidding has also affected the auctioneer's chant. The old style of bidding was known as "bidding on the quarters." Until the mid-fifties, bids ascended in quarter-cent gradations from one to fifteen

cents, half-cent gradations to twenty-five cents, and one-cent gradations after twenty-five cents. This system is complex, and it takes time.
As Louis Love says, "It takes a lot of bidding to move the price from
seven cents to twenty-five cents bidding with quarters." According to
Joe Currin, a retired tobacco buyer, the auctioneer would use filler
phrases during this slow bidding process: "If they'd say something
funny it would make things a little lighter and keep the buyers' attention. [chants] 'See that girl coming down the row, with her stockings
hung so low.' Something like that."

Today the bids ascend in one-cent intervals, a practice that results
in faster selling and reduces the need for filler phrases. The government-support price for tobacco, introduced in 1939, ensures a minimum price for tobacco. The support price, according to Louis Love,
has caused the auctioneer to further streamline his chant. "You didn't
have to beg someone to buy the tobacco." If there are no offers above
the support price, the tobacco is sold to the government-sponsored
cooperative. With more tobacco to sell and less time to sell it in, the
tobacco auctioneer no longer has the time or need to fill out his crying the bid with clever rhymes.

Government regulation has also had other effects on the auctioneer's style. Attracting the farmer was once a factor that influenced
the development of the spectacular, ornamented style of auctioneering.
An auctioneer who "put on a good show" would draw trade from the
farmers. However, since 1960 government regulations have required
the farmer to designate which warehouse will sell his tobacco months
before it is ready for market. Thus the showmanship of the auctioneer
no longer influences the farmer; it only slows the sale.

An expanding market, changes in the bidding system, and government regulations have all had their effects on the tobacco auctioneer's
chant. But it is not so easy to show how a change in the "atmosphere"
of the tobacco auction has affected the chant of the auctioneer. In
earlier days the sale of tobacco was a dramatic time in the agricultural
year. The price the farmer received for his tobacco would determine
whether the year would be one of plenty or deprivation, so the sales
created a great deal of suspense. The sale of tobacco also represented
a break in the monotony of farm life. In her monumental work *The
Bright-Leaf Tobacco Industry*, Nannie May Tilley says of market
season:

No episode of the year furnished such a pleasant time for the farmer. . . . It was one period during the year, outwardly at least, when the farmer became an important personage. . . . Nor were farmers, warehousemen, and buyers alone in their enthusiasm [for the market season]. People of other pursuits were also affected by the increased tempo accompanying the rapid release of cash. . . . Merchants decorated their windows with gaudy goods and hearty welcomes for the farmer. The entire town became exhilarated.[25]

In major tobacco-producing areas, the opening of the market season was marked by parades, speeches, square dances, and all kinds of celebrations.

At the center of all this excitement was the auctioneer, crying the bid, commanding the same attention and respect as the ringmaster at the circus. Most auctioneers played this role to the hilt. An account of auctioneer A. J. Ellington's arrival at a warehouse early in this century reveals how auctioneers perceived themselves: "Captain Ellington dressed for the sale. . . . He wore a hard plug hat, of the type worn by Pierpont Morgan. He wore gloves, a cutaway coat and striped trousers. There was usually a flower in his buttonhole and the morning newspaper was rolled up into an impromptu baton for the sale. Captain Ellington formally shook hands with all around him, gave a rakish tilt to his hat and embarked upon [the sale]."[26] While not all auctioneers were as pretentious as Captain Ellington, many of them had nicknames to denote their special status. In the not-too-distant past, men like "Tom Cat" Jones, Cary York ("The Mockingbird of Pine Tops"), or "Genial Gene" Simmons lent a festive air to the auctions.

But now that the carnival atmosphere has for the most part left the present-day tobacco auction, the tobacco auctioneer has simplified his chant. Improved agricultural techniques, government regulation of tobacco production, support programs, and sophisticated farm-market reporting networks make it possible for the farmer to know how much money his tobacco will bring before he ever goes to market. His prior knowledge eliminates much of the suspense and drama of the auction. Also, many farmers no longer come to the auctions. Warehouse owner Dave Mitchell has said: "The farmer just hasn't got time for it anymore. It used to be that selling tobacco was a trip to town. But now they load their tobacco into their truck, get on the highway, drive to the warehouse, and they're back home in fifteen minutes. It's just like everything else today, rush, rush, rush." The decline in auction attendance means the auctioneer has no audience to play to; he is less inclined to "put on a show." Auctioneering only for a small crowd of buyers, his voice need not carry as far, so the auctioneer's chant also has a less musical tone.

The tobacco-allotment program, which controls the amount of tobacco grown, has also undercut the role of the auctioneer. Dave Mitchell succinctly explains the situation: "Now there's only so much tobacco, and no one buyer wants all of it, but everyone wants some of it. So it's up to the auctioneer to see that the buyers get the tobacco they want. A good auctioneer knows how much tobacco a man wants and makes sure he gets it. A real good auctioneer keeps the buyer satisfied." This represents a remarkable change. The auctioneer's primary concern is no longer getting the best price for the farmer and attracting his business but making sure that the buyer fills his daily quota. A Danville auctioneer claims that the auctioneer is no longer an auctioneer but a "rationer." "In my day, I sold it to whoever bid the most. Didn't matter who put his hand up. It's not like that any more."

Since the late nineteenth century the tobacco auctioneer has held a highly visible and important position in the warehouse system. No doubt the prominence of his role encouraged the development of his flamboyant auctioneering style. As the significance and visibility of the auctioneer has declined, so has the ornamental style of the chant. With no audience to perform for and no substantive reason to ornament his chant, the auctioneer cries the bid faster and in a plain, unadorned fashion. No longer are clever rhymes inserted between the bids to keep the buyers bidding and amuse the farmers.

Only occasionally can the old-style auctioneering be heard. According to Dave Mitchell, auctioneers will often "cut up" on the last sale of the day. In this brief moment time is turned back to the "good old days" when the "clarion tones of the auctioneer is [sic] heard throughout the land."[27]

Although still functional, tobacco auctioneering seems in danger of losing its traditional status. Present market conditions are such that warehouse managers cannot afford the time to "break in" novice auctioneers. Unable to gain experience on the job, would-be auctioneers may well turn to the auction schools. As agriculture becomes agribusiness, the population of the tobacco community becomes smaller. As the population of warehousemen and tobacco farmers grows smaller, the number of potential auctioneers also declines.

But the greatest threat to the traditional auctioneer lies in the possible elimination of the auction system. In order to cut the cost of production, tobacco companies have begun dealing directly with the farmer, a process that eliminates the need for the warehouse and the auctioneer. One auctioneer now predicts the end of tobacco auctioneering altogether: "This auctioneering is about played out anyhow. Why, it won't even be around in another ten years."

Of Individuals

6. The Solitary Memory:
A Greek-American's Recollections of the Folk Play *Panáretos*
John A. Porter

Collectors of ethnic folklore in this country base their work on the premise that ethnic groups maintain and transmit tradition to the extent that they remain coherent, cohesive communities. The religious or nationality groups that manage to remain coherent and cohesive are generally those that preserve and nurture their native folk traditions most successfully. That is one of the reasons why folklorists find fieldwork among them so rewarding. As a student in the Curriculum in Folklore at the University of North Carolina, I collected among Greek Americans in the Chapel Hill-Durham area, concentrating on ethnic jokes told by first-, second-, and third-generation men (mostly restaurant workers) and miracle tales of saints and icons narrated by first- and second-generation women.[1] In both cases I was impressed by the vitality and flexibility of oral tradition, which I attributed to the intercourse of ethnic Greeks within the tightly knit Greek-American community.

In 1977, however, I made the acquaintance of an old Greek man who had emigrated to the United States in 1900 and who, despite the fact that he has lived in relative isolation from other Greeks and Greek-Americans, has nurtured a seemingly inexhaustible fund of song and poetry from his native land. In his case, it appears that the lack of community has played a positive role in the maintenance of certain moribund traditions that otherwise would long ago have been lost. Chief among these is a village play, *Panáretos,* whose familiar words and the memories they evoke comforted him and provided for him the connection to his homeland that he needed, particularly as a young man, in order to survive in a foreign and often hostile environment.

Harry Chepriss was born Aristotélis Antoníou Tsiapoúris on 15 August 1886 in Karpeníssi, Greece, a provincial town nestled in the mountains some three hundred kilometers northwest of Athens. The death of his father (a muleteer drowned while crossing a swollen river) coupled with the region's chronically depressed economy mired the family in poverty when Aristotélis was still a small child. "We didn't have nothing," Harry recalls. "I walked barefooted, by golly, till I was nearly twelve years old. My feet [were] like leather. And we eat nothing but cornbread. If we get light bread, we thought we eating chicken!"[2] Many of the anecdotes that he tells about that time are of stealing food. Others illustrate the mischief that he was fond of causing. More than once he was helped out of a tight place by his godfather, who happened to be the mayor of Karpeníssi.

His mother raised her four children—two girls and two boys, of whom Aristotélis was the youngest—alone. The older brother left home at an early age to join the guerrillas fighting the Turkish occupation forces in Kardítsa, to the north. (Although Greece had won its independence from the Ottoman Empire in 1826, the Turks remained in Thessaly, Epirus, Macedonia, and Thrace until 1913.) When Aristotélis was ten years old, his mother sent him to stay with his brother and learn the shoe-making trade. In 1897 he returned to Karpeníssi and went to work for a shoemaker to help support the family. "My mother had hard time," he says. "She work out in the fields with the oxen, hoeing corn, and the corn over there never get big. That land is poor. . . . Natural, you look for future of your life."

At his mother's urging, he wrote a letter to a distant cousin in the United States. "I was twelve or thirteen when I first thought of coming to this country," Harry explains. "It was hard times and we didn't have nothing to eat. My mother, she wants me to come here to send her some money." His cousin obliged by providing passage from Piraeus to New York, and a train ticket from there to California, where he was working in the mines. But in those days an immigrant also had to have twenty-five dollars to declare at Ellis Island. To raise that money, his mother mortgaged the house and livestock for one year. It was understood that Aristotélis would send back enough of his wages to pay off the mortgage.

The boy was only fourteen years old when he left home in the summer of 1900, a frightened adolescent who until then had slept in the same bed with his mother. "I was crying when I left," he admits, "but I tough it out." The crossing took thirty-six days, and the train

Figure 6.1. Harry Chepriss, Asheville, N.C. (photo by John A. Porter).

ride across the continent another six, and when Aristotélis finally reached the destination written on his ticket he learned that his cousin had left to go back East. After several months of working in the coal mine and shining shoes to make the expected remittances home, he followed the trail to Bowling Green, Kentucky, and then to Asheville, North Carolina, finding each time that his cousin had moved on.

In Asheville, surrounded by mountains that reminded him of home and realizing that winter was setting in, he decided to stay. The only other Greek in town at the turn of the century was a man named Trákas, who owned a wholesale produce house, and Aristotélis (having been given his new name, "Harry," by a Greek restaurateur in Bowling Green) sold bananas for him in the street. The local people had never seen bananas before. They called them " 'naners." "Hey, foreigner!" they would shout at the young Greek boy. "How much them 'naners?" "Nickel a dozen!" Harry learned to reply, in a heavy accent that he has never lost. Some of them tried to eat the yellow fruit skin and all.

His next job was selling weiners on the sidewalk. When someone else undercut his prices, putting him out of business, he looked for employment, but all of the small town's merchants "had their own people working for them." He was forced to take handouts or steal food, and to live through a cold winter in the woods, where he slept bundled in newspapers on a bed of pine needles. "Them days was hard times," he remembers. "I try to get job everywhere, [but] they don't give you no job, especially if you can't speak the language. . . . They tell me, 'Get out of here, foreigner!' "

Harry went to Greenville, South Carolina, several times to work in cafés owned by Greeks, but he didn't stay. In 1908 he and a compatriot pooled their modest savings and made a down payment on a café in Waynesville, North Carolina. After only a few months two drunken, gun-wielding lumberjacks frightened them back to Asheville, where Harry opened a small barbecue place. Later he sold that and bought a café, then went into the furniture business, had a junkyard, and ran a poolroom. All the while he sent money regularly to his mother and his sisters, for whom he provided a dowry. When the banks closed in 1929 he claims that he lost eighty thousand dollars. After that he became a jackleg plumber, did yardwork for ten cents an hour during the war, and sold real estate on commission. In 1960 he began collecting social security payments.

The early years made the most lasting impression. "You know, the years passing by and I forget," he says. "Except I remember the times when I can't get no job and can't get nothing to eat. That's what make it hard." Life in the United States proved no easier than he remembered it in Greece, and the separation from his family seemed practically unbearable. After 1910, when other Greeks from Karpeníssi and Sparta began to arrive, a small community formed, and in 1912 a Greek Orthodox church was established in Asheville. Harry was an active member until 1922, when he married outside of his religion, taking for his wife a fourteen-year-old local Baptist girl of German and Irish ancestry named Daisy. Parish bylaws required that members be married in the Orthodox Church, and denied the sacraments to those who chose not to comply. Angered, Harry severed his connections with the church. At about the same time a local chapter of the American-Hellenic Educational Progressive Association (AHEPA) was organized. Harry still believes that he was not invited to its social functions because his café served blacks as well as whites. His exclusion further alienated him from the growing Greek community.

He worked, meanwhile, in isolation from all but his occasional Greek business partners. He and Daisy lived in a remote area outside of town (now part of West Asheville), and visited mostly with her family. Greek friends from Greenville and recent immigrants from the "old country" alike made themselves unwelcome in Harry's house by their repeated abuses of hospitality. As for the post–World War II wave of immigrants, they did not—in Harry's view—appreciate the hardships and sacrifices of their predecessors. He resented the apparent ease with which they established themselves in business—usually with the help of the older generation—and bridled particularly when on his visits to their restaurants they would not even offer him a glass of water. (When Harry owned a café, he claims that he always fed his countrymen free of charge.) But even more than the lack of traditional hospitality, it was Harry's belief that "they thinking I'm hungry" (i.e., looking for a handout) that stopped him from going back. On his weekly trips to town, he now stops only at the businesses of several non-Greek friends and at eateries run by two Greek "old-timers."

Although Harry Chepriss has had closer ties—first out of necessity and later out of preference—with non-Greeks in Asheville than with his own compatriots, his long sojourn in this country has not by any means erased his Greekness. He still speaks his mother tongue with greater ease than he does English, and he cherishes the memory of his homeland (to which he has been able to return but twice for brief visits, in 1912 and 1927). After better than eighty years in self-imposed exile, Harry might be expected long since to have forgotten the lore and traditions that he learned as a boy. The disjunction between life in nineteenth-century rural Greece and twentieth-century existence in urban, industrialized American society would seem so great as to render the former anachronistic and irrelevant. But that is most emphatically not the case for Harry. He has lovingly nurtured his identity as Aristotélis Tsiapoúris, and carefully cultivated his heritage on his own in the United States, giving compelling evidence of the efficacy of even apparently outmoded traditions to render the environment of his adopted home not only tolerable, but conducive to a productive, well-adjusted life.

I met Harry in the summer of 1977, when Dr. Louis Silveri of Assumption College in Worcester, Massachusetts, and I interviewed him for the Oral History Collection of the Southern Highlands Research Center at the University of North Carolina's Asheville campus. The character of his memory was evident from the beginning of our talks. "I think I can tell you every president of the United States [since I arrived here]," Harry announced shortly after we sat down together for the first time on the front porch of his house. "The first one, he was McKinley. Then Roosevelt. . . . Then come Taft . . . and then come Wilson. [After] Wilson come Harding, and [after] Harding come Coolidge. From Coolidge come Hoover. [After] Hoover then come Roosevelt, and [after] Roosevelt come Truman. From Truman then he come. . . . What is the name? I can't call his name. . . ." He needed prompting to recall Eisenhower and his successors, but his long-term memory was clearly excellent. (Actually, Harry's short-term memory is hardly impaired, if at all. The fact that names of recent presidents do not come readily to his mind is attributable, I think, to the infrequency of his opportunities to talk politics, and his consequent loss of interest in it.)

One evening in the spring of 1978, while I was recording the songs and song fragments that Harry remembers from his boyhood in Greece, he mentioned a "performance" (*parástasis*) which he called the "performance of *Panáretos*" (πανάρετος). Without any pause or hesitation he began to recite from memory the opening lines of a play:

> Στρατεύματα καί ιτρατηγθί, είς προιοχήν ιταθείτε.
> Soldiers and generals, stand at attention.

> Ο χάρυς επληιίαίε, καί μήν παραζρομείτε.
> Charon has arrived, so make no careless move.

For the next fifteen minutes I listened as he recited, in Greek, lines from a drama staged annually in Karpeníssi at the end of the nineteenth century. (For a text in the original Greek, see note 4.) The story concerned the fate of a young general (Panáretos) who incurs the wrath of a king by falling in love with his daughter.

I subsequently recorded Harry's version of the performance of *Panáretos* on a number of different occasions stretching over a five-year period. This gave him a chance to "flesh out" the plot line, and me the opportunity to compare variants. With time, Harry approxi-

mately doubled the length of the first variant by recalling other supporting characters in the drama, speeches or fragments of speeches,
and additional lines spoken by major characters. Listening to him, I
found minimal variation in plot, attribution of lines, or line composition. Although the narrative tended to emerge piecemeal and not always in what appears to have been its original chronological sequence,
it nonetheless seems to have remained more or less intact in Harry's
memory over the better part of a century. This stability attests on the
one hand to the vitality of the poetry (and the story itself) for him,
and on the other hand to its removal from the influence of oral tradition. In its present context and under present conditions, Harry Chepriss's version of *Panáretos* is moribund; it will die with him. He has
transmitted it to no one in the community, nor will he.

According to Harry, the staging of *Panáretos* was a project undertaken by local shopkeepers in Karpeníssi, who put up the money to
cover the major expense, costumes. This seems to have been their contribution to the annual celebration called *Apókries*, or the *karniváli*,
several days of merry making in Greece prior to the beginning of Lent
on the Greek Orthodox calendar. The play itself was given on "Cheese
Sunday" (*Tiranís*), the Sunday before the first day of Lent (*Katharí
Deftéra*, or "Clean Monday"), because the Sabbath "was the only time
people [were] not out working." After morning church services, spectators flocked to Karpeníssi from the surrounding villages to gather in
one of the two town squares (*plateía*), where the first performance was
given. Harry remembers that as many as five hundred people gathered
around. They sat on the ground, or in chairs, and boys climbed up into
the trees to get a better view. There was no charge for admission.

Thirty-six actors took part, all of them men.[3] Those with speaking roles, however, numbered only twelve or thirteen. The rest were
soldiers, all dressed identically: short skirts (*fustanéllas*) that resembled Scottish kilts, sandals of the type that one strapped to the calf
(*tsaroúchia*), and peaked helmets (*perikefalaíes*) "like Alexander the
Great wore." Each carried cartridge boxes (*paláskes*) on a bandolier,
a sword (*xífos* or *yatagáni*) that "shined like aluminum" in one hand,
and a spear (*kondári*) in the other. Three of the soldiers had trumpets
or bugles.

Harry recalls that when the play began the king (*o Vasiléus*), his
counselor (*o Sýmvulos*), and the queen (*e Vasílissa*) were seated in

chairs facing the audience, with the king in the middle. Off to one side stood the princess (*e Vasilopoúla*), and opposite her was Panáretos. All three seated characters were portrayed by "old men." The king was the largest and had the deepest voice. He wore a full beard, which he stroked constantly, and an "old-timer" military uniform, decorated—like the other costumes—with colorful strips and pieces of paper. His pasteboard crown lay on the ground beside him. The counselor was a kind of "vice president," who "told the king what to do and what not to do." He wore a *fustanélla* and sandals. The actor who impersonated the queen was dressed in black and adorned with jewelry, a long plaited wig, and a kerchief.

A sergeant-at-arms (*o Epilohías*) named Karembaloúkis (probably the name of the actor who played the part) formally opened the action by demanding the audience's attention, whereupon the king delivered the first speech.[4]

> My beloved people, listen and hearken well to me.
> I who speak to you am the king,
> the most high king of all the kingdoms.
> I wish to speak to you, so hearken well,
> because one greater than us all is coming from the heavens.   5
> Because I want you to know that[5]
> my old age cries out that I speak the truth,
> and that my counselor sits here to tell fairy tales.
> My beloved, at attention—
> I wish to speak to the soldiers.[6]   10
> Soldiers and generals, stand at attention.
> Charon has arrived, so make no careless move.

From behind appeared Charon (*o Háros*), conveyer of the dead, carrying a sword. Harry remembers him as a frightening figure whose countenance made the audience gasp and recoil. He wore a rubber mask (*prosopída*), which was apparently painted like a skull, and had teeth that protruded menacingly. A rope was tied about his waist, holding up "tight red trousers," and from it hung "real bones" and small bells (*kyprélia*) that jingled when he walked. His shoes were "like sandals." On his head was a red pasteboard helmet. But the most remarkable part of his costume by far was his wings. They were attached in such a way that when he moved his shoulders they swished through the air, making a whirring sound. Harry recalls that they looked like silk and that people said they had come from China. At any rate, he has variously described them as "dark white" (gray) and brown, and says that they nearly touched the ground. Charon's first speech is as follows:

> Listen to me, fearless ones, with my hard heart and
>   malicious din!
> Bones, bones, crashes of thunder!
> Today I opened the black earth and came up from Hades.   15
> If I find anyone alone I take him up by the roots.
> I, then, am the one who blackens blood,
> who takes youths by the hair, old men by their beards,
> and even the smallest children stacked on my saddle!

This speech so frightened many members of the audience—particularly children—that they began to cry. For that reason, Harry explains, a buffoon (*o Paliátsos*) was provided for comic relief. This was a young boy (Harry himself played the part for two consecutive years, 1898 and 1899) who wore shorts under a skirt made of strips "like a hula dress," high socks, and a paper cap. In his hand he carried a whisk broom, with which he dusted the ground behind Charon while uttering his single line:

> And me on top!   20

The audience laughed at this, and Charon chased him away. During the rest of the performance the buffoon sat on a small stool or went around pestering the soldiers to amuse the onlookers. Meanwhile, Charon resumed his speech.

> Tomorrow morning, as soon as I rise, and as soon as
>   day breaks,
> I shall put to death this Panáretos, this only daughter,
> this queen, and this cruel king.

With this, Charon withdrew and Panáretos approached the princess. The role of the princess was played by a young man "twenty-five to thirty years old, well built, [with] a fine face, in women's clothes." He had to be short and have a high-pitched voice. Harry does not remember the details of his costume, but he does recall that red lipstick was used for makeup. Panáretos was also a youth, but taller and more robust in appearance. The word that Harry uses again and again to describe him is "handsome" (*ómorfos*). He likens Paná-retos's costume to that of an *evzone*, a member of a select infantry corps of the Greek army, whose uniform consists of *fustanélla*, ruffled shirt with baggy sleeves, and knee-high stockings. As supreme commander of the king's army, Panáretos was distinguished from lower-ranking officers by a helmet with three pasteboard peaks. He also carried a tridentlike spear and a sword slung from his belt. Harry says that he "had a date" with the princess, which is to say that he was her suitor. He addressed her first.

> Princess, my lady, on whom the sun rises and sets,
> three daggers have pierced my heart!   25

She replied:

> Panáretos, Panáretos, how much love I have for you!
> And I trust in God that we will be wed!

After this exchange, Panáretos returned to his original place.

Another general, whom Harry refers to as "the traitor" (*o Pro-thótis*), now approached the king, who was still seated. This general was "two-faced, . . . an enemy [who] made like [Panáretos's] friend." He was in uniform, and wore a helmet with twin peaks. Harry recalls the following brief conversation between them.

> *Traitor:* My lord, something is going on between your
> daughter and General Panáretos.
> *King:* Go and find out all that you can about what is
> happening.
> *Traitor:* I am unable to go, my lord. But I can send Aspro-   30
> potamíti.[7]

Aspropotamíti was an officer whom the general—ashamed of betraying his friend—could order to do his dirty work. Nonetheless, he went first to speak to Panáretos himself.

> Panáretos, though we are friends, a massacre is going to
> happen.

According to Harry, Panáretos "understood" the meaning of this, because "he was very smart."

> Friend, friend, I am grateful for your good manners.
> But once a thing is done, it cannot be undone.
> With him to whom you do it, there can be no reconciliation.

When he heard this, the traitor departed "with his head down." Aspropotamíti then gave the soldiers the order to bind Panáretos and take him before the king.

> My soldiers, make yourselves ready all   35
> to seal off the doors of Panáretos's tent.
> Guard, hold ready the manacles and follow at our command.
> (And you, too, Sergeant Karambeloúkis.)

They approached Panáretos, who protested.

> Never will I surrender to the king!

Aspropotamíti replied:

> Panáretos, Panáretos, humble yourself, I say.   40
> Give up your sword and spear.
> The king commands it, and it must be done.
> As the proverb says, The king commands, and the dogs are
>   tied.

The unfortunate young man was persuaded. He had but one final request:

> Leave me only to kiss my beloved,
> and you can take me at last.   45

He went and kissed the princess, then spoke to his captors.

> If that is the way it must be, put on the manacles,
> and let us go before our lord.[8]

After he relinquished his weapons, the guard fastened the manacles (or "handcuffs," as Harry calls them) on his wrists and they led him to the king, whom Panáretos addressed.

I have heard your summons, your highness,
and I have come to learn, my lord, what is your command?

The king answered:

Welcome to the worthy groom, 50
for today will I consummate the unseemly wedding.

Panáretos then became indignant.

Why have you chained me and had me brought before you?
As I die, so too will you.[9]
And thus I demand my rights!

Saying this, Panáretos broke the manacles from his wrists and flung them to the ground. The king rose to his feet in a rage.

Dog! I praise God, who brought you before me! 55
I will lay my sword upon you before I lose my life!

He raised his sword and struck off his offender's helmet, symbolizing his beheading. Panáretos fell, and as he lay at the king's feet, a red substance resembling blood issued from his clothing. Harry recalls with consternation that it did not stain the costume. Meanwhile, Charon came and, spreading his wings so as to enfold the body, dragged the slain general away, leaving only his helmet behind. Upon the death and departure of Panáretos, Harry says that the three soldiers played a solemn tune like "Taps" on their horns.

The king then summoned his daughter, who appeared before him and said:

I have heard your summons, your highness,
and I have come to learn, my father, what is your command?

The king greeted her as he had earlier greeted Panáretos.

Welcome to my daughter, greatly beloved,
for today will I consummate the unseemly wedding. 60

Seeing the manacles and the helmet, the princess took a step back.

Oh! What is this I see? What manacles broken,
and whose the head here cut off and lying?

Her father explained:

> It is that of your secret lover, cruel daughter!
> Today have I cut it off with my own right hand!

She inquired further:

> And where is the rest of the dead man's body?   65

The king's reply was as follows:

> It has become food for dogs and surfeit for lions!

> The stricken girl was moved to mourn her slain lover.

> Panáretos, Panáretos, how could you allow Charon to win?
> And how with the beauty of your body reveal the unsight-
>   liness of Hades?
> And how can I live now alone in this false world?
> Have pity on this ill-fated one, and accept my body!   70

With this she drew a dagger and plunged it into her heart. Charon came immediately and dragged her away. The trumpets sounded once more. The queen, who had watched all this from her seat nearby, rose and lamented the princess's death.

> The only daughter that I have in this world
> has gone and left me.[10]
> How can I live alone now in this false world?
> Have pity on this ill-fated one, and accept my body!

She too killed herself with a dagger. Charon whisked her away, and again the trumpets sounded.

> The traitor, who felt "remorse" for his betrayal of Panáretos, stepped forward at this point and brandished his sword at the sun.

> Ach, Mother, sweet Mother, ach, Mother, dearly beloved!   75
> Why are you not here today to weep your black tears?
> Heavens so high, look down below.
> Sun, Sun, why do you not bestow your light,
> and—fine as you are—not go along your way?
> Who is it that weeps, who laments,   80

who fills the house with tears and comes not outside?
Heavens that are so high,
hurl down a lightning bolt and burn this cruel king!

At this the soldiers all turned against the king and beheaded him.
Charon came for the last time and claimed his body. All the players
joined together to dance and sing a song to a *"Kalamatianó"* tune.

Panáretos, Panáretos, how sad I am for you!
With all my heart I grieve and suffer with you!   85

There was more, Harry says, "but I don't remember it."

The fulfillment of Charon's prediction, culminating in the beheading of the king, had a profound effect on the spectators. "People
were crying," Harry recalls. "It's so pitiful. They see all that, looked
like blood, down there [on the ground]. It's sad when you hear it,
when they are men we know." But there was, according to him, a
lesson to be learned. "You see," he explains, "Panáretos, he not supposed to court the king's daughter. . . . [He] was plain." The play
demonstrated "which way the king's daughter should marry." It "gives
you an example how, in those days, before Christ, the princess had to
marry another king, a king from another place." But the princess was
"plain," too, like Panáretos, and so their relationship became, for
Harry, a kind of parable of social equality. "Like here in America," he
says. "Here you can be a millionaire and they don't care whether you
are rich or poor. Equal! Like it is now in Russia. . . . In Russia, they
say, all are the same. In Greece, you get on the train and there is first
class, second class, and third class. [That's] no good! All are plain
Sammy!" When asked if it was to point this out that the play was performed, Harry shakes his head. "The businessmen of Karpeníssi did it
to entertain the people." He guesses that "something like that . . . happened," but concludes that the performance was staged "just to have
a play."

Having completed the performance in the town square, the troupe
moved on to the homes of the wealthy,[11] and of town officials such as
the mayor, the judge, the prosecutor, and "the chief of police," performing the play in courtyards or in the street. The spectators—many
wearing masks—apparently followed from place to place, throwing
confetti, dancing, and singing as they went. They adapted lines from

the play to the music, and improvised their own. Harry has from time to time sung the following:

> Panáretos, Panáretos, how sad I am for you!
> And with all my heart I grieve and suffer with you!
> And the beauty of your body reveals the unsightliness
>   of Hades.
>
> I too want to go down to Hades, and to Paradise,
> to meet and talk with Charon, and to plead with him.
> My Charon, give to me burning arrows.

Harry recalls being particularly impressed by the actors' voices as they walked from one house to the next. Musical accompaniment was provided by gypsies with a mandolin, a flute, a violin, and a guitar, as well as what he calls a "*latérna*," or a large, heavy music box that had to be wound. The actors and musicians took no money for their work. Instead they were offered at each house a glass of wine or other refreshment. Harry remembers that toward the end of the day, after numerous performances, they were "high, but they behave nice." The final performance was given late in the evening in the other town square.

According to Greek folklorist Mihális Meraclés, *Panáretos* (or *Panáratos*) is another name for *Erofíli*, a dramatic work written at the end of the sixteenth century by Yiórgios Hortátzis, a Cretan, and published in Venice in 1637.[12] The relationship between the two is so close as to be unmistakable. In *Erofíli*, Panáretos is the name of a boy orphan who is adopted and raised by a king of Egypt, eventually becoming commander of his army. His misfortune is that he falls in love with, and secretly marries, the king's daughter, Erofíli, and for that transgression is beheaded by the king, who is in turn trampled to death by a "Chorus of Maidens."[13]

Yiórgios Hortátzis studied in Italy and introduced the theater into Crete when he returned to the island. In the opinion of Línos Polítis, professor of modern Greek literature at Oxford, the prototype for *Erofíli* was the *Orbecche* of Giambattista Giraldi, the first Italian classical tragedy of the Renaissance.[14] Hortátzis's plays—and particularly *Erofíli*—achieved widespread popularity in Crete during the author's lifetime, and along with *Erotócritos*, the long verse romance by Venétzios Cornáros, constituted the high point of the golden age of Cretan literature during the seventeenth century.[15] When the Ottoman Turks captured Crete in 1669, refugees fleeing the island carried Cretan literary tradition to the Venetian-ruled Ionian islands along the western coast of Greece.[16]

At about this time, the Italian commedia del l'arte (which, according to Polítis, was unknown in Crete) had begun to flourish in the islands, and particularly in Zákinthos, with the result that the themes of Cretan popular literature were adapted to elaborate performances with masked actors. These performances were originally given in Italian but gradually became hellenized between the seventeenth and nineteenth centuries. They took place annually during the carnival that immediately preceded Lent. The extent to which these *omilíes* (literally, "speeches"), as they came to be known, became a part of oral tradition is difficult to say. In the case of *Erofíli* (which over the course of time became known in its new form by the name of its protagonist, Panáretos), the existence of a written, published text undoubtedly militated against complete assimilation into oral tradition. But the text itself seems to have been unavailable in some places, and as a result, the spirit of Hortátzis's work was more faithfully adhered to than the letter. At any rate, the play gained wide acceptance on the mainland, to the astonishment of many commentators. Writing in the preface to his anthology entitled *Medieval and Modern Greek Poetry*, C. A. Trypánis wonders, for instance, "how this melodramatic play captivated the imagination of the Greeks, and how some of its verses have passed on to the people. It seems as though it were the glorification of faith in love that secured its popularity."[17]

Comparison of *Erofíli* and *Panáretos* demonstrates that although they tell essentially the same story, they are significantly different in particulars.[18] Likewise, examination of two versions of *Panáretos*—the one from Karpeníssi at the turn of the century and another collected in the nearby town of Amfilohía in 1957[19]—lends further credence to the view that the play was affected by oral tradition as it passed from one place to another, and from one generation to the next. At the same time, though *Panáretos* unquestionably freed itself of fidelity to and reliance on the written text of *Erofíli*, it seems never fully to have entered oral tradition. The informant who narrated the Amfilohía version, for instance, confirmed that the actors "used to read it from a book" (presumably in rehearsal), and Yiórgios Zóras speculates that "this is apparently a reference to the circulation of a popular edition of 'Erofíli' " as late as the first half of this century.[20]

Harry Chepriss recalls a "book" used by the performers during their rehearsals, which started two or three months prior to the presentation of the play and were held in a "big hall" in Karpeníssi. If the actors indeed memorized their lines from a written text, the results surely preclude the possibility that it was a text of Hortátzis's *Erofíli*. Perhaps *Panáretos* itself was written down. If not (and I have found no reference to any such text, published or unpublished), it seems likely that the "book" at issue was in fact *Erofíli*, and that the actors merely consulted it from time to time to "correct" or "refresh" their memories.

Harry's earliest recollection of the play dates from 1896, when he was ten years old. "My mother would ask me, 'Where are you going, my child?' 'I'm going to the market, Mama, to see *Panáretos*.' " Other than *Karagiózi*, a shadow play of Turkish origin that toured the Greek countryside, there was no theater in Karpeníssi at the turn of the century. In 1898 Harry was chosen to play the part of the buffoon. The reasons for his selection over the other children are not entirely clear in his own mind. He was, by his own admission, a poor student and something of a troublemaker in the classroom. "In school I was nocount," he says. "I don't know why I couldn't learn arithmetic. I was thick headed. Now stories, I remember them. But the teachers then were hard-boiled eggs, and they would beat me with a ruler. They took me out and put me with some other boys to sing." He dropped out of school after the third grade and was working for a shoemaker and a plumber. Meanwhile, his mischievous antics endeared him to most of the rest of the community, including the play's sponsors. "They liked me because I was funny," Harry recalls. "I was full of life. . . . The doctors, the lawyers, all them mens liked me, because I answered right away. . . . They took someone who had the guts, not just anyone."

Because his part was so small, Harry did not have to rehearse with the others. Although he knew about the "book," he never saw it himself. Consequently, it appears that he learned the play on the day of its performance by listening to the other actors. This becomes more credible if one remembers that the play was only twenty to thirty minutes long, and that it was given as many as fifteen times during that Sunday afternoon. If we grant the likelihood that Harry was familiar with the play as a small child and that he participated in or at least witnessed several rehearsals in the two years that he was a participant, and if we consider that he may have heard the performance as many as thirty times in those two years, then we can perhaps understand how its lines would have been so firmly and deeply etched in his impressionable young mind, to be recalled often when he suddenly found himself far from home, and all alone. "If you see it one time—oh, golly!" Harry says. "That's why people come over there again and again and they remember. That's why I remember."

But surely more is required than a good memory and a memorable line for so much to be remembered so clearly and so well. Harry longed for home and took comfort in whatever evoked it for him, whatever could temporarily provide the illusion that he was back in Greece, secure among family and friends. *Panáretos*, which brought the whole community together and in which he—of all the children in the town— was given a role, had warm, even glowing associations. In his early years in this country, he says, when he was alone, he recalled the sung lines. As Harry explains it, the process was cyclical: "I remembered and I would sing it sometimes while I was working here, and I remembered it." He attributes his power of recollection to God, who "gave me foresight (*próneia*), it seems, so that I can remember."

7. The Banjo-Song Genre: A Study of "High Sheriff," Dink Roberts's Man-against-the-Law Song

Cecelia Conway

In the twentieth century the banjo thrives in the upland South and is an emblem of the white mountain folk; but this has not always been so. Blacks brought the banjo to this country from Africa, and the instrument remained with them for many years. The first report of a banjo player in North Carolina was set down in 1787 in the journal of a man who dined in Tarboro with Andrew Grier and after dinner "saw a dance of Negroes to the Banjo in his yard."[1] In the twentieth century black banjo players have been difficult to locate, even on archival sound recordings. When I began my fieldwork in 1974, the Library of Congress Archive of Folk Song contained recordings of fewer than a dozen old-time black banjo players. But several Afro-Americans continue to play in this tradition in the North Carolina Piedmont. Given the vitality of their playing, the rhythms of this tradition must have been intricate, syncopated, and steady at the turn of this century when the repertoires of these men were being formed.

Of the Piedmont Afro-Americans still playing, Dink Roberts has the most varied, complex, and competent playing style; his style seems to embody the most archaic traits. His recorded repertoire is, likewise, more extensive and striking than that of the others and apparently more closely linked to the early, and thus formative, Afro-American banjo tradition: "I tell you, I learned them old pieces lookin' at the other people play. I had the music on my mind, you know. I'd go to town and hear somebody playing, you know. Walk up—I'd say, 'I'll play that.' Get out by yourself, you get out by yourself and you can play it. But if you get with someone else—they cut you off." Roberts, who is now in his nineties and lives near the town of Haw River, learned music

Figure 7.1. Dink Roberts, Haw River, N.C. (courtesy of Lenny Rogoff).

from blacks in Alamance County and elsewhere, including at least one medicine-show performer and others who are no longer living:

> *Roberts:* I learned from them. See, they old, way older than me. I'm 79. God has blessed me. That's the truth. Going now [to play] in a few minutes. Gonna drink this one. Y'all ain't in no hurry? . . . I played with John Arch [Thompson]—he was an old man like me—[for] gatherings and frolics and things like that.
> *Conway:* Square dances?
> *Roberts:* "Hands up eight and don't be late." George White played banjo [like me]. Everybody plays music got a different sound. He could go. He married my first cousin, George White did. Oh Lord, [we played] in different places, different places. In people's houses, people's houses.[2]

Roberts learned the "Coo Coo" from a fellow that he met at a dance in Greensboro, and he learned "Mame," "Black Annie," and other pieces from a local performer named Mince Phillips. Clearly Roberts's travels in the upper Piedmont helped form his repertoire.

The bulk of his repertoire, however, Roberts learned as a youngster from his family members near Haw River in the Little Texas com-

munity of blacks. The first song that Roberts learned on the banjo was
the "Fox Chase." He remembers that his father used to play it when
they lived in Chatham County. But Roberts learned a different version
from his mother's family later. His maternal uncle George Roberts
played banjo, fiddle, and guitar, and a number of George's children
picked up music from him and sometimes played for young Dink:
"Laid Poor Jesse in His Grave" is a song Roberts learned from his
cousin Johnny Roberts, who was much older than he. Today Roberts
carries on his tradition by continuing to play the banjo for his wife,
son, and grandson, who dance and occasionally sing or play themselves.

Roberts plays the guitar as well as the banjo and knows several
sacred songs and early blues (for example, "Motherless Child" and
"Mame"). But his repertoire consists primarily of pre-blues songs that
he accompanies not with the guitar, but only with the banjo. All of
his banjo performances do entail song lines, and many of his songs are
surprisingly similar to a vast number of banjo songs played throughout
the upland South by both blacks and whites: for example, Tom Ashley's and Hobart Smith's "Coo Coo," Fred Cockerham's "Roustabout,"
Burl Hammons's "Sugar Babe," Rufus Crisp's "Shout Little Lulie," Roscoe Holcomb's "Hook and Line," Doc Boggs's "Reuben's Train," John
Snipes's and Odell Thompson's "Georgie Buck," Lucius Smith's "New
Railroad," etc.[3] This apparently heterogeneous body of songs does not
fit comfortably into either the work-song, the blues, or the ballad categories. Instead, these songs seem to me to form a distinct genre, the
banjo song.[4]

Although at least three types of banjo songs seem to have emerged
by the early 1900s,[5] the old Afro-American traditions that initially
shaped the genre in the upland South still are audible in the songs of
blacks and whites alike. Typically they have song texts that are puzzling, brief, and elliptical:

> Go tell my loving wife,
>   "Cut him down."
> "See here Mr. Garfield,
>   I'll take a cigar."
> Go tell my loving wife,
>   "Ain't dead,
>   Ain't dead,

>   Ain't dead; laying mighty low."
> "Well Mr. Garfield,
>   I'll take a cigar."
> Go back and tell my loving wife,
>   "Ain't dead,
>   Ain't dead; laying mighty low."

This "Garfield" song, like others in Roberts's repertoire such as "John Hardy," "Jesse James," and "John Henry," has a central character widely celebrated in song and perhaps inspired by a historical person.[6] Some might interpret these songs as deteriorated or incoherent fragments of longer narrative songs about a public figure or historical event,[7] but I do not. Roberts consciously and intentionally performs these texts; his family enjoys them as they appear and considers them satisfying and complete; and, as I will show, their structure is meaningful and cohesive.

The social context of Roberts's music encourages the performance of such brief and emotionally charged songs. Nowadays he usually plays these pieces for his family or friends. The performances are casual: his wife sometimes inserts sung or spoken lines into his performances, and during them she and her son James often dance. In the hubbub of a visit, the apparently fragmentary lines float by amidst intricate musical rhythms. Some of Roberts's songs have fairly static texts of one or more stanzas, but he does not present his music formally as a sequence of distinct pieces. He sometimes interpolates a song fragment in his conversation, and he often incorporates spoken commentary into a song without breaking the continuity of his performance. In fact, a visitor in Roberts's home witnesses a single performance that lasts from arrival to departure. The performance is orchestrated by Roberts and moves unpredictably through a variety of lines, paces, topics, and moods.

The characteristics of spontaneity and play that are common to Afro-American tradition[8] are especially pronounced in Roberts's song performances. Rather than performing, he is at play. At a folk festival in 1976, for example, Lily Roberts chatted throughout the banjo workshop and burst into Roberts's performance several times without his invitation or objection. Both Dink and Lily reflect an old Afro-American approach to performance, little influenced by the white inclination to

Figure 7.2. Dink and Lily Roberts, Haw River, N.C. (photo by Cecelia Conway).

create a sense of removal between the performer and the audience. These characteristics indicate further that his texts are an old conversational style, worthy of special attention. I believe he essentially puts on the mask of the speaker in the song. He merges with the persona to express himself conversationally and dramatically rather than referentially and symbolically.

Not only do the song texts and fragments function as significant parts of the complete social performance, but some of the abbreviations are themselves demonstrably meaningful to Roberts. He frequently sings, for example, just a line of "Motherless Child," a traditional sacred song for which he knows at least three verses. This particular line is not, for Roberts, simply an allusion to a hypothetical experience or to a public event. Although the fragment easily reminds listeners of his full song, the one line also serves the man as a reference to the lasting emotional impact of a particular experience of his own. When Roberts was nine, his parents died, and his maternal uncle raised him along with his own eight children. Dink Roberts refers directly, emotionally, and repeatedly to this entire experience when he sings the fragment "It's hard times when Mother's gone."

Roberts's singing of this line suggests a way to understand the nature of Roberts's texts and their variations. Whether one line or twenty, it is not a fixed text that Roberts learned (or what he can remember of it) that determines the length and content of a single performance of one of these songs, but what the man desires to express in a particular social moment. This approach implies that his singing is a direct expression of himself; it is the spontaneous refashioning of a variant, not the transmission of an appealing fixed text.

Using this approach, I began to search for the emotional, rather than narrative, content in Roberts's fuller texts and discovered recurrent patterns. His apparently fragmentary lines convey, I found, fully coherent and powerful meanings formed with careful craftsmanship. The following example—Roberts's performance of a one-stanza banjo song "High Sheriff"—illustrates a set of textual characteristics found in many of his songs and will help us identify one type of banjo-song text.

"High Sheriff," like other songs in Roberts's repertoire, is not a narrative ballad but a lyric. His song is typically short and simple, but puzzling. In essence, the song presents the emotional response of an unnamed speaker to a threat set up in the early lines of the song:

> Well ah
> > High Sheriff and police
> > > riding after me.
> > What's gonna 'come of me?
> Yeah,
> > down the street a-coming,
> > down the street a-coming,
> > down the street a-coming Monday morning.
> Well ah
> > What's gonna 'come of me?
> > > Ain't that right. [spoken]

The response, however, is not a dramatic action; the speaker neither escapes, gets caught, nor turns on his pursuer. The song mentions none of his prior actions, states no motives of the high sheriff, and develops no chain of events. Indeed, the speaker does not physically react to the dramatic threat that introduces the song. Instead, his response—"What's gonna 'come of me"—is verbal. The line is phrased like a question, but it is more exclamatory than inquiring, for even the speaker's uncertainty about what will become of him remains unanswered. His words are not narrative or inquiring, but lyric. They express his uncertain, if not fearful, feelings in response to the posed threat.

The details of this song, presented from a first-person point of view, reflect upon and characterize the speaker. Although the public roles of the high sheriff and police make them imposing figures, they are not as important within the song as this speaker. In this confrontation, the speaker's experience of his antagonists—his being pursued and threatened with capture—is emphasized more than they or their actions.

Three basic characteristics (the participant-persona, the threat, and his response) constitute the recurrent formal pattern not only in Roberts's performances of "High Sheriff" but also in the other Afro-American performances of this same song. They appear, for example, in a text taken down in the Pee Dee region of South Carolina in 1891:

> Yonder come de high sheriff,
> Comin' atter me,
> Comin' atter me,
> Comin' atter me;
> Yonder come de high sheriff
> Comin' atter me,
> An' no one to stan' my bon[d].[9]

Both variants show further formal similarities in their preference for certain parts of speech: nouns, verbs, and verbal modifiers. Particularizing by means of adjectives or figures of speech is not characteristic of these songs. Both texts refer to individuals other than the speaker by class alone; they do not contain proper names. For example, it is only the sheriff, not angry redneck Sheriff Jones, who threatens. "High Sheriff" is, of course, just a title, but the adjective "high" intensifies the threat.

In a song world of minimal connotations, one that avoids adjectives and metaphors, verbs carry the burden of imagining. Indeed both of these songs are presented in and unified by imagery of motion. Present participles ("riding" and "a-coming") are the dominant verbal form.

They are used to modify nouns denoting the antagonists and to designate their threat. Adverbs and adverbial prepositional phrases often indicate distance or position and sometimes elaborate the motor imagery. In the South Carolina variant the initial adverb, "yonder," calls attention (like "high") to the space within the song world. It confines the motion within the limits of eyeshot (and therefore to a face-to-face community) as it introduces the antagonist. The adverbial phrases "after me" and "down the street" bring more specific direction to the antagonist's movement within the abstract landscape.

Even the verbal phrases modifying the antagonists, however, emphasize the speaker by aiming the motion of the antagonists at him. In Roberts's phrase "riding after me," the movement is aimed at "me." The threatening impact of this experience is reinforced by the later line "What's gonna 'come of me." The double repetition of "down the street a-coming" prolongs the description and draws the pursuit by the high sheriff onto the fugitive persona even more emphatically than the unrepeated phrase "riding after me." The word choice and the syntax of the line have the speaker acted upon, rather than acting. They characterize him as one who acknowledges that unpredictable and often uncontrollable and disastrous events loom before him.

That the listener or the singer empathizes with the persona is not demonstrable, but the invitation is there.[10] The songs, then, express the speaker's emotional response to threat, not in a careless reflex, but in a considered manner that reflects his continuous temperament or disposition. They, thus, evoke empathy for his state of being. In the line "What's gonna 'come of me," the abstractness of the word "what," as well as the verb "become," draw attention away from the outcome of events and stress the persona's viewpoint. The line questions the speaker's future and present state of existence, that is of being.

In both variants of "High Sheriff" the speaker is alone and uncertain, if not fearful, and the response line unifies the song. At the same time this direct-address response line distinguishes the speakers in the two variants of the song. In the South Carolina song the speaker assumes that he will be caught; he is forlorn and feels that no one will stand bond for him. The future possibilities for Roberts's persona—that is, whatever may become of the speaker after escape or seizure—are more uncertain. Yet, the open-endedness of the song characterizes the unaided speaker as irrepressible. When the song ends, the opportunity to dodge confinement has not been blocked. The contrast between these two statements shows that in these lyrics the response line distinctly characterizes each speaker at the same time that it presents the emotional core of the song. This line is the one that indicates each performer's personal contribution within the borrowed formulaic structure.

One such line occurs in the film *Born for Hard Luck*, which documents the later years of the hobo and veteran medicine-show performer Arthur Jackson. At the end of the film, after performing in a South Carolina store in his stage persona, "Peg Leg Sam," Jackson thanks his audience and then says, "High Sheriff on my heels. I better be on my way, yes!" Jackson speaks these words playfully in conversation in a manner similar to Roberts's, and enough of the "High Sheriff" elements occur in this scene to warrant comparison with the song. In the first person, Jackson states his experience ("on my heels") of the threat of capture represented by the antagonist ("high sheriff"). Then he gives his response. At the same time, Jackson's response line is personalized. His unaided persona expresses less uncertainty than Roberts's and greater irony about the need for flight; the line is more understated and casual—"I better be on my way, yes!"[11] Jackson's creation of an imagined situation like the one in Roberts's song suggests the currency of this dramatic concern in the culture and repertoire of these performers.

Considered in its historical and cultural context, the response line fully expresses the concerns of the black experience. In this secular "High Sheriff" song, blacks directly address the power and threat of the white social structure in the form of one of its contemporary representatives, the sheriff. After slavery, freedom, and reconstruction, they might well ask in the midst of segregation, as Roberts's song does, "What's gonna 'come of me?" Despite impending threat, however, the lyrically emphasized persona is further characterized by the ironic understatement of the performer's verbal response to the dramatic situation. He is as concerned with his way of being in the world and with clear self-understanding and self-expression as with what the high sheriff may impose.

The same distinctions hold in a two-stanza variant of "High Sheriff."[12] This variant uses the identical line-stanza structure found in the previously discussed South Carolina song text, and the core line also gives an individualized response to the standard antithetical situation:

(1) Yonder comes the High Sheriff ridin' after me.
Ridin' after me, Yes, ridin' after me.
Yonder comes the High Sheriff ridin' after me,
Oh, it's captain, I don't want to go.

(2) Been down to Frankfort,
servin' out my time.
Servin' out my time,
Yes, servin' out my time.
Been down to Frankfort,
servin' out my time,
Oh, it's captain, I don't want to go.

Although this is the first of these variants to include more than one stanza, the response of the speaker—"I don't want to go"—provides the unity for the second, as well as the first stanza. In the second stanza, Frankfort—no doubt the location of jail—is an appropriate emblem for the law and an equivalent for the high-sheriff antagonist. ("Captain" also refers to an authority figure.) The ironically understated response of the speaker in this example emphasizes his personal feelings rather than his activities—emphasizes what he does and doesn't "want," rather than his going or staying. Like the other response lines, this one particularizes the speaker but does so by revealing his reluctance, rather than his isolation.

The stanza and song type illustrated by "High Sheriff" is embodied in a much wider group of songs performed by Roberts and others, and I believe that it is a specifically Afro-American song pattern. The only Anglo-American variant of the "High Sheriff" known to me supports this claim. This variant, the first stanza of the song "Police," recorded by the North Carolina mountain fiddler Tommy Jarrell, differs from the black variants in crucial ways that heighten the dramatic action:

Police come. I didn't want to go this morning.
Police come. I didn't want to go this morning.
Police come. I didn't want to go.
I shot 'em in the head with my .44 this morning.

The order of the structural elements is the same in this stanza as in the black variants. The speaker describes a threat with maximum economy in the initial two words "Police come." The second structural element is, of course, the spoken response of the persona: "I didn't want to go this morning." However, grammatical alterations minimize this persona's *experience* of the threat and emphasize his reluctant response. No verbal phrase is used or repeated to stress that he is threatened or pursued as a fugitive. No present participle implies a continuing chase.[13] Instead, repetition serves to hold the antagonist and the persona in opposing balance, sentence for sentence, for most of the stanza, rather than to extend the presentation of the speaker's view or experience of the threat.

But the most radical turn of the Anglo-American text is the extra response line, for it introduces a new thematic element—the speaker's *reaction* to the confrontation: "I shot 'em in the head with my .44." The persona becomes a protagonist: action dominates the concluding line and overshadows the verbal emotional response of the speaker.

Nonetheless, all variants of "High Sheriff" are lyrics,[14] rather than third-person narratives, the form of older British ballads preserved in the American South. This lyricism controls the form, the tone, and the point of view of the songs. Their form is paratactic rather than sequential in structure; the songs are characterized by abrupt juxtapositions and the independent arrangements of phrases without connectives.[15] Their tone is sympathetic to the main character or speaker. Their point of view is often first person.[16]

These songs, thus, share what I may now call the defining characteristics of the banjo-song genre. Furthermore, the threat-and-response structural elements of this type of the model help clarify for us the lyrical meaning of each individual text by providing an easy means for comparing their themes. In all the variants of "High Sheriff," a persona is threatened by the law. In each of these texts, this threat is represented by an antagonist (the sheriff) who is an agent of the law. In the variant with two related stanzas, the law is represented in the second stanza by a place of law enforcement (the local jail). Since it is the law that threatens in these variants and since there is not a structural slot to indicate whether the man is innocent or guilty, the central character seems subject to and tormented by a law that is alien to him.

Rather than act—strike out against this injustice as the Anglo-American persona does by shooting the police—the Afro-American persona simply speaks; he endures this arbitrary reality, saying with ironic understatement, "What's gonna 'come of me" or "An' no one to stan' my bon' " or "I don't want to go." Figuratively the antagonist appears and threatens with motion; the persona remains passive but expresses himself verbally and emotionally. This pattern is reinforced by the content of all the Afro-American responses.[17] The very fact that threat is built into the song model characterizes the speaker of the black and white variants as vulnerable.

In sum, the banjo-song genre reaches an artistic complexity that reveals the interweaving of the formative rhythmic black influence and the later more melodic white influence. The songs are lyrically and narratively complex even in elements as fundamental as point of view: some mix the subjective emotional "I" with the narrative use of named characters who dramatically speak their lines.

Thematically the songs reveal the historical climate of the times, especially in the upland South. They show concerns in the lives of black folk at the turn of the twentieth century. Slavery, represented by "massa" and "missus," was no longer the primary danger for blacks.[18] Instead, the antagonist was the law. The laws, written by the dominant class, better served whites (especially rich and powerful men) than the common man. Songs in the banjo-song genre became popular at a time when populism was dwindling and the Jim Crow laws were being tightened to suppress blacks again. The banjo songs, unlike the still-popular spirituals, do not expect or call for divine help.[19] Instead the songs reveal the secular values of the black community: the use of clear and distinctive emotional expression and the expectation of support and solidarity among friends and relations.[20] These community values remained in place against the threat of the law and then industrialization[21] for several decades. Soon after this time the guitar became readily available and the blues emerged to express new concerns in even more assertive ways.

8. The Narrative Style of Marshall Ward, Jack-Tale-Teller

Charlotte Paige Gutierrez

The story of "Jack and the Beanstalk" is widely known throughout the United States and England; Jack's exploits in the land at the top of the magical vine are preserved in oral tradition, children's books, and popular cartoons. However, few people outside the southern Appalachians realize that the Jack of "Jack and the Beanstalk" is also the hero of dozens of other wonder stories. These stories, called "Jack tales" by the folk, are especially numerous and well formed in the Beech Mountain area of Watauga and Avery counties in northwestern North Carolina, where they have been kept alive by such skilled tellers as Jane Gentry, Ray Hicks, R. M. Ward, his brother Miles Ward, and Miles's son, Marshall Ward.

Various elements of the Old World *Märchen* or "wonder tales" traveled with the early settlers from many parts of Europe to the southern highlands, where they fused into a cohesive cycle that centers on the thoroughly Americanized farmboy-hero, Jack. The Beech Mountain Jack, unlike the heroes of the European wonder tales, assumes a well-founded personal identity; he is a recognizable individual who moves with equal ease through clever stories and magical stories. Although the Beech Mountain Jack tales share common defining characteristics, the tales nevertheless are subject to the manipulation and modifications of each narrator. Marshall Ward was one of the most active and innovative contemporary tellers of Jack tales in the Beech Mountain tradition. Furthermore, Ward is an apt subject for intensive study because unlike other tellers, his entire Jack-tale repertoire his autobiography, and supplementary biographical information from interviews are all available.

Marshall Ward was born on 10 December 1906 in Beech Creek, North Carolina; he died in nearby Banner Elk on 12 December 1981 at the age of seventy-four. He grew up in a log cabin on a farm and attended a one-teacher school at the age of eight. He began helping with farming chores before he entered school and continued to farm all his life. Marshall had two older sisters and five younger brothers. When Marshall was thirteen, his mother, who was always sickly, died of pneumonia. When he was sixteen, he left home to work for a lumber company, but, not unlike Jack, he later returned to his father's farm. His personal autobiography ends at his sixteenth year; it includes no mention of his marriage or teaching career.[1]

Ward never served in the military and never lived outside his native area. He attended what was then Appalachian State Teachers College in Boone (now Appalachian State University) and taught fifth grade in Banner Elk for thirty years. He also farmed during this time. "I did as much farming," he said, "as a lot of people that farmed all day." He retired from teaching at age sixty-five, but he continued to farm. He told me in 1974, "I've got a notion to quit and let somebody else do it [farming]. You need a hobby or something to do to occupy your time, but you don't need to work too hard after you get past sixty-five. I'm sixty-seven. Be sixty-eight in December. If I didn't have arthritis I'd be pretty strong."

In later years Ward lived with his wife in a modern ranch-style house in a rural area near Banner Elk. His house was situated at the foot of Little Beech Mountain. He was a member of the Bethany Baptist Church and taught shape-note singing both at church and in school. He had three children: a son and two daughters. His son served in Vietnam and both daughters are schoolteachers.

As a direct descendant of Council Harmon and a lifelong resident of northwestern North Carolina, Marshall Ward was a recipient of the Beech Mountain Jack-tale-telling tradition.[2] Ward claimed that he learned his entire repertoire of Jack tales by the age of five. He did not remember being encouraged to memorize them: "They just come natural to me. I'd hear 'em a time or two, and I could tell any one." Ward was born into a family in which Jack-tale-telling is a particularly strong tradition, yet none of Ward's brothers and sisters told the tales. "Had nephew that would tell 'em in school—charm the children and they'd miss the bell—when he was little. But now he won't tell 'em. Says he forgot." Marshall Ward also told the tales when he was a child:

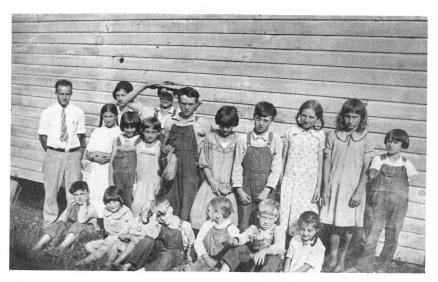

Figure 8.1. Marshall Ward with his first fifth-grade class at the Presnell School, Banner Elk, N.C., in 1932 (courtesy of Thomas McGowan).

"When my classmates would spend the night, I'd tell 'em till they were snorin'. Then I'd quit." But, unlike his nephew, Marshall Ward did not quit telling the tales when he grew up. Since Jack tales are usually told to children by adults, it is necessary that some adults do not quit telling the tales if the tradition is to survive.

What factors influence a person to learn tales and continue to tell them for a lifetime? Ward said, "I like telling 'em. That's the trouble. It's kinda part of me. It's kinda a habit you get into. But I like it because other people like it. I have never turned anybody down that wants a story, if they come see me." We may hypothesize the reasons Ward enjoyed telling Jack tales. Ward's proclivity for Jack-tale-telling was probably related to his choice of a career in teaching children (figure 8.1). The way in which Ward spoke about children reveals his close feeling for them; he referred to the children in his classes as "his" children and spoke of "getting to know them" as a better way of judging their progress than testing it. Since Jack tales are a children's genre, it is only natural that a person who likes children would like to tell the tales. Moreover, Ward's autobiography only covers his childhood, thus indicating the importance to him of his own childhood. Ward was a good Jack-tale-teller and had the ability to charm his listeners since childhood. Surely a favorable audience reaction must be flattering to a teller, whether he be child or adult. If Ward's Jack tales contributed to his popularity as a child, then this association of tale-telling and social acceptance may have been instrumental in Ward's continued life-long interest in tale-telling.

Richard Chase may also have had an effect on the development of Ward's narrative skills. Marshall Ward was the person who first told Richard Chase that Jack tales existed.[3] Ward was also present when Chase collected the tales from older members of the Ward family. He accompanied Chase on subsequent folklore-collecting trips in the Beech Mountain area, serving as a liaison between Chase and the folk. Thus Ward became aware of the value of his tradition from the folklorist's point of view. It must have been flattering to have an outsider write a book about one's family; Ward's pride would show in his face and voice when he referred to Chase's The Jack Tales. In recent years Ward actively contributed to the preservation of the Jack-tale tradition by performing for local primary and secondary schools, colleges, folk festivals, and interested individuals.

An individual tale-teller like Ward is more than a preserver of traditional material; he is also a creator in that he brings his own interests, values, and personality into his tale-telling. The mark that an individual performer makes on traditional material may be referred to as the "style" of the individual narrator. Ward's creativity did not limit itself to the area of style: he also contributed new, original tales to the Jack-tale repertoire and expanded its context. It is these three areas—style, repertoire and context—in which Marshall Ward's own contribution to the art of Jack-tale-telling is highlighted.

When Marshall Ward told a Jack tale, his face and body became quite animated.[4] Although he remained seated while speaking, he did not hesitate to use his body to express or emphasize the action taking place in a tale. For example, when Jack cuts off the cat's paw in "Sop Doll!" Ward made a sweeping, cutting motion with one hand, symbolically cutting off his other hand at the wrist (figures 8.2 and 8.3). When a shrewish wife in "Jack and the Heifer Hide" shrilly tells her husband that a certain trunk is valuable because "my great-great-grand-

Figures 8.2 and 8.3. Marshall Ward telling "Sop Doll!" on the front porch of his house, Avery County, N.C., 1978 (courtesy of Thomas McGowan).

pappy give it to my great-grandpappy and my great-grandpappy give it to my pappy and my pappy give it to me," Marshall rhythmically pounded his fist against his hand as each of the woman's progenitors was rhythmically cited. Ward's facial expressions changed in accordance with the mood of the tale. When Jack is happy, Ward beamed. When Jack is sad, Ward looked sad. When a character is surprised, Ward jumped back in mock amazement as he spoke. In using dialogue, he seemed to be talking to an imaginary person slightly to his right and in front of him. He rarely looked at his adult audience when I heard him perform, but rather looked forward and to his right. In telling tales to children, however, he occasionally changed this stance in order to address individual children at particularly exciting parts of tales or when he noticed distracted listeners.

Ward was a skilled mimic. Thomas Burton and Ambrose Manning of East Tennessee State University recorded his animal imitations and animal calls.[5] Ward incorporated these into his narrative whenever appropriate. He changed his voice to suit the personalities of different characters. Ward's witch's voice was high and cracked. His giant's voice was gruff, loud, and very low pitched. In "Jack and the Heifer Hide," Ward did a superb imitation of an intoxicated husband, complete with a slurred rendition of "She'll Be Coming around the Mountain." Like any good Jack-tale-teller, Ward changed the speed and tone of his voice to suit the action. He talked faster when describing a fight between two bulls, and then slowed down to describe Jack's grief that his bull has been killed.

Since Ward is the only teller of Jack tales I have actually seen perform, it is impossible for me to compare visual aspects of his style to those of any other tale-teller, and it is possible for me to compare his vocal style only to that of Ray Hicks and Maud Long.[6] Maud Long uses her voice like Ward, but Ray Hicks's vocal style is quite different. Ward said of Hicks's tale-telling style: "Ray Hicks tells it—droll, long voice—he doesn't tell nothin' like I tell 'em—almost a different story. The way he tells 'em is different. I don't know which one's changed 'em." by "droll, long voice" Ward was probably referring to Hicks's not using as much modulation of tone and tempo to express action and emotion. Since Long and Ward together with "animated" narrators such as Council Ward and R. M. Ward were all distantly related to each other and to Hicks, the contrasting vocal style represents either a personal trait or differing stylistic traditions in various branches of the family.

Ward's tales were also distinctive in being longer than those of other tellers. Part of this length is due to Ward's frequent use of repetition. For example, in "Cat 'n Mouse," at the end of the tale Jack tells his parents everything that has happened to him while he was away from home; in effect Ward was repeating the entire tale in abbreviated form. The length of Ward's tales also resulted from Ward's frequent insertion of details of everyday life. In "Jack and the North West Wind" Ward described the everyday chores of a farmer: "Well, it was awful hard in those days to make a living. Jack had to work all the time to keep the cow fed and the hogs slopped and keep everything a-goin'."[7] Ward often gave spatial measurements, such as the height of a tree or giant, or the distance from Jack's house to the king's house. Ward also very frequently mentioned the time of day. He told us when Jack wakes up, when he eats, and when he goes to bed. This excerpt from "Jack and the Bean Tree" illustrates Ward's concern with the details of daily living:

> He began to climb that tree and in about a month he's back up at the top of the tree. And you know that tree is a circle vine, and you could go up that tree just like you go up a pair of steps. And Jack he'd sleep whatever time it come night. He'd get tired and lay down and sleep. And he'd just eat all the beans he wanted. It's just full of beans. People come around there from everywhere just picking beans. They just wanted beans—they'd pick up off that big tree. They didn't have to climb high on the tree to get all the beans they wanted. They big'uns. And Jack he just eat beans and went on up. And they had enough juice in 'em for all the water he wanted, so it worked out fine.

Ward's narratives contained practical information. The above passage considers the practical aspects of having a giant bean tree: you can get all the beans you want. In "Jack and the Blue Bull" Ward described how Jack makes a sleeping compartment in a tree by cutting limbs and fastening them to the larger branches. In "Jack's Hunting Trips" he described how Jack packs meat "just right" for future use. In "Jack and the Blue Bull" Jack uses his medicinal skills for the wounded bull:

The blue bull he was bleeding in several places where the red bull had cut him with his horns. Jack took him down to a little creek there and got him in the water and washed all the sore places up. There was some bambuli [bamboo?] trees growing along the little creek. He went and climbed up the bambuli trees and got him some buds and mashed them up and made a kind of salve out of it. He rubbed it on the sore places and cut places and the blood stopped. Then he went over there and tapped a great big rawsom [resin?] tree which was a pine tree. He let the rawsom run out, and then he rubbed it over the sore places, the rawsom all around. That rawsom draws the soreness out and helps heal up cuts and wounds.

In the same story Jack exhibits good woodsmanship; he knows to follow a creek, because a creek has a natural path beside it that is "good for travel."

Ward combined his practical thinking and imagination to let Jack get more mileage from his magic objects. In "Jack and the North West Wind" Jack is given a magic "playaway" club that will beat people or objects on command. In the versions of this story by Jane Gentry, R. M. Ward, and Marshall Ward, Jack uses the club to force thieves to return Jack's belongings. Jack then returns home with his magic club. Gentry and R. M. Ward ended the story here. Marshall Ward, however, elaborated on the practical potential of a magic playaway club:

Jack was [home] just a-gettin' along the best you ever saw. And there was great big poplar trees a-standin' up there—about four feet through, a hundred and fifty feet high. He says, "Playaway club and jump on them big poplar trees and build us a fine house." And that playaway club jumped on them big poplar trees and in a little time had a big house built—a poplar house, made of big poplar trees, real fine. Then Jack, he cleaned up all his land with the playaway club. He'd scrub tree stumps, pile rocks. It'd do anything Jack told it to do. It was a sight to see what it could do in a day. So Jack got everything fixed up real nice.

One day he was sitting out there. And a little creek went down by his house, and he said, "Playaway club, build me a big lake so I can put fish in it, swim in it, and have me a good place to play and boat." It wasn't no time that that playaway club had dugged a big hole out the earth and built a big lake; must have been a fifty acre lake. And Jack had that to swim in, raise fish. And he could just do anything he wanted to with that playaway club.

He said, "Playaway club, I want you to go and get my dad and bring him in." It wasn't two minutes that that playaway club come in with his dad a-setting astraddle of it. He said, "Playaway club, I want you to go after Tom and Will." And in about three minutes he had Tom and Will there. And they all lived together, happy ever after, getting along just fine.

Ward used his Jack tales as vehicles to convey his own personal values and sense of ethics. He inserted into the tales passages that reflected his beliefs about the right way to live. For example, in "Jack and the North West Wind" the unruly, eighteen-member Hicks family has stolen Jack's magic hen. Jack has since acquired a magic tablecloth that produces unlimited food. Jack must pass by the Hickses house. He knows the Hickses have stolen from him, yet he feels sorry for them: "Well, Jack looked around. They didn't have much to eat. Jack knew that. He thought it'd just be nice to give them one good square meal like he'd had." Jack commands the tablecloth to produce food. The Hickses' table manners leave something to be desired:

> Lo and behold, that tablecloth was spread plum full from one end to the other. And that old man and woman and the boys and girls jumped into it with their hands. They didn't take time to use forks and spoons to be mannerable. Jack thought they ought to have a blessing, but they didn't take time. And such eatin' you never saw! They was a-eatin' like they'd never seen nothin' like that, and I don't think they ever had. Jack he sat there and watched them eat for about two hours. They eat looked enough like to kill anybody. And then they just stretched out. They couldn't do no more playing. They couldn't do anymore talking, they'd eat so much.

When Jack sets his playaway club against the Hickses, he will not let it stop beating them until old man Hicks says, "I'm sorry! We did steal it! We had no right to steal it!" Jack has been presented as mannerly, kind, and generous. The Hickses have been presented as unintelligent (they try to cut wood with a dull saw), thieving, unmannerly, ungrateful (they don't say a blessing), and greedy. The message of the incidents is that one should try to be like Jack and not be like the Hickses. Marshall Ward was the only Beech Mountain teller who developed the ethical implications of this story.

Ward also had a tendency to "clean up" tales in which Jack harms people. Such tales are rare in the Jack-tale tradition. Yet in one of the more popular Jack tales, "Jack and the Heifer Hide," Jack is responsible for the deaths of three people. Tom and Will are jealous of Jack's success. They tie him in a sack and prepare to throw him in the river. When the older brothers are distracted by a fire, an old man comes by and asks Jack what he is doing in the sack. Jack says that he is waiting for the angels to come throw him into heaven. The old man gladly takes Jack's place in the sack and even gives Jack a herd of sheep in exchange for a trip to heaven. Tom and Will return and unknowingly drown the man. At this point Marshall Ward interjected, "Well, we don't know if the old man was saved. We hope he was." Jack returns to Tom and Will's house with a herd of sheep that, Jack claims, he caught in the river. Tom and Will immediately decide that they will catch sheep by jumping in the river. In most versions of the tale, Jack gladly helps Tom and Will into sacks and throws them in the river. Marshall Ward was obviously uncomfortable with this development and tried to soften Jack's trickery as best he could:

> "Well," said Jack, "I tell you boys, now I don't want to dis-encourage you boys [from jumping in the river]. I want you boys satisfied with what sheep I've got. I tell you what I'll do. I'll give you boys a thousand head of sheep. We all can own the horse and ride it. All of us can use the dog. You boys pasture the sheep here for me—three thousand sheep—and we'll go in thirds on it."
>
> "No!" said Tom. "We don't want none of your old sheep. We don't want your old dog, and we don't want anything to do with your horse. We want what we want for ourselves. If you get three thousand sheep out of the river, and here you come back with three thousand sheep, a fine horse, and that dog, we gonna get 'em out of there for ourselves. You're gonna throw us in!"
>
> "Well," Jack says, "I've made you a good offer and a good deal." "No deal," said Tom and Will. "We want ours by ourselves." "Well," Jack said, "if nothing else won't do you boys and

that's the way you want it, I'll take you to the river and pitch you in."

Well, Jack didn't want to do this, but they's making Jack do this. Jack hated to do this, but he knew he had to do this or they gonna kill him and take what he had, and he'd been fair. He tried to do everything he could for the boys.

In all versions of "Jack and the Doctor's Girl," Jack is forced by robbers to steal oxen from a farmer. Jack is paid for his work by the robbers and is allowed to return home. No thought is given to the poor farmer who lost his oxen. But Marshall Ward worried about the farmer. We hear that Jack goes to the trouble to see that the farmer is compensated for his loss: Jack buys an expensive wagon and team of horses and sells it to the farmer for a low price. The farmer is elated because now he can sell the wagon for more than the stolen oxen were worth and pay for his wife's much-needed operation.

Through his telling of a Jack tale, Ward often addressed social issues and problems. For example, in "Answer the King's Daughter's Question" the king is an evil slave driver. When Jack becomes king he frees the slaves, "gives them a home, and lets them marry." In his introduction to "Jack and the Doctor's Girl," Ward touched on the rich man's exploitation of the poor man:

> One time Jack lived in a community where his father lived, and he was poor class people and had to work to make a living. There was an old doctor lived in this little village, or town, and he just run everything. In fact, he just about robbed the people of everything they had. In fact, he overcharged them for medicine, for going to see sick people, and he just about got all the wealth and money of that town. He was the banker—just about everything outstanding he was. He run the church, he was head of the church. People done about everything the doctor wanted them to do in that town, because he had more wealth than anybody.

This introductory section of the tale brings into play factors not explicitly or even implicitly stated in the versions of Ray Hicks and R. M. Ward. To begin with, we have a particular type of villain. A doctor is supposed to be someone who helps people, but here he takes advantage of people. He has used his position to gain control of the economic and religious institutions in the isolated community. An incident later in the story proves the doctor to be a hypocrite: when he thinks wrongly that he has murdered Jack, his first concern is not with his wrongful deed, but with the possibility that the people in Sunday school might see the bloodstains on his clothes. A greedy, hypocritical person is particularly distasteful when he holds a position of responsibility and uses this position to hurt the very people he should be helping. Given the nature of the doctor, Jack's fight for the girl becomes also a fight by the little man for fair treatment in general.

Ward did not like other aspects of the society portrayed in "Jack and the Doctor's Girl." Referring to the fact that Jack's marriage had to be approved and arranged by her father, Ward said that "in that day and time you didn't get married like you do in America." "In America" the prerequisite for marriage is usually romantic love, an ideal that Ward found desirable. In the tales in which Jack wins his wife, Ward did not allow Jack to marry his fiancée until they have dated several months, gotten to know each other, and "fallen in love." Ward thus revealed his rather modern belief that people should marry for love rather than for convenience, status, or money.

More than any other Beech Mountain teller Ward concerned himself with the emotional state of characters and with relationships between characters. For example, in "Jack and the Doctor's Girl" Jack and his father are very close. Jack discusses his problems with the doctor with his father, and Jack's father weeps when he fears that the doctor will harm Jack. Ward's insight into the doctor's guilt feelings was especially sharp. Jack tricks the doctor into thinking he has killed a man. When the doctor realizes what he has done, he stands there for five or ten minutes before saying, "Well, I guess I'll not be worried with him anymore." He says this with a tinge of fear and regret in his voice. These emotions build as time passes and become more prominent in the doctor's voice and in Ward's facial expressions. By the end of the story we can see the doctor as a real person struggling with his feelings. He is not the flat villain of many folktales. So we are prepared when Jack finally relieves him of his burden by telling him that the man he "killed" had already been dead for three days.

Ward's stylistic addition to the Jack tales—that is, his moralizing and insertion of practical information—was probably related to his

Figure 8.4. Marshall Ward in his classroom at the Banner Elk Elementary School, 1978 (courtesy of Thomas McGowan).

expansion of the natural context of Jack-tale-telling. I have noted that Jack tales are usually told by older relatives to children. Ward, however, incorporated Jack-tale-telling into his fifth-grade curriculum. Every Friday Ward and his pupils told Jack tales (figure 8.4). Sometimes Ward would instruct the children to illustrate the tales as part of their art class. Surely Ward was not unaware of the importance of his position as educator of mountain children. Although the tales are somewhat educational in their natural family setting, Ward, as teacher, capitalized as much as possible on the educational nature of the tales. He did so by inserting moral values and practical information into the tales.

Ward also added to the Jack-tale repertoire by "making up" new Jack tales. For example, Ward composed a tale called "Jack and the Watermelon" in which Jack grows a giant watermelon, digs his way through it, and becomes king of the watermelon people. Ward's "Jack and the Log Cabin" is the story of how Jack builds his mother a house from a single giant log.[8] Ward told two tales from Chase's *The Grand-*

father Tales, "Jack and the Outlaws" ("Robin Hood") and "The Three Pigs" (Jack is the youngest pig).[9] Since these tales are not included in the repertoires of the other major Beech Mountain tellers, I suspect that Ward learned them from *The Grandfather Tales;* he said that he had read this book. Ward also told a version of "The Princess on the Glass Mountain," which he also entitled "The Clover Patch Mystery." His tale "Jack's Travels" is a mixture of original material, Ward claimed, and portions of *Gulliver's Travels.* Chase notes that one of Ward's uncles read *Gulliver's Travels* and was responsible for its incorporation into the Jack-tale tradition.[10] Regardless of the original sources of Ward's additions to the Jack-tale genre, these tales still conform to the definition of the Jack tale. With the exception of "Jack's Travels" these tales have the "lack/lack liquidated" structure common to most Jack tales. The hero Jack—whether he be a young pig or an Appalachian Robin Hood—is the same "traditional nonconformist" Jack as the Jack of the more widely known Jack tales.[11]

We have seen that Marshall Ward modified the Jack tales in accordance with his own values and interests and that he expanded the context and repertoire of the Jack tales. Thus the Jack tales that Ward passed on to the next generation of tellers are not exactly the same as the Jack tales that he received from an earlier generation of tellers. If the children who have heard Marshall Ward's Jack tales in turn pass these tales on to their children, it is likely that Ward's modifications of the tales will be passed on as well. For example, if the only version of "Jack and the Doctor's Girl" ever heard by a child is that of Marshall Ward, the child will assume that Jack's payment to the farmer for the stolen oxen is a traditional part of the tale. The Jack that Ward's pupils are familiar with is by nature a Jack who would be expected to worry about the fate of the farmer. The concern with honesty in "Jack and the Doctor's Girl" will become an integral part of the telling of this tale. A pupil who is familiar with Ward's repertoire would surely be aware—either consciously or unconsciously—of the emphasis on Jack's virtues. Jack's honesty, kindness, hard work, and good manners are repeatedly highlighted in Ward's tales. Since these virtues have been so thoroughly integrated into Ward's Jack tales, a transmitter of Ward's tales would hardly ignore or forget this aspect of the tale-telling. If a child passes on Ward's version of the tale, then Ward's modifications are on their way to becoming "traditional" material.

We can assume that some of Ward's other modifications will remain a part of the genre simply because they are interesting and entertaining. For example, Jack's practical use of the playaway club in "Jack and the North West Wind" is a fascinating and memorable addition to the tale. His humorous description of the Hickses' table manners is likely to catch the attention of a listener and be remembered. Jack's medicinal skills in "Jack and the Blue Bull" may be of particular interest to Ward's more practical-minded listeners. And, of course, Ward's original tales will become part of the inherited repertoire of any of Ward's pupils who choose to become Jack-tale-tellers.

Ward's particular tale-telling context gave him an edge in assuring that his individual narrative idiosyncrasies would be picked up by a relatively large number of potential Jack-tale-tellers. We have seen that traditionally the Jack tales are told within one's family. Under usual circumstances this limits the number of people for which a given teller may perform. But as a teacher Ward told tales to children outside his own family; in fact, he told tales every Friday for thirty years to every local child in the fifth grade. Therefore the Ward family tradition, along with Marshall Ward's own modifications on that tradition, has made its presence felt within an entire community instead of only within one family.

While the older tale-tellers associate Jack-Tale-telling with family work and entertainment, the pupils of Marshall Ward associate the tales with school. Instead of strengthening the bonds between grandparent and grandchild, Marshall Ward's tales may have strengthened the bonds between teacher and pupil. Instead of lightening the burden of farm chores, Ward's tales may have lightened the burden of schoolwork. Ward described the reaction of one of his pupils to the Jack tales told in school:

I had a little old boy pupil—he wasn't right bright. He got to the fifth grade and didn't want to go no further. He said he'd rather stay in my grade as long as he went to school. When he got to be sixteen he was gonna quit anyway. He said he wanted to hear them Jack Tales. He called me up—it wasn't six months ago—and he said, "Mr. Ward, you still tellin' them Jack Tales?" I said, "Yeah, I tell 'em." He said, "I'd like you to come tell me one." I said, "Just come up to my house and I'll tell you one anytime you come." I

said, "How old are you, Willy?" He said, "I'm forty-four."
[Laughs.]

Although Willy, who "wasn't right bright," was apparently not very
interested in being in school, we can assume that he at least learned
practical information and moral values from Ward's Jack tales. Though
school may have been generally boring for Willy, Ward's tales provided at least one point of interest for the child, thus making the ordeal
of school more tolerable.

Ward's manipulation of Jack-tale-telling and its context served to
draw the genre away from the folk tradition. Or to be more precise,
Ward's Jack tales mark the transition between an "old" Jack-tale tradition and a "new" Jack-tale tradition. For example, the old tradition
allows Jack to steal or kill occasionally. The new tradition, which had
been exposed to modern education theory and its distaste for violence
in children's tales, does not allow Jack's occasional wrongdoings to go
unquestioned. Although part of Ward's censorship of violence in his
tales may be the result of his personal views, I am assuming that his
bachelor's degree in elementary education had exposed him to more
theories concerning child psychology than the average teller is exposed
to. It is interesting that "Jack and the Doctor's Girl" and "Jack and the
Heifer Hide" have been told in various forms in northwestern North
Carolina for many years, yet until Marshall Ward no major Beech
Mountain Jack-tale-teller seemed to care about the victims of Jack's
pranks. Rather, the tales were valued for their humor; the fate of the
victims was irrelevant. In concerning himself with the ethical implications of these tales, Ward lessened the impact of the humor of the tales.
For example, when Ward interrupted his telling of "Jack and His
Heifer Hide" to say that he hopes the drowned man is saved, the mood
of the tale is changed from humorous to serious. It is harder to laugh at
Jack's pranks when we are repeatedly reminded that they cause suffering. The old way of telling the tale may be better or it may be worse
than Ward's new way of telling it. Ward's new way was, however,
more appropriate to his sensibilities and to the sensibilities of modern
elementary-school teachers.[12]

It is possible too that the values reflected in Ward's Jack tales are
partly a result of the modernization of his home area. Until the last

decade the Beech Mountain area was one of the most isolated regions of the Appalachians. Ward said that when he was younger there was only one road into Watauga County, and his description of his childhood illustrated the lack of modernization of his area. When he broke his legs, they were set in splints by a neighbor. When he cut his foot at school, his cousin carried him home "about three miles right across a big mountain and down another hill, across two or three hollers, across three barbed wire fences and four or five rail fences over to my house where I lived."[13] Yet in his later years Ward lived in a modern house not unlike that of an average middle-class American. Ward's alma mater has become a moderately large university, and Watauga County has developed some light industry and become a popular center for winter and summer tourism. The development of Beech Mountain has also brought many outsiders into the area. As this poor, rural section of northwestern North Carolina gradually becomes a middle-income, semi-urbanized area, we can assume that the traditional frontier value system will be modified. The values in Ward's Jack tales—honesty, hard work, good manners, kindness—are values we would expect to find idealized by the less regionally defined "middle class." Because the recognition of violence as an unavoidable part of life is not uncommon in a frontier setting,[14] we can hypothesize that Ward's softening of violence in his tales was partly due to a weakening of the frontier value system in his native area.

The publication of Jack tales by Chase and others has probably had a further effect on the modernization of these tales. One example of this effect is Richard Chase's editing of the tales. Chase changed the phrase "Old Stiff Dick, killed fifty-six with one lick" to "Strong Man Jack, killed seven at a whack" in order to make "Jack and the Varmints" palatable to the average American reader. More important, the very fact that the Jack tales are in print makes them a part of middle-class culture. Although the oral tale-telling tradition may survive in some areas for a while longer, we can predict that in the future, if not in the present, more Jack tales will be read than heard. Just as old-time fiddling has reached the middle class mainly as amplified bluegrass, we can expect the Jack tale to reach the middle class in a form acceptable to its new listeners. Marshall Ward was, in fact, one teller who significantly contributed to this process.

9. Symbols from Ribbons:
Afro-American Funeral-Ribbon Quilts in Chatham County, North Carolina
Mary Anne McDonald

One of the first times I visited Laura Lee, an elderly black woman who lives near Moncure in Chatham County, North Carolina, we sat in the front room of the house she shares with her son, her daughter, and her grandson, and talked about quilts—how she used to make quilts when she was raising a family, where she got her scraps, her favorite patterns, and her feelings for what makes an attractive quilt (figure 9.1). Lee is a wonderful narrator, and she described outstanding quilts she had made in the past (a stroke crippled her in 1976, and she is unable to do much sewing now). One of the quilts she talked about was made "from ribbons. Off of the flowers. Off of somebody's grave."[1] I had never heard of making a quilt from funeral-flower ribbons, and I couldn't imagine why someone would do such a thing or what the quilt would look like when it was finished.

On another visit a few days later, Laura Lee told me this story about a funeral-ribbon quilt: "Now that one that she has was made from the ribbons of Lawyer Harry Horton. . . . He's dead, but I mean his wife saved the ribbons. She knew I made [quilts], and so she saved the ribbons, she thought it was such a something for somebody to do, so she saved them and sent them to me. And brought them. And I made that one and I remember what went into that one. Well, he was a judge." Laura Lee went on to explain her long association with Judge and Mrs. Horton and how he, an influential white man, had benefited the black community. He was seen by the black community as a person of reason and fairness during the racially turbulent 1960s and 1970s. Lee had worked with him when she was a child-welfare worker for Joint Orange and Chatham Community Action (JOCCA) and says, "I learned a lot at his feet." While she was telling me about this quilt I thought that it was in the next room and that my curiosity would soon be satisfied with a look at it. Laura Lee spoke of this quilt as if it were present. However, it turned out that she had given the quilt away some ten years ago—right after she made it. Even when the quilt was not physically present, the memory of making it functioned as a symbol. For Laura Lee the funeral-ribbon quilt is a symbol of Judge and Mrs. Horton.

A year and many visits later, Laura Lee borrowed back a funeral-ribbon quilt so that I could see it and photograph it. It is brilliantly colored and has obviously been used, not stored away in a chest. Hearing about this and other funeral-ribbon quilts made me curious about this tradition. How could funeral-flower ribbons, so closely associated with the death of a friend or a loved one, be transformed into a useful and beautiful object? I wanted to find out if other women in the community made such quilts and if they did, whether these quilts had a symbolic function over and above their normal utilitarian and aesthetic functions.

There are no books or articles on the funeral-ribbon quilt, so it is

Figure 9.1. Laura Lee at her home, Gorgus community, near Moncure, N.C., in 1983 (photo by Mary Anne McDonald).

difficult, if not impossible to determine how widespread this tradition is, how common these quilts are in other communities, or how they function in other communities.[2] Because of the paucity of other sources, the data considered in this study must be viewed as specific, personal, and perhaps idiosyncratic. However, the funeral-ribbon quilt, although not well documented, is not a tradition found only in Chatham County. Even though there are no published data on funeral-ribbon quilts, folklorists have seen them in other Afro-American communities in the Southeast. Folklorist Laurel Horton says she has seen such quilts elsewhere in North Carolina while doing fieldwork. Tom Rankin says he saw funeral-ribbon quilts in black homes in East Tennessee in the summer of 1980 while he was a field-worker for the Tennessee state parks program.

During 1983 and 1984 I mentioned these funeral-ribbon quilts to many white friends and acquaintances. Whether southern or northern, rural or urban, middle-class or low-income, their reactions were the same: surprise, incredulity, and veiled disapproval. Clearly the use of material associated with funerals, and therefore death, as cloth for quilts is not expected or accepted in Euro-American culture. Funeral ribbons are the only quilt material I have found that is peculiar to Afro-Americans. All other sources for scraps mentioned by black quilters of Chatham are common in the white tradition as well. The flour sacks, mill-end scraps, sewing scraps, old blankets, and sample books used by the black women are also used by white women. Because funeral ribbons are used exclusively by Afro-Americans and excite such strong feelings among Euro-Americans, an examination of this tradition may reveal symbolic associations with death and the quilts themselves that are very different in Afro-Amercian culture from Euro-American culture.

Funerals, death, and associated inner feelings are difficult for most people to discuss. They are difficult enough for people to talk about within their own racial and socioeconomic group. How then could I expect to talk about such sensitive subjects with women who are so different from me? All these women are black, over eighty years old, and have spent most of their lives as low-income farmers' wives. I am white, twenty-nine years old, and was raised in a middle-class suburban area of northern Virginia. Certainly the differences in our situations affected the information I was able to collect. Although much separates me from these women, I have been visiting them on and off for over three years and they are familiar with me, my tape recorder, my camera, and my persistent questions. None of the women uses the term "symbol" when speaking of these quilts. I am cautious about imposing interpretations on people's actions that may reflect more about my feelings than theirs. Yet I think that by closely examining the transcripts and looking at how the quilts are used, we can draw some conclusions about the symbolic roles these quilts play in these women's lives.

The three women in Chatham County who make funeral-ribbon quilts represent three different aspects of this tradition. The strength of the symbolic content varies among them. To determine how the quilts function, I looked at several factors: where the ribbons came from, whether they were new or from a grave site; the expressed reasons for using the ribbons; the time when the quilt was made; and how the quilt is used now, both materially and symbolically. Through making comparisons, I was able to see the three women as representing three different levels of symbolic use of these quilts.

All three women I talked with who made quilts from funeral ribbons know each other. Bessie Lee and Laura Lee are sisters-in-law and live next door to each other in the black community of Gorgus, near Moncure. Both are acquainted with Jennie Burnett, who lives on the other side of Pittsboro. However, each woman claimed independent invention for the idea of using funeral ribbons in a quilt. All three women use cotton or polyester scraps to make quilts that are representative of the Afro-American quilt-making tradition. Afro-American quilts are characterized by large blocks or squares, bright highly contrasting colors, the use of strips, and an improvisational sense of design. Researchers have documented these characteristics in Afro-American quilts throughout the Southeast and as far north as New Haven, Connecticut.[3] The funeral-ribbon quilts made in Chatham do not differ in execution or design from the quilts the women make from more ordinary material.

Bessie Lee was born in 1897 on a farm in Chatham County near where she now lives (figure 9.2). Her mother was a quilter and Bessie Lee learned to quilt by watching her. She began quilting in earnest

Figure 9.2. Bessie Lee at her home, Gorgus community, near Moncure, N.C., in 1982 (photo by Mary Anne McDonald).

when she was about sixteen years old. When she married, she and her husband farmed cotton, wheat, and corn on land they owned. They raised six children.

Like other Afro-American quilters that I have worked with in Chatham County and elsewhere, Bessie Lee gets many of her patterns from newspapers and books. Her funeral-ribbon quilt shows her preference for colors that are bright and, as she puts it, "show up." She enhances color contrast by the way she places her pieces. She says, "you wouldn't put two darks together [but] light and dark." She pieces all her quilts by hand and uses material that people bring her; she doesn't buy new material for her quilts. Although she, like the other women, once used locally grown cotton for the linings of her quilts, she now uses worn-out blankets, old quilts, or polyester batting. Bessie Lee used to get together with other local women for quilting bees where all would help quilt the top, lining, and back together. However, she hasn't been to a quilting bee in twenty years. Many of the women she used to quilt with are now disabled (like her sister-in-law Laura Lee), and some have died. Most of the younger women work in town and do not have time for a quilting bee. Now she says, "This is my winter job, while it's snowing and snow on the ground I piece up quilts."[4]

Bessie Lee has made only one quilt from funeral ribbons. She says she can't remember how she got the idea to use ribbons. Her daughter in Burlington got the ribbons for her at an outlet store there. She has never used ribbons from the flowers on a grave, although she is aware of this tradition. She says she used the ribbons because they were shiny and pretty and available. She thinks she made the quilt around ten years ago, but can't remember for sure. She made the funeral-ribbon quilt as she would make any other quilt—its construction was not associated with the death of a loved one.

Actually what she made is only a quilt top. She has not quilted it up, so there is no lining and no backing. Her funeral-ribbon quilt is unfinished; it could not function as a warm bed cover. Bessie Lee has around fifteen quilt tops that she has not yet quilted up. She keeps them folded up in a suitcase and stored in an unused bedroom in her house. She stores the funeral-ribbon quilt top the same way she stores her other cotton quilt tops. She does not treat it as something special.

When Bessie Lee showed her funeral-ribbon quilt to me, she did not say anything to indicate that it was special in any way. Since the ribbons were not from a grave site but came from an outlet, to her they are really no different from other cotton material she uses for quilts. Her daughter often brings her cotton mill-end scraps from Burlington. Bessie Lee talks of this quilt as being made simply from scraps—that the scraps are funeral ribbons does not seem important to her. She did not have any stories associated with the quilt—it is not emblematic of a person or idea. From her attitude and her treatment of it, we can see that its function in her life is not different from that of any other cotton quilt top.

This is not true of the second quilter, Jennie Burnett. Burnett was born in 1892 on a farm in Chatham County not far from her present home (figure 9.3). She was raised doing farm work and learned to quilt by watching her mother. She has always loved doing handwork and making quilts. She says, "Whenever I could beat my parents from the field to the house, I'd sew for that little length of time, dinner hour."[5]

After she married in 1924, she and her husband bought ninety acres and farmed cotton, wheat, corn, and oats. She did the heavy farm work right alongside her husband: "No Lord, I went to *work* when I married, oh Lord. I ditched and cut briars, and cut wood. . . . I went

Figure 9.3. Jennie Burnett with her funeral-ribbon quilt at her home near Pittsboro, N.C., in 1983 (photo by Mary Anne McDonald).

to the field—my husband stayed there till I come in to cook dinner. While I was cooking dinner he was resting. He was a real farmer. And that's what we lived in was farming. [pause] I plowed one end and he plowed the other. Plowed right along side of him. I sure did." It was not an easy life, and she didn't find as much time for quilting as she would have liked. Jennie Burnett and her husband did not have any children of their own, but they raised several foster children.

Burnett remembers a few of her mother's quilt patterns, although she does not make them herself. One was called a "snake quilt," the other a "brick" pattern. Like other local women, she gets her patterns from books and magazines. Her funeral-ribbon quilt is pieced in the very common log-cabin pattern. Her visual aesthetic calls for high-contrast colors in a quilt, and in her funeral-ribbon quilt, yellow and purple, and yellow and pink stand beside each other (figure 9.4). When I asked her how she decided to put colors together, she answered: "Well, I just look and see what's pretty together." People give her material and she uses whatever she can find. She has even made a quilt from old neckties someone gave her. She says: "You see, honey, we couldn't go out and get what we wanted. We had to use what we had. Just use what you got."

Jennie Burnett stopped farming in 1967 when her husband died.

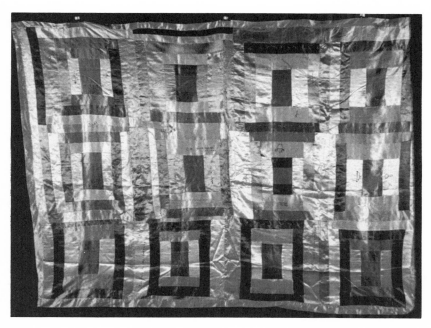

Figure 9.4. Pieced funeral-ribbon quilt, Afro-American, made by Jennie Burnett in 1971 (courtesy of the Ackland Art Museum, University of North Carolina at Chapel Hill).

Since then she's done some domestic work in Durham and Chapel Hill. Now, at ninety-two, she has time to do more quilting. She says, "See, I lives right by myself and I gets lonesome, I just set up and go to sewing." The sewing helps her pass the time.

Like Bessie Lee, Jennie Burnett has made only one quilt from funeral ribbons. She can't remember how she got the idea. Unlike all her other quilts, she bought the material for this quilt: "I didn't get them [the ribbons] off of flowers, but that's where I reckon they come from. I went to a factory place where they made the ribbons, and that's what that quilt is made of." She bought the ribbons in Burlington, perhaps at the same outlet where Bessie Lee's ribbons were purchased. Jennie Burnett has never collected ribbons from a grave site; her husband died in 1967, and she did not save his funeral ribbons.

Burnett did not say why she used funeral ribbons for this quilt. She does like the shiny silk and the colors of the ribbons. Although

Jennie Burnett is friendly and likes to talk, she does not have much to say about the tradition of making funeral-ribbon quilts or her reasons for making her own funeral-ribbon quilt. For example, when I asked her what made her decide to put the date of her husband's death on the quilt, she replied: "I just—I don't know. Just here by myself." She does not overtly evade these subjects, she just does not seem to have much to say about them. This reluctance to discuss her motivations could be caused by uneasiness due to our very different backgrounds. She might feel more comfortable explaining her reasons to her good friend Lillie Lee, who lives down the road. She may not feel as comfortable talking to me about these personal topics. However, she talked to me at length about other sensitive subjects, such as her husband's illness and death, KKK activities, problems she has with a younger woman who shares her house, and crime within the local black community. Her reticence about her reasons for making the quilt may be due to a lack of intimacy between us, yet it may also be attributed to the difficulty most people have in recognizing and articulating their deepest feelings about death and their motivations for actions related to deeply held beliefs.

Whatever her reasons for not directly discussing the symbolic content of the quilt, Burnett does associate this quilt with her husband. During an interview in November 1983 she mentioned the quilt to me in response to my question about the date of her husband's death. She said, "He died in sixty-seven. I got a quilt with that on there." Even though the ribbons she used were not from his funeral flowers, she did purchase funeral-ribbon material from the outlet. Moreover, Burnett treats the quilt with reverence, as special, and as symbolic of her husband and their life together. The ribbons she used stand in for the actual funeral ribbons—they are his by proxy.

Burnett made this quilt four years after her husband's death. In 1971 she moved from her old homeplace, where she and her husband had lived, to a new cinder-block house by the road. Perhaps this move, one of only three or four in her life, intensified her feelings of loss and loneliness. She pieced this quilt at a time of upheaval and change, and the quilt seems to have provided her with a way to link her past with her present. The quilt bears three other dates in addition to that of her husband's death. Two of the four embroidered dates stand as a testimony to significant moments of her married life: her marriage date and her husband's death date. The other two dates record the day she began making the quilt and the day she finished it. Thus, Burnett seems to be linking the making of the quilt with memories of her life with her husband. The embroidered dates are not simply significant dates in her life. She did not include her birth date, for example, or her date of baptism. Clearly this quilt concerns the life she and her husband had *together*, and the making of it was a commemorative act.

Other evidence corroborates this hypothesis. This is the only quilt Burnett has made using funeral-ribbon material, the only quilt for which she purchased material, the only quilt that she lists in her will (it is to go to her nephew, Rufus Goings, who looks after her as a son would). All of these denote its specialness. Furthermore, it is also the only quilt on which Burnett has done special embroidery. On it she has done free-hand embroidery of a baby chick pecking feed, a vase of flowers, a human figure, a fish, and a jug. These common objects evoke her life on the farm. She has also embroidered religious phrases such as, "The Lord is My Shepard," "I love the Lord," and most significantly, "God Bless My Home." The church is an important part of Burnett's life, and she associates its comfort and security with her husband and home. The quilt is a blend of the sacred and secular from which she gathers her strength. Although Burnett may not feel comfortable talking about her reasons for making this quilt, the quilt itself is an eloquent statement of her beliefs and values in a time of dislocation and concern.

Laura Lee is another black quilter for whom a funeral-ribbon quilt seems to have symbolic value. Lee still lives on the farm where she was born in 1900. According to Lee, her mother's family, the Seymours, were free blacks at the time of the Civil War and owned hundreds of acres of land in Gorgus.[6] Laura Lee still owns and lives on some of that family land. She spent some of her childhood in Aberdeen in Moore County, North Carolina, living with relatives who had no children of their own. While there she attended Sara Lincoln Academy, a Presbyterian school for blacks funded by Northern Presbyterian philanthropists. At age sixteen she returned to Gorgus and taught school for several years before marrying in 1919. She and her husband farmed and raised six children of their own as well as several foster children.

Laura Lee's mother was an industrious woman who taught her daughters to sew and quilt. Laura Lee had local women in to "quiltings" during the years when she was farming and raising her family. Like Bessie Lee and Jennie Burnett, Laura Lee gets quilt patterns from magazines, newspapers, and friends. Her quilts also exhibit Afro-American color combinations. Yet, while the other two quilters are articulate about their aesthetics of color and design, Laura Lee denies spending time considering the aesthetics of a quilt. When I asked her how she decided what colors to put together she replied: "No, I don't have time to sit up and ponder over how I'm going to do this. Just get it done, see how it turns out. You know, but be sure you get it done." She is more attuned to the utilitarian role of her quilts.

Service to the community has long been a central part of Laura Lee's life. After years of informal social work, she became a professional social worker in 1968 when she was hired as a child-welfare worker for Joint Orange and Chatham Community Action (JOCCA). She held this job for eight years until she was crippled by a stroke in 1976. Although the stroke put an end to her professional social work, she remains an informal social worker through her quilts. She keeps track of everyone's condition and sends old clothes and quilts to families who need them. Helping others is an impulse central to her personality. She says that she will be all right as long as she can do something to help someone.

Laura Lee's commitment to community service and her view of the quilt as primarily a utilitarian rather than an aesthetic object is reflected in her treatment of her finished quilts. She has one or two quilts on her bed and two unfinished tops stored away. All of the rest have been given away to relatives or to others in the community. This is why she is in such a hurry to finish them. When I commented once that I liked the large squares in her quilts, she told me: "Well I did this [made the pieces big] 'cause I told you I was always in a hurry, I had to hurry up 'cause I knew I was going to give it to somebody. And I *wanted to*—a quilt is a quilt when you're getting one." [Laughs] In contrast, Jennie Burnett must have twenty-five to thirty quilts stored in a closet and around her house. Bessie Lee has at least ten finished quilts and fifteen tops stored in her home. Laura Lee has made many, many quilts in her time, but she generally gives them away as soon as she makes them. I have only a few pictures of her handwork. I was able to document only one of the five funeral-ribbon quilts she made, and then only because she kindly borrowed it back for me to photograph.

Like the other women, Laura Lee views quilting as a salvage art, and for her, part of the challenge is to turn available discarded materials into something beautiful. Not only can she not afford the luxury of purchasing materials specifically for a quilt, but it would violate her principle of making use of things other people throw away. Her philosophy of salvage is her expressed motivation for using funeral ribbons in quilts. She says: "I went to a cemetery, just looking around. Where they had taken these wreaths off and all these beautiful ribbons were just strewn around the edge of the cemetery, you know, in the woods there, and it came to me that something could be made *beautiful* from those ribbons. And I begun to collect them. And then I begun to make little things. And then I had so much I said, well, I could make quilts. And I don't know how many that I've made. And I gave them away." Unlike the other two quilters, Laura Lee retrieved used funeral ribbons from flowers on graves instead of using new ones purchased from an outlet.

Laura Lee has made at least five quilts from these ribbons; this makes her the most prolific of the three funeral-ribbon quilt makers. For three of her quilts, she gathered ribbons directly from the cemetery. She says: "The first ones I made were some I just went to the cemetery and picked up the ones that they had thrown away. And I don't know, they were just a mixture of people. You know, I don't know how many people's graves they had come from. I don't have any idea. Because they had just cleaned up the cemetery and carried those old things out there and dumped them in a pile to haul away." The first quilts she made were of these assorted ribbons and did not have symbolic significance specific to particular persons.

Later she made a quilt (mentioned at the beginning of this paper) from ribbons from Judge Harry Horton's grave. Judge Horton's widow brought the ribbons to Laura Lee. Although the quilt itself was raffled off to benefit the church, Laura Lee frequently refers to it and to the experience of making it. Laura Lee has no idea where the quilt is now, yet even though the quilt is not physically present, its memory sparks stories about Judge Horton and his wife and their role in the community.[7] For Laura Lee, the quilt is a personal symbol of Judge Horton.

Laura Lee also made a quilt from her son's funeral ribbons. He died in 1973 and his wife, Eva Lee, brought her the ribbons. Laura Lee made the quilt soon after the funeral. I asked her if this was difficult for her to do. She replied: "No. Because to *me*, he was dead. He was gone. And I don't ponder over yesterday much. . . . I've had so many things that I've had to live through until I had to find a way to do it. That's the way for me. Just to think whatever it is that's happening now, it'll change. . . . But I made use of [the quilt], I know that. It wasn't thrown away." She is proud to have been able to turn part of her own misfortune and loss into a quilt that would benefit someone. She does not mention her feelings of grief at her son's death. Yet rather than avoiding the subject she frequently mentions the quilt she made from his funeral ribbons. This transformation from ribbons to quilt, from loss into useful object, enables Laura Lee to order her grieving within the framework of her life. For Laura Lee the quilt symbolizes her son, and also her triumph over tragedy through her ability to help others. As she says, she'll be all right as long as she can help someone. The quilt is a symbol both of her son and of her self-perception as one who performs services for others.

Funeral-ribbon quilts have differing symbolic values for these three quilters. Bessie Lee treats her funeral-ribbon quilt like any other quilt. She values its shiny material—ribbons that never entered a graveyard, and also never acquired an additional level of personalized meaning. For her the quilt does not function symbolically. The ribbons Jennie Burnett used in her quilt were never in a graveyard either, yet she endowed them with a commemorative meaning through her embroidery and her special treatment of the quilt. She transformed the ribbons into an embroidered record—a quilt that functions as a symbol of her husband and their life together and links that life to her present widowhood. Laura Lee is the only quilt maker who uses ribbons that served first as bows on funeral flowers. Two of her funeral-ribbon quilts are significant: the one made from Judge Horton's ribbons and the one made from her son's ribbons. Both function as symbols of these personalities, yet neither quilt is physically present. Laura Lee needs only the memory of making them, not the material objects themselves.

The symbolic use of the funeral-ribbon quilts in these women's lives reflects not only personal attributes or experiences, but also wider Afro-American attitudes toward death and burial. These attitudes can be seen in the Afro-American graveyard decoration of which John Vlach writes in *The Afro-American Tradition in Decorative Arts:*

"Black graves are made distinct by the placement of a wide variety of offerings on the top of the burial mound. Most of these items are pottery or pressed-glass containers, but many different objects are encountered. . . . Graveyard goods are a statement of homage; their function is to keep a tempestuous soul at rest."[8] The last objects used by the deceased have special meaning for some Afro-Americans. Telfair Hodgson, daughter of a wealthy plantation owner in Savannah, Georgia, writes in her memoirs, circa 1907: "Negro graves were always decorated with the last article used by the departed, and broken pitchers and broken bits of colored glass were considered even more appropriate than the white shells from the beach nearby. Sometimes they carved rude wooden figures like images of idols, and sometimes a patchwork quilt was laid upon the grave."[9] Vlach quotes several who explain these beliefs: "Sarah Washington of Eulonia, Georgia, commented: 'I don't guess you be bother much by the spirits if you give 'em a good funeral and put the things what belong to 'em on top of the grave'; and her husband Ben seconded her opinion: 'You puts all the things what they use last like the dishes and the medicine bottle. The spirits need these same as the man. Then the spirit rest and don't wander about.' "[10] The last objects used by the deceased contain power and occupy a special position on top of the grave. Vlach traces this custom to Africa. Decorating graves is still common practice in Afro-American communities today.[11] Daniel Patterson has documented this tradition in Hillsborough, North Carolina.[12] I have seen decorated graves in Chatham County and in coastal North Carolina—grave decoration is an active tradition.

In one sense the funeral ribbons are the very last thing to be associated with the deceased. This connection makes them special and powerful. The glass, broken china, and personal possessions used to decorate graves function to mediate between the everyday, material world and the spirit world over the grave where the body lies. Conversely, the funeral ribbons move from their liminal position on top of the grave to a role in the material world, as utilitarian household objects. Yet even in the everyday world, the ribbons still contain symbolic power through their association with the dead. The quilts can be imbued with special meaning, as Jennie Burnett did with her embroidery. Even when the ribbons have not actually been used as grave decorations, as Jennie Burnett's were not, the quilter seems to have made a special effort to obtain and use funeral ribbons to help endow the quilt with special importance. She and Laura Lee use these ribbons closely associated with death to make quilts that, more than quilts made from other fabrics, hold special meaning.

For these women, funeral-ribbon quilts can serve as a commemoration of a person, as does the quilt Laura Lee made from Judge Horton's funeral ribbons. They can commemorate an earlier, happier stage of life, as widowed Jennie Burnett's quilt reflects her married life. The process of making quilts may be a way to cope with distress: Jennie Burnett made her commemorative quilt when she was leaving her homeplace and starting a new life alone, and Laura Lee made a quilt from her son's ribbons shortly after his death when she was doubtless trying to come to terms with her loss. An Afro-American cultural heritage, seen also in the tradition of graveyard decoration, where connotations of power and significance are given to objects last associated with the deceased, underlies this use of funeral ribbons transformed into quilts. Because of the power and liminal qualities of the funeral ribbons, these quilts can become symbolic of the people, experiences, and ideals of the quilters' lives.

10. "Learnin', Though": Environmental Art as a Creative Process

Kathleen Condon

Words and pictures simply cannot convey the impression one gets driving down a street of mill houses in Bynum, North Carolina, and coming upon Clyde Jones's yard. Brightly colored wooden and cement animal and human figures, gourds, stuffed animals, mailboxes, birdhouses, lanterns, and other objects stand, sit, or hang from cedar posts throughout the yard. A herd of animals resting in the right sideyard faces the street, giving the impression they are about to begin a march. The first time I visited, a hand-painted sign bearing the figure of a man and the words "Jungle Boy at Work" (which I would later learn was a gift from an admirer) hung prominently over the primary grouping of objects.

Jones's yard would raise the curiosity of any passerby, but as a folklorist, I had very specific interests. I knew of the controversy among folklorists surrounding yards such as Jones's; in fact, I had first visited his yard with two folklorists, Cece Conway and John Vlach. In the past, folklorists have often shied away from the study of such individualistic creations, which do not fit well within the community-oriented models of the folklore discipline. Folklorists have left the study of such creations to other scholars, art commentators, and collectors, many of whom have labeled such creations "folk art" without coming to terms with thorny questions of traditionality.[1] Often they speculate wildly on the intended meanings of the works while ignoring the sometimes cryptic explanations of the makers.

John Vlach argues against defining such works as "folk art." "Too often," he writes, "the term 'folk art' is used as a convenient umbrella under which many orphaned objects find shelter." He feels the term should be restricted to art that "exists in communities and is expressive

Figure 10.1. Clyde Jones's home in Bynum, N.C., in 1988 (photo by Charles G. Zug III).

of collectively held values which direct and focus an individual artist's creativity."[2] Robert Crease and Charles Mann, in a path-breaking article on individuals they call "back-yard builders," concur with Vlach's position. Arguing that such artists set themselves apart from group values rather than embracing them, they note that "folk art says 'We are,' but the works of the back-yard builders cry, 'I am.'" Mark Bulwinkle, a California builder interviewed by Crease and Mann, offers his own opinion on the controversy, erecting a sign in his scrap-metal "jungle" declaring:

> I AM NOT A FOLK ARTIST!
> I AM NOT A FOLK!!
> I AM A BULWINKLE!!![3]

Within the last few years, folklorists and scholars in related disciplines have begun to turn their attention toward these unusual creations. In several recent articles, and especially in *Personal Places,* a collection of essays on "informal-art environments," authors consider the life histories and personal comments of these artists, carefully examining the traditional as well as the idiosyncratic aspects of the artists' works.[4] When I began studying Jones's yard in 1983, most of this writing was not yet in print, but my research preoccupations were very similar. I wanted to examine the artistic motivations of one of these individuals for myself, to find out what Jones was trying to express in his yard, and to see if this expression reflected the aesthetics and values of a particular community. During our first interview, I began to learn about Jones's life and his reasons for decorating his yard.

Clyde Jones was born in 1938 on a farm on the Rocky River, about ten miles from Pittsboro, North Carolina. As a youth Jones worked on the family farm and attended school intermittently. When he moved to nearby Bynum with his family in 1956, he began to work at the local cotton mill. Jones left the mill ten or twelve years later, and since then he has worked as a day laborer, helping landscaping crews, pouring cement for construction crews, and cutting wood.

While cutting logs one day in 1979, Jones dropped a chain saw on his leg. With his leg in a cast for almost a year after the accident, Jones was unable to work, and he searched for something to do to pass the time. One day he was sitting on the porch of his family home, looking at the three artificial deer he had placed in his sideyard: "And I saw them little deer in there. Well, I was out there, and you know how it is when you got a big cast on your leg. I was sitting out there in the yard, and them three deer—sitting by theirselves. And I decided I wanted something with 'em."[5] First Jones chainsawed a pig out of a wooden log. Next he tried an anteater, an animal he'd seen in a book. Then he made a horse and rider. As time passed and Jones recuperated, he continued to work on his new project. Two years after his first accident, Jones pierced his eye with a nail while cutting wood on his porch. This second accident once again prevented Jones from working steadily, and he devoted more and more time to his growing collection of objects.

After discussing the yard with Jones and several of his neighbors, I found that although his work had in part been influenced by his traditional background, it clearly did not reflect the values and aesthetics of his traditional community. Lifelong Bynum residents are often a bit perplexed by Jones's work. "I don't know," mused one neighbor when I asked her opinion, "I guess it shows talent. And imagination." Another neighbor commented, "If he just wouldn't paint them such queer

Figure 10.2. Clyde Jones in the yard of his home in Bynum, N.C., in 1988 (photo by Charles G. Zug III).

colors, it'd look right like animals." Jones has many admirers, but they come primarily from outside the local community and are intrigued by the eccentricity of his yard. Jones says he welcomes the comments of others because they give him "more ideas," but his work is not dictated by these suggestions.

Although yard displays are common and culturally acceptable in rural North Carolina, and indeed throughout the United States, Jones's yard does not fall within this tradition. Varick A. Chittenden has found that many yard displays throughout rural New York State express the value placed on family, religion, and nature.[6] Although Jones's interest in nature was fostered by his traditional farming background, his intense fascination with animals and with wood is more an idiosyncratic personality characteristic than a learned cultural value. Jones sees himself as unusual and different in this respect, as an "oddball." Jones's original yard display of three commercially manufactured deer and several stone and cement flower beds was well within the commonly accepted tradition of rural North Carolina yard ornamentation, but his yard now shares little in common with these more modest, often highly idealized, pastoral displays.

Although Jones, like many other yard artists, uses skills from his occupational background to decorate his yard, his art does not have its roots in an artisan tradition.[7] Many individuals can use a chain saw or pour cement, but Jones did not learn to make the figures that decorate his yard from any of them. When I asked Jones if he had ever seen or heard anything that had inspired him to begin his work, he replied, "Nope, nothin' but them three deers sitting there in that yard; that's all why I took it up there." Jones's work remains his own—the term "folk art" sheds little light on his highly idiosyncratic endeavor.

Once I decided what Jones's work was *not*, I was faced with a much more difficult question: What *was* it? To find an answer, I began asking Jones questions to elicit his perspective, to uncover what he was trying to express in his yard. I visited Jones many times before I began to realize that although I had been careful not to assume that Jones's art was "folk," I had been wrong to assume that he was trying to express anything through it. In considering Jones an "artist," I had assumed that he was primarily motivated by the desire to express a concept or a vision in finished form. Everything I had read had conceptualized built environments similar to Jones's as expressions of highly personal visions. Crease and Mann describe the builders they study as "individuals untutored in art or architecture who worked tenaciously for years to transform their personal visions into habitable worlds in the confines of their yards."[8] Elinor Horwitz also sees these works as motivated by the desire to express something: "The total environmentalists are people for whom a very private vision became an obsession, and the desire to create found an outlet in a project of enormous scope which took years—even decades—to fashion."[9]

Simon Rodia, the creator of *Watts Towers*, the world's most celebrated informal art environment, has been credited with a variety of expressive motivations. Horwitz describes his work as "the creation of an artist who was obsessed with a stunning and singular fantasy and had the skill to carry it to fruition."[10] Yet Horwitz does not describe the content of Rodia's "fantasy." Rodia abandoned his awe-inspiring construction after thirty-three years of back-breaking efforts, never to explain the "meaning" of his work. When admirers tracked him down living in Martinez three hundred miles to the north and asked him the meaning of *Nuestro Pueblo,* his title for the towers, he cryptically replied, "Lot-sa things, lot-sa things." When pressed, he retorted, "Don't you understand? It's the end; there's nothing there."[11]

In the absence of any definitive statement from Rodia, Roger Cardinal has speculated on the creator's intended meaning: "It might be held that the Towers are a challenge to triviality and ugliness, a 'something big' that is not mimetic of American bigness, but a brilliant alternative to it in the way it exploits the very things that America discards."[12] Perhaps Cardinal's interpretation is partially correct, but more recent research by the folklorist Dan Ward has provided convincing evidence that the towers and boats of Rodia's spectacular work were inspired by similar structures, made of wood and papier mâché, that are carried through the streets during St. Paulinus feasts in Rodia's native Italy.[13]

The desire to execute a specific vision in a finished work has clearly motivated some of these builders, although the exact nature of their visions is not always clear. James Hampton seems to have been expressing a very personal vision in *The Throne of the Third Heaven of the Nations Millennium General Assembly.*[14] The Woodstock, New York, stone mason Clarence Schmidt once wrote to a friend explaining that he had constructed his *House of Mirrors* because he had always "dreamed of creating something that would live forever in the minds of men."[15] Although these men seem primarily driven to express themselves, not all builders are. In insisting on seeing all such builders as expression oriented, and in positing intended meanings in the absence of statements from the artists, we may be missing the primary meaning of some of these constructions for their creators.[16]

Elinor Horwitz has written, "Few folk artists seek fame, and many speak deprecatingly of their work. They tell you it's 'just whittling,' 'just something to pass the time.'"[17] Horwitz assumes that these individuals are expressing themselves despite their own statements to the contrary. Like Horwitz, I discounted comments from Jones such as "Well, it's just a hobby to me. I don't care what anybody calls it, I call it a hobby. I love to mess with it," or "It's just good sports to me" as the self-deprecating words of a very modest artist. The first time I visited Jones's yard, a man driving by had commented, "Yeah, he's got his mess out." At the time, I interpreted this man's comment as insensitive, not guessing that this man was probably much closer to understanding Jones's work than I.

In my first conversation with Jones, I strove to understand what Jones was trying to express in his work. The prominently displayed words "Jungle Boy at Work" had led me to believe that his expression must have something to do with a jungle, and I asked Jones if this was the name of his work:

Jones: What, the whole thing?
Condon: The whole thing, yeah.
Jones: I just call it a jungle and let it go.
Condon: When did you start calling it a jungle?
Jones: Well, some of these people give me the ideas. A lot of people call it a little zoo.
Condon: A zoo?
Jones: Yeah.
Condon: But you like "jungle"?
Jones: Either way's all right by me.

This was my first major clue that Jones was not thinking of his work in the same terms as I, and my first encounter with Jones's habit of assenting—"I'll go along with that"—to any assertion I made about his yard. At first I found this habit extremely frustrating, hell bent as I was to elicit Jones's own ideas on his yard. It was not until I began to see Jones's work as he saw it—as a hobby to occupy his spare time and to satisfy his urge to try new things—that I began to understand his singular lack of interest in forwarding his own interpretation.

Jones is not interested in formulating a finished concept of his work; the process of creation is much more important to him than an expressive end product. When I asked him why he worked on his yard, his response was always similar: "Lady, I got a crazy head, and I take up on a lot of wantin' to try things. I just like to do that kind of work. See what I can and can do and can't, you know. I just get interested in it, I guess. What counts, I love it. That's what counts, messin' with it. I'm gonna build it one of these days. I'll get it. Might be ten years. I don't know. Who knows, by that time maybe I'll be learnt." This process of "messin' with it," of learning, of seeing what he can do, is

what Jones is "up to" in his yard. As he hints, perhaps his work will be
finished only when he's finished with the process of learning through it.

Jones does envision finishing his creation: "But I'm gonna fool somebody one of these days, what I'm gonna make out of it. I'm gonna get
there. Taking a long time. Who knows?" But when asked what this
finished work will be, Jones is evasive. Only once during our conversations did he ever forward an organizing theme for his yard:

Jones: I'm gonna come up with it one of these days.
Condon: What's "it"?
Jones: Well, it's kind of hard to explain it. It's a long way from
what I had in mind.
Condon: What'd you have in mind?
Jones: It was actually a little old zoo, or something. You know,
the animals all around and all that.
Condon: How's it different now?
Jones: Some of the animals aren't coming out like I wanted 'em to.
They're not good enough, I guess. But like I said, I'll get there.

Yet, when I questioned Jones on this zoo concept months later, his response was noncommittal:

Condon: You told me when you started you kinda had in mind a
little zoo. Do you still think maybe—or, what do you think about
it now?
Jones: Well, nothing wrong with that, I guess.

Jones still has no name for his work, and when I last asked him if he
thought he ever would, he said, "Lady, that's something I don't know.
Yeah, I got a name for it right now—a mess. I got a name."

The comment is not self-deprecating—Jones likes to think of his
yard as a "mess" because the absence of a fixed organizing concept
gives him the freedom to try new things and incorporate the ideas and
gifts of others into his process of "messin'." In the spring of 1984, Jones
made eight or nine fanciful human figures. When I commented on this
new development, Jones replied, "That's just somethin' I'm doin' right
now." Jones was not expressing anything new by including human
figures in his yard—they were simply the objects that he was preoccupied with trying to make at the moment. In the past, Jones was more
interested in making fish:

Jones: I did mess with a lot of fish.

Condon: Like, are there any here?

Jones: No, I let 'em go. I just messed with 'em. Let people have 'em. I don't want 'em in here.

Condon: How come?

Jones: I just don't want no fish in here. It'd been better off, I reckon, if I kept 'em.

Jones is constantly trying something new—one of his latest additions is a display of hanging lanterns. Jones also often incorporates objects that others give him, such as the stuffed animals children bring to him or the hand-painted signs given to him by admirers.

Jones frequently rearranges the objects in his yard according to current whims and does not seem terribly interested in finding a permanent resting place for any of his individual creations. When I asked Jones if there was any order to the way the objects in his yard were arranged, he replied:

Jones: I keep 'em placed like I want 'em.

Condon: And how do you decide?

Jones: Well, I just hit ideas, and want 'em in line sometimes, you know . . . just scatter 'em all over the place.

Condon: Like, is it better if some are next to others?

Jones: Yeah, I just scatter 'em out, and a row of this and that. Mix the little ones with the big ones.

Condon: The little ones with the big ones?

Jones: Yeah. Once in a while when I move 'em.

I once asked Jones why he had moved some new orange-and-yellow felt banners from one object to another between my visits. He laughed and answered, "You oughta come back next time, and every one of 'em sittin' back up yonder." A painted cow skull that once rested on the ground later hung from a tree along with some plastic monkeys— by now it is probably somewhere else. Jones most frequently rearranges the pieces placed closest to the street, the ones most often seen by passersby. In the spring of 1984 Jones began placing more pieces in the left front corner of his sideyard, but now he has replaced these with new works, moving the original grouping to the rear of the right side-yard.

Figure 10.3. A cluster of creatures (giraffe, "snappers," deer, and goat) arranged by Clyde Jones in a neighbor's yard in Bynum, N.C., 1988 (photo by Charles G. Zug III).

In the last few years, local interest in Jones's artwork has led to the exhibition of some of his wooden animals outside his yard. A number of them now fill the lawn of Bynum's antique-and-gift shop—the blue ribbons tied around the necks of most animals signify that they are not for sale. At Crook's Corner, a Chapel Hill restaurant and bar, Jones's animals perch atop the roof and peek out from behind plants in the outdoor dining area. Individual animals have been featured in exhibitions at the North Carolina Museum of Art and at the student center of the University of North Carolina at Chapel Hill. When I asked Jones about these exhibitions, he said simply, "Yeah, I let 'em go down there," speaking almost as would a father allowing children to attend summer camp. Although Jones is proud of these pieces and would not want to part with them, they are not "missing" from his yard while they're away because he has no set place for them within a grand scheme.

Nor does he have any interest in "finishing" any of his individual objects. He approaches them much as he approaches his yard—he gets involved with the continuing process of seeing what he can do with an object. When I asked Clyde how he got the idea for an animal, he replied, "I don't know, I make a mess when I first start with it, and then I go from there." On another occasion, Jones reiterated this same sentiment, "You know, I've got to make so much mess, and then start from there. That's me." Sometimes Jones knows what the animals will be when he starts, sometimes he does not, and sometimes he changes his mind along the way.

This process doesn't end when Jones places the objects in his yard. Jones often "culls" pieces he has become dissatisfied with:

> *Jones:* See, I'm going through this thing, placing some of this wood, now. I'm gonna take some of the cull wood out, and replace a lot, when I find what I want.
> *Condon:* What do you mean by "cull wood"?
> *Jones:* Well, it's not what I like.
> *Condon:* Do you mean that it's not quite finished, or . . .
> *Jones:* Well, I don't ever finish none of 'em—I just make a mess.

Jones often takes out individual pieces and puts them in his work area to rethink them:

> *Jones:* I set it over yonder. You see, I'm gonna take that and cull it. I'm gonna take the good out and put it with—over yonder, now I work with my bad . . . But I'm seein' some ideas I like, right now. I didn't like that piece of wood until I set it out by itself.
> *Condon:* Do you do that sometimes—just set it out by itself?
> *Jones:* Yeah, I get out here and sit down when it's dark, at times, and look at it. I do it.

Jones often repaints and refurbishes the objects in his yard. When I first visited Jones's yard, his horse and rider was painted a dark gray. Six months later Jones commented to me that the rider was looking ragged, and soon after he painted the horse and rider white with pink polka dots. Later still he repainted it silver and gave the rider a new gun. Jones says he applies additional coats of paint to many of the other objects to protect the wood. However, some paint jobs are clearly more decorative than preservative, such as the artificial deer he spray painted with orange blotches and later painted white again.

This process of change goes beyond mere ornamentation; sometime Jones will totally change the identity of an object. Sometimes he forgets what he had wanted a particular animal to be. Then, he says, "I just take my saw and make something else out of 'em." Jones often sacrifices old objects in the service of new ones. The sign "Jungle Boy at Work," first displayed above the major portion of animals, was later posted on a tree in the left-hand sideyard. Later he used the back of this sign as a placard to display photographs of his work that people have given him. Clearly Jones is more interested in the process of creation than in finishing his individual pieces.

Are other backyard builders driven by these same motivations? Looking back at the literature on other builders, I find that many of them also seem motivated by the desire to occupy spare time with the process of trying to make things rather than by the desire to express something. Ralph Lanning, a shipping clerk for Burlington Industries in Denton, North Carolina, makes and places wooden animals in his yard that look remarkably similar to the animals made by Jones. Lanning also began his work during a period of enforced leisure time when he was working part-time one spring. First he kept himself busy by constructing wooden fences on his property. And then: "I'd get tired and sit down and stare at these trees. . . . I'd begin wondering what they'd look like if I turned them different ways. I'd see them taking on different shapes, and I'd see faces in the root systems. So, you might say this thing started off from sheer laziness. If you sit in one place long enough and let your mind go to work, you can make something out of almost nothing."[18] Like Jones, Lanning seems inspired by the process of seeing what he can do rather than the desire to express something in making his animals.

Miles Carpenter, famous for his painted wooden watermelon slices, began carving animal figures in earnest after the death of his wife: "When my wife passed away I was real despondent. I guess that's when I really took to carving more and more. It's a big help when you're real despondent to be able to do something like this."[19] In making his carvings, Carpenter was driven to see what he could do with a root rather than to express something: "I started making things out of roots because I seen something funny in them. I would look at roots from a tree that fell down, or I'd pull some up, and I'd look at all those long and short and thick and thin and tangled parts, and I'd just begin to see something funny. . . . You have to be able to see something in a root—then you just fix it right."[20]

Walter Flax, a man who has created a fleet of model naval ships in his yard in Yorktown, Virginia, is not interested in creating a finished work. He does not preserve the ships that he has already constructed; in fact, he often uses pieces from old ships to create new ones. Flax gets satisfaction simply from making these ships; he told Horwitz, "I'm gifted thataway. Sometimes you got something you can do—other people *can't* do it."[21]

Emanuele "Litto" Damonte evaded questions about his reasons for constructing a "hubcap ranch" in the hills north of San Francisco when he spoke with Crease and Mann. "The question of motives," they noted, "made him uncomfortable and he would automatically change the subject." "I don't know myself why I started," Damonte told Crease and Mann. "People come, they bring hubcaps, and I hang them up. I didn't have no idea it was going to turn out like this."[22] Damonte, like many of these other builders, seems motivated by the desire to see what he can do with a particular building material—and for Damonte that building material is hubcaps.

It seems, then, that Jones is not alone in his orientation toward a process rather than an end product. In concentrating our efforts on discerning what these builders are expressing, we miss the point. If we look and listen closely, these builders remind us that human creativity is a complex phenomenon that cannot always be reduced to our own preconceived notions of "art" or "artistry." If these builders are expressing anything in their work, it is simply their passion to create.

Of Communities

11. In the Good Old Way: Primitive Baptist Tradition in an Age of Change

Brett Sutton

This century has seen the arrival in the southern highlands of outsiders of every variety—humanitarians and philanthropists, educators and folk-lorists, politicians and businessmen. Challenged by the region's problems and attracted by its physical and cultural resources, these outsiders have often had something to give and have just as often looked for something in return. From the early mountain folk-and-craft schools to the garish commercial developments fostered by the tourist industry, their projects have brought rapid change and a new mix of values to the mountains. Some of the newcomers have worked to preserve traditional mountain culture; others to refurbish, repackage, or replace it; few have been willing to leave it alone.

For those of us interested in American folklife, the evolution of Appalachian culture over the course of the century constitutes a fascinating case study in modernization. Much has changed since English folklorist Cecil Sharp's first ballad hunt in the mountains in the early 1900s. Although Sharp's ground-breaking efforts provided the model for the collecting expeditions that followed, he could hardly have foreseen the effect that publicity and mass media would have on indigenous highland culture. It is doubtful that early students of Appalachian folklife would have predicted that the local fiddlers' conventions of their day would eventually become nationally popular youth gatherings.

It is not surprising, or even improper, that Appalachian folklife should have strong appeal for modern people feeling trapped by a throwaway, hypercommercialized, technocratic society. We cannot escape our culture, but we can turn to folk art for a reminder of what is durable and enlivening in our past. Almost everyone benefits from a revival of interest in folklife. Even the people of the mountains themselves, though they have seldom been the primary recipients of the material rewards of national attention, have at least found a source of pride in their role as bearers *par excellence* of the Anglo-American folk tradition.

Such attention has not been without its price, however, as the force we turn to folk art to escape threatens to dominate it in the end. Popularity breeds popularization, transformation by the mass market, and sometimes commercial exploitation, and for fifty years the fruits of popularity have helped shape the course of Appalachian culture, creating a public image of the mountaineer and his culture that often degenerates into stereotype. Some of the fruits of the folk revival are worthy extensions of the original forms; others are grotesque parodies, as a visit to some of the gift shops along the Blue Ridge Parkway will confirm. And at a time when "authentic mountain toys" are mass-produced and old-time fiddling contests draw more urbanites from the Northeast than natives, we are led to ask what aspect of mountain folklife, if any, survives in its original form.

Nothing, of course, can resist modernization, but there is one mountain institution that has been relatively untouched by commercialization and cultural revivalism, and consequently, remains relatively unchanged, and that is the traditional religion of the region. One of the sturdiest examples is the subject of this essay, the Primitive Baptist church. That an institution of such vitality should have escaped the attention of the folk revivalists is surprising. It is perhaps a consequence of the instinctive avoidance of serious religious issues by a secular-oriented culture, or a function of protective elements within the tradition itself. Whatever the explanation, such protection from public scrutiny has preserved not only the forms, but also the substance of an earlier era. The purpose of this essay is to examine those forms and the context in which they thrive.

Primitive Baptists believe in predestination and unconditional election. Salvation is granted only to the elect chosen by God before the world was founded, who may be made aware of their election through the gift of grace. Good works and mere human will are totally ineffectual in obtaining salvation, so the church does not actively seek new members. Grace is a beautiful mystery.

The experience of grace is at once an elevating and humiliating event, creating simultaneously a feeling of satisfaction and a feeling of alienation from the world. One member stood before the church at a meeting and expressed it succinctly: "The Lord laid his hands on me one morning. Ever since that day I been pointed fingers at and called the child of God."[1]

There is a deep ambivalence about the world among Primitive Baptists that is characteristic of the faith. The church's sober, some would say gloomy, perspective on the world stems in part from its frank recognition that suffering is basic to the human condition. No one is immune from sin, and all human effort is powerless against it. Feelings of humility and alienation—universal in human experience—are understood as natural proof that only God's transcendent power can save souls. Although this realization gives the Primitive Baptists a basic acceptance of powerlessness and travail, it does not encroach upon their humble joy in the unearned and unmerited gift of grace. Theirs is an honest, simple outlook, somehow truer to the reality of daily life than the superficial optimism of many contemporary churches. A Primitive Baptist hymn acknowledges this curious balance:

> Mixtures of joy and sorrow I daily do pass through,
>> Sometimes I'm in the valley—then sinking down with woe;
> Sometimes I am exalted—on eagles' wings I fly;
>> Rising above Mount Pisgah, I almost reach the sky.
>
> Sometimes my hope is little—I almost lay it by;
>> Sometimes it is sufficient if I were called to die;
> Sometimes I am in doubting, and think I have no grace;
>> Sometimes I am a shouting, and Bethel is the place.[2]

Although on some points they appear strict Calvinists, the Primitive Baptists trace their history through a long line of nonconformist sects directly to the apostolic church described in the New Testament.[3] The church's doctrine is founded on a literal interpretation of scripture; they believe that rickety man-made additions to biblical commandments are false, and they especially object to the doctrine of free will, which teaches that people can save themselves by choosing Jesus. The Free Will dogma gained popularity in America as the cornerstone of the early nineteenth-century revivalist movement, and it was in resistance to that movement that many churches consolidated their forces into what became the Primitive Baptist church.

Figure 11.1. Black Primitive Baptist church near the Virginia border, 1976 (photo by Brett Sutton).

Upon this group of churches fell the duty of preserving the seed of the "good old way" against changing times. Virginia and North Carolina were major focal points of the creative activity that produced the Primitive Baptist church, and remains today a center of the church's strength. The commitment to the autonomy of the individual church, along with relative geographic isolation, has produced a heterogeneous array of Primitive Baptist churches throughout the mountains of southern Appalachia and along the eastern slopes of the Virginia and Carolina Blue Ridge and in the adjacent Piedmont, including both black and white associations, as well as unaffiliated independent congregations. Because of their autonomy and distrust of institutional structure, no single description of doctrine is applicable to all. The most conservative churches continue to reject all deviations from a strictly interpreted biblical Christianity, including missionary movements, revivals, Sunday schools, radio ministries, church choirs, musical instruments in church, national governing bodies, seminaries, infant baptism and lavishly decorated church buildings (figures 11.1 and 11.2).

Primitive Baptists have not made themselves popular by dragging

Figure 11.2. Interior of a black Primitive Baptist church (photo by Brett Sutton).

their feet in the face of religious modernization; their unwillingness to help baptize the heathen and their refusal to acknowledge the ecumenical spirit of the times has occasionally made them the target of unreasonable criticism. And in recent years some critics have accused the church of hanging onto ignorance and illiteracy and blocking needed social change in the mountains. But the image of the church being dragged screaming into the twentieth century is a myth. Although conservative in piety, members of the Primitive Baptist church are not backward in any sense of the word. They are modern people with a contemporary understanding of their world, who do not stubbornly resist all change for its own sake. What they do resist is any force that threatens the religious foundation of their worldview.

Since the Bible teaches that God chose the members of the church before "the foundation of the world" and will gather them in His own good time, Primitive Baptists reject revivalism; they reject the whole concept of church growth. They see no point in campaigning for lost souls, and they neither cajole nor coerce sinners to join the church. Once in the fold, however, members are highly committed and not likely to weaken. They may occasionally stumble into sin, as any mortal must, but such an experience seems to bring them closer to the church rather than drive them from it. One member put it this way: "And I don't say I joined the church, because if the church don't join you first, there ain't nothing to it, the way I look at it. 'Cause I can join the church, and I can unjoin, but if the Lord join me to it, then I'll stay there."

One product of such stability has been the maintenance of the social cohesion so necessary for the generation and preservation of folk tradition. Because religion is not merely a compartment of life, but life's entire justification, the church's influence encompasses the whole community. Church business sessions, held the Saturday before the monthly Sunday services, are occasions not just for the discussion of business matters related to the church, but for the airing of general problems troubling the community. The church members as a body are effective against forces that threaten to divide the community. If necessary, they can exclude defiant members from the fellowship of the church; more often they offer spiritual and material comfort to the suffering. Church funds are directed where the need is greatest: an ailing sister, a family hit by hard times, a visiting preacher who has traveled a great distance at his own expense (church leaders themselves accept no salary). Community attention and community resources are directed not outward to foreign missions or national associations, but inward to the community itself.

This concern for the local community, along with a determined resistance to change, has deflected the modernizing forces that have swept unimpeded through so much of secular mountain culture. Potent vehicles of change, such as radio and television, mass publication of church literature, printed music, and the professional clergy, are excluded from church activities as human inventions that are neither spiritually necessary nor sanctioned by God. The only mass media used to a significant extent by the church members are religious periodicals, and these are peripheral, because doctrine emphasizes the importance of the direct, personal experience of grace above all written material. Locally designed traditional forms predominate in worship and practice (figure 11.3).

At the heart of all Primitive Baptist expressive forms is the spoken word, normally uninhibited and improvisational. No written text other

Figure 11.3. Primitive Baptist river baptism (photo by Brett Sutton).

than the Scriptures, no published Bible commentary or tract, no recita-
tion of memorized prayers or creeds, no formal responsive readings—
none of these appear in the Primitive Baptist service. The primary medium for the expression of spiritual truth is spontaneous expression,
supported by all the creative vigor of 150 years of oral tradition. Worship is not standardized, but draws from each member whatever testimony, prayer, sermon, or song has been given through divine inspiration. In practice, all members are not totally free to express themselves
as "God commands." In black Primitive Baptist churches women may
occasionally give testimony in church and often are responsible for the
leading of hymns, but in neither black nor white churches are they
permitted to serve as elders, lead prayer, or preach.[4]

Oral historians have noted the extent to which people in rural
communities cast the continuum of their lives into dramatic episodic
narratives. There is no better illustration than the Primitive Baptists'
narrated experience of conversion and grace, the most finely formed
product of their oral tradition. Although such conversions occur initially as mystical private events, they are cast ultimately into verbal

form, since no personal experience is really complete until it has been shared and, to an extent, validated through public testimony. One of the most memorable visionary experiences I ever heard was told to me by an elder who was one of the most respected members of his church. I had asked him to explain how he came to join the Primitive Baptist church, and after a moment's pause, he described this experience:

> I never will forget it. I was in West Virginia, in a coal-mining camp. My brothers, they went in the mines to work. I didn't feel like going out to work that morning. I thought I was natural sick. I said, "I'll stay at home, stay at the house here. You all go on to your work." They didn't want to leave me, but they went on to the work.
>
> Long about nine o'clock, I laid down across the bed. And being laying there, a man appeared over me. He was just as white, as white as snow. And he walked right up over me, astride my legs, and looked right down in my face. And his hair was as white as lamb's wool, flowing out over his shoulders. And he had a white cloth over his head. And his eyes was just flashing like fire. And he was white, he was so white, his garments were so white. And I felt myself getting numb down in my feet, and death crept on up, crept on up. I was just sure I was dying. This man, he kept looking me in the face. And his eyes was revolving, just like fire in his eyes. I couldn't get my eyes away. I wanted to turn my head, but I couldn't. I had to look right at him. Death come on up. I knowed when it hit my heart, I'd die, I thought. But it passed on up to my eyes. My eyes, they felt like they was full of sand, and I was about to close them. He reached right under there and he got a spear out. It flashed like lightning. A little dagger about that long. And it was gold, and it just flashed like lightning. He come down on me with it.
>
> I didn't know nothing then for a long time. I laid there, I don't know how long. When the Lord brought me to, I was laying on a little bench all the way across the room. And I heard a voice, and it come from somewhere over my shoulder, and it spoke like this: "Arise now and shine, for the light has come, and the glory of the Lord is risen in you." By that time, I was able to walk out on my own. It was a dark and dreary morning when I went in my room,

but when I come out, everything looked new, everything was summertime, and the trees was green all around. The little birds was sitting out in the ends of the twigs of the trees, chirping just like they were offering thanks to God. I ain't never seen a morning so bright. About that time, I heard angels begin to sing, going back into the western part of the world. I heard them sing, "He done died one time, ain't gonna die no more."

Such narratives are widespread in the Primitive Baptist community, although few are as vivid and dramatic as this one. They have many elements in common. Spiritual beings abound—there are men in white, angelic messengers, monstrous horses that carry the mortal on tours of heaven and hell. There are cool mountaintops where the sinner is taken to reflect, lonesome roads where voices whisper hymns in the wind, stern commands coming from angry skies, miraculous natural signs, divine revelations of the future. Each is the product of an individual member's spiritual experience and an emblem of his participation in the church. Yet they are not artifacts self-consciously polished by individual storytellers so much as overwhelmingly personal experiences that become community property in the retelling. Even as they reflect the individuality of a spiritual experience, they become the raw material for a rich shared oral literature, the vehicle by which personal grace becomes community grace.

The visionary experience may be central to Primitive Baptist belief, but the sermon is the heart of Primitive Baptist practice. Since congregations may hear five or more sermons at a single meeting lasting three or more hours—depending on how many elders are present—churchgoers tend to develop a connoisseur's taste for the preacher's art. Each sermon is both a personal manifestation of the spirit and a highly organized rhetorical form that calls into play all the verbal, dramatic, and even musical skills of the preacher. God does not call a man to the pulpit without granting him the gift of inspiration that makes him a worthy outlet for the spirit. Sermons are never prepared in advance, even in outline form. To rely on notes is to admit faithlessness.

A man who has been truly called by God to preach is transformed by the spirit the moment he steps into the stand. Church members tell of a local elder, now dead, who was afflicted with a severe stutter that left him only when he mounted the pulpit and began to preach. Under the divine intervention of God, his words flowed powerfully and smoothly, and not until the sermon ended and the spirit left him did his stammering return.

Aflame with the gift inspired by God in the holy setting, a preacher may narrate his own conversion experiences or draw on communal material by rendering the experiences of others in his own words. He may create dramatic retellings of Biblical events, illustrated with gestures and expanded by the addition of contemporary parallels. Each sermon is, to an extent, a personal statement, but there is much sharing of style and content among the preachers of a particular circle of churches. Many elders of black congregations I visited, for example, tended to draw on the same body of proverbial phrases:

> I ain't got nothing to brag on, but I feel like I got something to die on.

> Salvation is a gift, not a get.

> If the devil is out there in the road, make him get in the back seat. If you let him in the front seat, he'll want to drive, and there's no telling where he'll carry you.

> Come one, come all, come great, come small.

> A preacher is like a radio: somebody's got to turn him on.

> Our doors this morning are hanging on welcome hinges.

As the man in the pulpit warms to his labor, his prose may become melodic and poetic, flowing in a rhythmic chant that can be notated like music. It is not unusual, in fact, for the preacher to incorporate hymn stanzas into the already rhythmic text of the sermon. In the black church, the congregation may actually participate in such a sermon, shouting and singing in harmony with the elder. Conventional categories are useless to describe such an event; here, song and sermon flow together as one.

The spoken word is one key element of the Primitive Baptist service. Song is another. And there are times when song serves better than speech to convey the spirit, as this deacon explained:

> A man can preach all day long, and if you don't feel it, it don't do you no good. That's the way that is. And you can sing, and if the

Lord give you a spirit to sing, that singing is just as good as preaching. It fills you up all over; you get just like a new person in there. Yes sir, you get to where you just can't hardly sit on your seat. Make you feel right. That's right! Now, I have seen people preach, oh, I don't know how long, look like it didn't have a good effect on you. Just preach, didn't warm you up. And then a woman in there can just sing a song, and it just gets all over you. That's right! That's strange—it's a strange thing to say about it. It look like they can just sing a song, somebody can just pick up a song-book and sing a song, look like that song just feeds you, and just fills your soul, right now. And that's the good part of it.

The Primitive Baptists are still using the same hymn texts that formed the backbone of the repertoire when the church was founded in the early nineteenth century. The two standard hymnbooks, Benjamin Lloyd's *Primitive Hymns* (1841) and D. H. Goble's *Primitive Baptist Hymn Book* (1887), each one containing texts but no music, are still in print.[5] The books contain hymns written up to the original dates of publication, but the core of each collection consists of the stern hymns of eighteenth-century Christianity, many of them composed by such great English divines as Isaac Watts, John Newton, and Samuel Stennett. Among some of the more liberal Primitive Baptist associations, lighter-hearted, buoyant gospel hymns have gained a toe-hold, but in most places they have not managed to drive out these sturdy old workhorses.

Thumbing through one of these little hymnbooks, one does not find songs of complacent happiness or aggressive optimism, but rather hymns that express humility and fear before a powerful God, the leaden feeling of moments before grace, the terrible fear of damnation, the inscrutable mystery of God's ways. Texts that have long since been purged from regular denominational hymnbooks because of their pervasive gloom retain their importance for Primitive Baptists:

> Hark! from the tombs a doleful sound!
>   My ears, attend the cry:
> Ye living men, come view the ground
>   Where you must shortly lie.
> (Goble, p. 139)

> The time is swiftly rolling on
>   When I must faint and die;
> My body to the dust return,
>   And there forgotten lie.
> (Lloyd, p. 475)

> Lord, what a wretched land is this,
>   That yields us no supply.
> No cheering fruits, no wholesome trees,
>   No streams of living joy!
> (Lloyd, p. 296)

> When sorrows encompass me round,
>   And many distresses I see,
> Astonished, I cry, Can a mortal be found,
>   Surrounded with troubles like me?
> (Goble, p. 203)

Such hymns are sung slowly in unison, without musical accompaniment, to doleful tunes drawn from the collective memory of the singers. A large number of these tunes are unison versions of the three- or four-part hymns found in the shape-note songbooks published in the South during the nineteenth century. George Pullen Jackson has shown that the southern songwriters who contributed to these published collections drew heavily on the tune stocks of the Anglo-American folk tradition,[6] a tradition that also produced the Primitive Baptist music. But it cannot be automatically assumed from such circumstantial evidence that the Primitive Baptist versions were learned *from* the books. The overlap in the two repertoires may simply reflect the fact that each had its origins in the same oral traditions of the early nineteenth century.

Whether the Primitive Baptist tunes have survived purely in oral channels, parallel to various written extensions, or whether they have enjoyed the stabilizing support of written collections at various points, they nevertheless survive today without benefit of musical notation and are subject to the shaping influences of regional and temporal variation. Some of the tunes are variants of secular tunes: one such tune used with the text "When I can read my title clear" is a member of the tune family associated with the ballad "The House Carpenter." Given the strength of Primitive Baptist singing, the large current repertoire may contain once-popular secular tunes that now exist only in the sacred versions, preserved under the canopy of the church.

Since the words are printed and the tunes sung from memory, texts and tunes tend to float. The same tune, usually nameless, may be used for many texts of the same metric pattern and, on different occasions, a particular hymn may be sung to several different tunes. Such flexibility is particularly noticeable in the black church, where old hymns have been grafted to spirituals, yielding hybrids of great vigor.[7]

In many churches in the nineteenth century, it was common for hymns to be "lined out": the song leader chanted one or two lines, which the congregation then sang, and so on through all the verses. This practice, once a necessity in congregations where books were scarce, was abandoned by most churches as soon as books became more plentiful. For the most part, however, Primitive Baptists continue the practice as an honored tradition; it still thrives today among black congregations in general and is common among white churches located in some parts of the mountains.[8]

It is particularly interesting to note white and black versions of the same tune. As with many southern denominations before the Civil War, slaves and masters attended the same churches, and it was not until the late nineteenth century that Primitive Baptist associations divided into black and white branches. If we can assume that there was a common repertoire of tunes up to the moment of division, then the contemporary divergence between black and white versions is fascinating evidence of the shaping power of cultural contact on tune evolution.[9] In general, the black versions are slower, more elaborately ornamented, and more heavily rhythmic; the white versions, stronger in melody and more subtly ornamented. The size of the tune repertoire is smaller in the black community (counting only the old hymns and omitting spirituals), possibly because their tunes have never been preserved in printed songbooks.

Figure 11.4 illustrates three versions of the same tune—one printed arrangement and two separate performances by black and white Primitive Baptist congregations. The transcriptions are placed together here to facilitate comparison.

"Kentucky" is the name identifying the tune in John R. Daily's *Primitive Baptist Hymn and Tune Book* (1918). But the Daily book is

Ingalls

white congregation
(original key: F♯; ♩ = 26)

black congregation
(original key: D; ♩ = 20)

Grace, 'tis a charm- ing sound,

Grace, 'tis a charm- ing sound,

Grace, 'tis a charm- ing sound,

Har - mon - ious to the ear.

Har - mon - ious to the ear.

Har - mon - ious to the ear.

Heaven with the ec - ho shall re - sound.

Heaven with the ec - ho shall re - sound.

Heaven with the ec - ho shall re - sound.

And all the earth shall hear.

And all the earth shall hear.

And all the earth shall hear.

not used by the congregations whose performances are rendered here, and the tune is rarely given any name at all by the singers; it is unlikely that most members have a name for it. The earliest source for the tune is probably Jeremiah Ingalls's *Christian Harmony*, where it is called "Delay."[10] It is Ingall's version that is reproduced here. Daily's version, though formally more directly related to the Primitive Baptist church, is written in ¾ time, which is used less frequently among Primitive Baptists than common time. The text here is not the only one used with this tune; any short-meter text will fit it.

In the printed versions this tune is rather plain, but in actual performance, the singers enrich the simple melodic outline with flourishes and ornaments that are reflected only partially in these transcriptions. The black versions in particular are difficult for even the most painstaking transcriber to reproduce on paper.

Both versions are performed very slowly, at a pace that allows for greater ornamentation but tends to obscure the relationship between the performed and printed versions for the casual listener. The white group averages about twenty-six syllables of text per minute; the black group, a much slower twenty syllables per minute. The pacing is so slow that bar lines seem inappropriate, so I have omitted them altogether. To facilitate comparison, I have also transposed the performances into Ingall's original key of C.

Each live performance was given by a group of several dozen singers in rough unison without musical accompaniment. But since each verse produced a slightly different variation of the tune, and since each individual singer injected personal variations, these two transcriptions constitute only a generalized schematic approximation of the tune, not an exact rendering.

This century has seen the modernization of Primitive Baptist hymn singing. It really began with the local and itinerant singing-school masters in the last three dacades of the nineteenth century,[11] but in the 1910s and 1920s singing schools increasingly found a receptive audience among many of the mountain people. These schools, in which the teacher charged small fees for conducting week-long workshops in re-

Figure 11.4. The tune "Kentucky" as recorded in an early tunebook and as performed by contemporary white and black Primitive Baptist congregations.

ligious part-singing, were not sponsored by the Primitive Baptist church and were frequently interdenominational. But they attracted numerous church members, and with their rising popularity, musical literacy spread and generated a demand among some Primitive Baptists for fresh material. Temptation came in the form of little paperback songbooks published in the same easy-to-read shape-note system of notation used in the schools. The books were sometimes sold by the teachers themselves, who occasionally served as agents for hymnbook publishers seeking to open new markets by introducing musical literacy in rural areas. (It is important to note that these collections were significantly different from the old shape-note books, which had never been used in Primitive Baptist services. The songs, the musical style, even the shape-note systems, were different).

It must have been exhilarating for singers to find a brand new repertoire suddenly opening before them. The new books contained hymns that differed considerably in style and content from the traditional Primitive Baptist music, and seem to have had at least a superficial attraction that initially won over Primitive Baptist conservatism. The old unison folk tunes had been built on the modal scales of British oral tradition, but these newer songs, many of them recently composed gospel hymns with lively tunes and sentimental words, tended to be in major keys and were straitjacketed melodically by the tempered-scale harmonic demands of the piano on which many of them had been composed. Despite staunch resistance from traditionalists, the new hymns gained enough general popularity that "official" Primitive Baptist hymnbooks began to be published and adopted by some of the churches. The books included both words and music, and contained mixtures of new songs and favorite traditional hymns, which occasionally received new four-part facades that made them quite unlike their former selves.

The singing school was thus one commercial wedge that succeeded in loosening the hold of religious folk traditions among the Primitive Baptists. Significantly, it was a relatively superficial modernization and did not constitute a change in doctrine. And as it turned out, its success was only marginal. The new books never succeeded in driving out the old texts. The habits of tradition die hard, and having neither the accompanying piano (instruments were still prohibited in church by doctrine) nor the high musical literacy to bring off the four-part harmonies, which were the main feature of the newer gospel songs, many congregations simply reverted to the unison, modal, ornamented style of the past. Some congregations that have committed themselves to music books have found that the old skills can dissipate quickly when neglected. But others, in the tradition of Primitive Baptist conservatism, have resisted the change, and have refused to allow "note" books into the church. In such groups, the traditional music is still alive, and the chilling old melodies are still delivered strong and full.

Primitive Baptist song is beautiful, but that is not the main reason it survives. The tradition resists change because it is part of the spiritual life of the church, and its beauty is a product, not a source of that life. Complimented on their singing, Primitive Baptists will often hasten to point out that sacred singing is no mere ornament to the service, but an essential vehicle for the spirit. One elder illustrated the point with this story:

> There's a lot of difference in singing. There's pretty singing, and then there's good singing. And good singing is better than pretty singing. I'll give you an illustration. A son had left home, and his father couldn't sing a tune. He could not sing a tune. In a few years, he returned home. And he greeted his mother and said, "Mother, where's Dad?" "Down at the barn, doing his work." And he went down, and when he got in hearing, his daddy was going over the words:
>
> > Amazing Grace, how sweet the sound,
> > That saved a wretch like me;
> > I once was lost, but now am found,
> > Was blind, but now I see.
>
> And he said he walked around, and as he turned around beside the barn, his daddy had his head over, and he could see the tears dropping, each time he went over those words. Now, he said, it wasn't pretty, but it was the best singing he'd ever heard in his life.

There is no better evidence or explanation for the survival value and the expressive power of the old Primitive hymns than the fact that the songs live not just in the church but in the community at large. Just as Primitive Baptists have resisted the compartmentalization of religion, they have made the singing of its hymns a part of daily life. To hear preaching, you have to get to the church, but the songs are portable and accessible even if you don't have a Bible handy. It is a rare member of the community who doesn't know, hasn't heard, or doesn't enjoy Primitive Baptist hymns, even if he no longer attends that church. The old hymns are part of the earliest memories of church members:

> Most of the music in the home was just singing. Dad would sing in them old hymn books. Many, many mornings in the wintertime, we'd get up before day, he woke me up singing some old hymn. Just about every morning, he would get up and get the fire started, and sing a hymn or two before breakfast. And then, during the day or during the night, he'd take a notion—and he'd have us children to help him at night sometimes—we'd gather around a little table with the oil lamp, and we'd all try to help. And that singing wasn't just in the house. We had neighbors who lived half a mile away, lived on a farm, and you could be out—there was no noise, no airplanes, no automobiles, or anything to destroy the sound— and you could hear people singing sometimes, I guess, for a mile. The ladies'd be out sometimes about their work, and the men, and you could just hear that singing just echo from one hill to the other.

Because so much attention has been lavished on the secular folk music of the Appalachians, it is easy to forget that there were many families whose entire lives, including their music, centered on faith. The singing of the old hymns and the reading of the King James Bible accompanied church people literally from the cradle to the grave. There would be prayer meetings held in the evenings at members' homes, and invalids and the dying would request songs of their children who gathered around their beds. But the songs were not always used in such somber, religious contexts. At times they were parts of lighter social occasions. Bean stringings and apple peelings provided an opportunity for people to get together and sing recreationally—not always or only the familiar ballads and secular songs, but sometimes the folk hymns that were used in the churches. Long trips by wagon, and later by automobile, were passed in group hymn singing. Though Primitive Baptists objected to the use of musical instruments in church, they felt no proscription against their use elsewhere in the community, and the hymn tunes occasionally found their way into string-band arrangements. One local musician, Elder Golden Harris, recorded a pair of Primitive Baptist hymns in 1931, singing and accompanying himself on the fiddle.[12] There are even reports from the black community of the hymns being used as work songs during wood chopping and plowing.

It is important to remember that these hymns, as units of oral tradition, were subject to the same forms of dispersion as other genres of mountain folklore. Traveling elders and song leaders, those who had special skill for remembering tunes and building large mental repertoires, were the primary agents of song transmission. Musical trading occurred with hymns as with fiddle tunes. An elder visiting another church as a guest preacher might carry with him a favorite tune, and leave it behind when he left, having himself picked up a new tune or new way of singing an old one. The large annual association meetings, which brought church people together from a large area, functioned, in fact, as the ecclesiastical counterpart to modern-day fiddlers' contests. Song exchange continues today, the only concession to modernization being that some tunes are captured not by the memory but with a portable tape recorder.

The Primitive Baptist hymns are not just songs that must stand or fall on their own musical merits. They are integral components of a deeply internalized worldview, and have a special staying power unmatched by even the best-loved secular songs. The expressive range of the repertoire is broad, and there is always a hymn one can turn to for special comfort in times of distress. Some of God's gifts, in fact, come in the form of music:

I'd been somewhere and was way in the night coming back. I was coming, and the moon was shining so bright, it was mighty nigh . . . you could pick up a pin almost. I was coming along ridge and wood, leaves and things all off. I was walking and singing. I never will forget the song I was singing was "Blue Moon of Kentucky." The moon was shining so bright, that just struck me, you know, in my mind. And don't you know, as clear as it was, something got over the moon. A dark cloud just overshadowed it, and I couldn't see nowhere. And a voice spoke to me out of that cloud. You know what it said? Called me by name, said, "You quit singing that song. The song for you to sing"—he pointed it out to me—"is 'The time is swiftly rolling on when you must faint and die.' " And that scared me. That frightened me. I didn't sing no more of that other song.

But I'm glad He took it away from me. I ain't got no more charm for them kind of songs.

Another elder tells of two angels hovering overhead as he lay in bed, singing him one of the old hymns as a special message of salvation. Another heard the faint voice of a dead grandmother singing a hymn in the air around him as he worked in the field. Such "gift songs" are valued as emblems of grace, and none who receive such blessings will ever lose the sense of their special symbolic meaning.

Songs received from divine sources stand an improved chance of surviving in the oral tradition. But other factors are also influential. A song treasured as a spiritual gift by a member and always led by him in church becomes a memorial to him after he has passed away; it is sung at his funeral and for years afterward in his memory. On the wings of such hymns, great church leaders achieve a kind of immortality in the oral history of the community. In one recent case an energetic elder painstakingly reconstructed a tune that had once been the favorite of an elder now deceased, but that had since become virtually dead in the oral tradition. He consulted with those who knew scraps of the tune, and by applying his own musical skills, eventually patched them together. He brought the restored tune back into the tradition, to the joy of all, not only because a great old tune had been saved from extinction, but because the memory of a great church leader had been preserved as well. The tune now bears the name of the elder who had carried it for so many years.

It is hard for any so-called folk tradition to survive the rigors of modern life, and the Primitive Baptist community is no exception. But the Primitive Baptists have maintained stability and withstood the altering effects of time better perhaps than most communities with functioning oral traditions in the formal arts. As traditional expressive forms, the conversion narratives and the Primitive Baptist hymns have the same ingenuous vitality we admire in their secular counterparts, but are fed by a stronger root system. By adhering to the doctrine that personal contact with God is superior to any artificial or secondary communication, the church has placed itself beyond the reach of the mass media and shielded itself against the commercialization that transformed the surrounding secular culture. In addition, the church values the old ways and considers them inherently superior to the products of a progressive mentality. It deplores change for change's sake. And finally, the Primitive Baptist community itself has remained strong and thus nurtures the process of oral tradition as well as its forms. Primitive Baptists have kept folklife strong by keeping the original religious commitment intact.

12. Banjos and Blues

Kip Lornell

During the 1930s and 1940s Durham, North Carolina, was a leading center for blues music in the southeastern United States. Durham is located
in the heart of the important tobacco-growing region of the state. This
and its closeness to the main highways and railroads made it a principal
industrial center in the Piedmont South by the 1920s, and so Durham's
population rose from 6,679 in 1900 to 69,683 in 1940. The percentage
of Afro-Americans in the population consistently remained between 30
percent and 40 percent during this forty-year period of extreme growth,
and in 1940 stood at approximately 35 percent.[1] Most of the black migrants moved into the Hickstown, East End, Hayti, and Walltown sections of Durham, and it was in these areas that blues musicians lived and
performed.

During the 1930s an impressive number of musicians played blues
music in Durham. There were blues pianists such as Jesse Pratt, Hubert
Sears, Murphy Evans, Duncan Garner, and "Stovepipe." Harmonica
players Sonny Terry and Jordan Webb could be heard at local house
parties. It was the guitar, however, that was the favorite instrument of
Durham blues musicians, and many important blues guitarists were associated with the city. The two best-remembered musicians from this
era—Blind Gary Davis and Blind Boy Fuller—were both unusually
adept guitarists, and Davis was arguably the most accomplished blues
guitarist in the Piedmont style ever to record. Both men were full-time
musicians as well as recording artists, supporting themselves playing for
functions throughout Durham and the surrounding countryside.

Many other fine guitarists played in Durham's "Black Bottoms"
and streets during the 1930s, never gaining more than local recognition.
Scrap Harris, for example, was thought by some to rival Gary Davis's

guitar prowess. This list of otherwise unknown guitarists includes Johnny Moore, Robert Donnigan, Budd Johnson, Marvin Lynn, Tom Rivers, Artis Johnson, and two brothers, Opal and Arthur Lyons.

The music played by these black musicians was extremely diverse, though it was certainly primarily blues. The only primary sources available are the 78-rpm records made from the mid-1930s through the early 1940s by a handful of the active Durham musicians—Blind Gary Davis, Blind Boy Fuller, Brownie McGhee, Richard and Willie Trice, Bully City Red, Sonny Terry, Jordan Webb, and Floyd Council. These recordings suggest that their repertoires consisted of blues or blueslike songs and religious songs.

It is a fact that Durham was a focal point for blues singers in the Piedmont, but the underlying reasons why blacks performed blues have never been adequately explored by blues scholars, ethnomusicologists,

Figure 12.1. Durham bluesman Willie Trice at his home in Orange County in 1975 (photo by Kip Lornell, courtesy of the Blue Ridge Heritage Archive, Ferrum College).

or folklorists. Most would agree that the blues is an emotional music. Michael Haralambos suggests that "As a definition of blues music, the phrase 'blues is a feeling' is used by singers and blues fans alike. Blues does more than tell a story, it articulates a mood, a state of mind."[2] Although blues songs are ostensibly personal expressions of unhappiness over private troubles, most scholars argue that they are also vehicles for relating moods that have hung over black America. Bruce Bastin, for example, argues that "the bluesman also echoes the feelings and frustrations of his friends and others in his community, who may be less able to express their emotions but who respond to, and identify themselves with, his songs."[3] These themes also appear in Paul Oliver's important study *Conversation with the Blues* as well as several other works concerned with traditional blues.[4] Some scholars have suggested that blues also developed out of an intensely racist social setting and imply that racism has been a significant force motivating blacks to perform blues.[5]

These observations regarding the communicative and emotional power of blues and the forces that motivate blacks to sing this music are valid. But this essay will suggest that specific regional conditions in Piedmont North Carolina during the 1930s are significant for an understanding of blues here—and probably of blues in general.

An overwhelming majority of the musicians in the blues center at Durham utilized their musical skills on weekends or in the evenings, after they finished the full-time daily jobs that had lured them, like other blacks, into Durham from "the fields sharecropped by their parents and to seek a more profitable means of living." They typically "held a series of low-paying menial jobs." Usually the music was "a part-time activity that promised nothing more than a little spare change and guaranteed entrance to house-parties and dances."[6]

For the blacks in Durham, many of whom enjoyed the same economic and social status as the blues musicians, this music served the social function of entertainment. There were three prime sites for blues activity in Durham, and all three involved entertaining blacks and whites who were willing to pay the musicians. These sites were the weekend house parties, the tobacco warehouses, and the city's street corners. The advantage to "scuffling" on the streets was the ease and speed with which the musicians could pick up money. Fridays and Saturdays were the best days to work the streets because many of the musicians' compatriots were paid at the week's end and were more

Figure 12.2. The urban landscape: the tobacco warehouse section of Durham, N.C., October 1940 (Howard W. Odum Sub-Regional Photographic Study, courtesy of the Southern Historical Collection, University of North Carolina at Chapel Hill.

likely at that time to part with cash. To reach their goal of picking up money as quickly as possible, musicians stationed themselves in front of business establishments such as barbershops, cafés, and poolrooms, or in residential areas where neighbors would congregate to play checkers, drink, and talk.

Tobacco warehouses provided another and more lucrative place for the city's musicians to perform. These warehouses were situated near the center of Durham and were filled each fall with visiting farmers and merchants. This was an extremely important annual event for everyone. The farmers got a chance to sell their tobacco and visit the city for a few days, local businessmen near the warehouses did well, and the blues musicians enjoyed a large receptive audience with a great deal of cash in hand. Willie Trice explains what it was like for blues musicians at that time: "The tobacco pickers and farmers would bring the tobacco into the warehouse. We'd go down there to play music for them while they sold their tobacco and get to feeling good, you know, drinking some. They'd tip us a heap of change to play some music."[7]

The musicians who chose to play at warehouses during the tobacco season could easily earn ten dollars or more in a single evening of playing a guitar, beating a washboard, or blowing a mouth harp, which was as much as they could earn at many jobs laboring for several days. Naturally many musicians made it their business to play at the warehouses during the height of the tobacco-selling activity. According to Durham musician Arthur Lyons: "You could go down there about 9:30 in the evening and play until 2:00 or 3:00 in the morning and make some change. All day on the weekends, too."[8]

The third and most important context for this music was the house party, which offered employment for musicians nearly every weekend, year round. There were two basic types of house parties. The first was organized by individuals who opened up their homes for a weekend night of dancing, drinking and gambling. Few held house parties on a regular basis, but in any of the black sections a house party was usually being held somewhere. These informal house parties, sometimes referred to as "fish-fries" because the host often made extra money selling food and drink, were important outlets as they provided a place where people could relax after a week's work. Sometimes, however, when the drinking got a little heavy these parties became rough, as Sonny Terry recounts: "I'll never forget this one night we was playing at this fish fry. Everybody was having a good time when this gal they called Razor-Toting Sally jumped this guy and started cutting him. She'd cut on a man if he looked at her hard, that's how she come to get her name. This fellow was hollering, trying to get loose of her. . . . I find out later the man almost died, he was in the hospital nearabouts six months. They never did nothing to Razor-Toting Sally."[9]

Bootleggers ran a second variety of house parties, which were staged every weekend at the same house or "joint" and were strictly a money-making venture. Illegal alcohol and other concessions were sold by bootleggers for a great profit, and gambling was commonplace. Whereas at informal house parties blues players performed for tips and all the liquor they could drink, the bootleggers paid the musicians a set fee for playing from midevening until early in the morning. Jessie Pratt, a blues pianist active during this era, explains what it was like for the musicians: "We had good times, good times! Mighty seldom that people got to fighting too bad. The music sounded real good. You usta dance to the music we was playing. Hillian Davis usta play guitar with me. He could put a guitar behind his back, way up here [gestures to his shoulder]—kept playing it, dance with a girl, all at the same time! We got all our drinks free and about $15 or $20. We had to play from near about 8:00 until 3:00 or 4:00 in the morning."[10]

The diversity, excitement, and dangers of life in Durham are evident in these recollections, but what was life like for blacks in small towns or farming communities in Piedmont North Carolina? A look at nearby Cedar Grove, North Carolina, helps to answer this question.

During the 1930s Cedar Grove was a typical small, rural Piedmont community of approximately thirty-five hundred people, which relied heavily upon farming as its major source of employment. Situated in northern Orange County, Cedar Grove lies twenty-five miles to the northwest of Durham, and approximately eleven miles northwest of Hillsborough, the county seat. Fifty years ago Cedar Grove had the only post office in Orange County north of Hillsborough and was considered the important trade center for northern Orange County.[11] During this period two general stores, Ellis's and Oliver's, served the community, while the local physician, Dr. Hughes, operated the area's only drugstore. The community also supported its own blacksmith and two churches, Cedar Grove Methodist Church and Eno Presbyterian Church.

According to the 1940 census, Orange County had a population of 23,072 with a racial breakdown of 15,911 whites and 7,161 blacks, or a ratio of about two to one. Cedar Grove was an exception to the rest of the county, as it was virtually racially balanced with 1,753 blacks and 1,671 whites. Numerically there were more blacks in Cedar Grove than anywhere else in the county, except for the more densely populated Chapel Hill area, where the black population numbered 2,917.[12]

Cedar Grove's large black population was heavily involved in agriculture. Each of my informants reported that he was farming during the 1930s, as were most of his friends and relatives. This information is supported by government statistics, which state that in all of Orange County there were 503 black-operated farms, and that 239, or almost one half, were located in Cedar Grove. There were also 267 white-operated farms in the township, only twenty-eight more than their black counterparts.[13]

In summary, according to the 1940 census all but 91 of the 3,424 persons living in Cedar Grove were considered to be part of the "rural farm population."[14] It was also a relatively poor farming population. Nearly two thirds were tenant farmers, as compared with a countywide average of 30.6 percent. Doubtless a high percentage of the blacks were among the tenant farmers.[15]

This was the racial and economic setting in which blacks lived and played music in Cedar Grove during the 1930s. Unlike Durham blacks, their secular music was played primarily on fiddles, banjos, and guitars for square dances, and quite a few Afro-American musicians living in settlements or communities close to Cedar Grove traveled to the community expressly to participate in these dances. This group included banjoists Jimmy Nichols and Willie Criss of Hurdle Mills, banjoists Minnick Poteat and Dink Bradshaw from Caswell, and Bruin Moses, a fiddler from Mebane. John Arch Thompson, his brothers Jake and Walter, and their friend Charlie White were probably the most important black musicians around Cedar Grove at the time. Most of the musicians from this cadre were equally adept at fiddle and banjo and during the course of an evening would play either.

Little specific information about any of these musicians is available, as nearly all have been dead twenty years or longer. It is possible, however, to reconstruct the social setting and milieu for this music. These musicians frequently played at their own homes for small gatherings like picnics, or at neighbors' homes on weekends, but the most important event that called for string-band music was the dance. These times when neighbors and friends joined together are most vividly recalled by the older residents of Cedar Grove. These dances were known as set dances, square dances, or, most commonly, barn dances. We cannot be certain precisely how long the black square-dance tradition existed in Cedar Grove, but from the information gathered from residents it can be reasonably asserted that blacks were following this tradition in the 1880s and possibly earlier.

Such dances were directly tied to the agrarian cycle of planting, working in the fields, and harvesting. When the farm work was completed in late autumn, then the black community in Cedar Grove held its dances. The beginning of the season for barn dances was signaled by a corn shucking, as Odell Thompson explains: "When you gather the corn out of the field and haul it into the barnyard, you put it in piles.

Figure 12.3. The rural landscape: black and white farmers at an all-day cornshucking in the northern Piedmont in 1939 (Howard W. Odum Sub-Regional Photographic Study, courtesy of the Southern Historical Collection, University of North Carolina at Chapel Hill).

After they get it all together, they'd call a bunch of hands to shuck the corn. That's what they call that corn shuck. Then that night they'd pull off a dance."[16] This occurred sometime between the middle of October and the beginning of November and marked the end of the intensive agricultural activities for the year.

Barn dances were held in Cedar Grove virtually every Saturday night during the winter months. Christmas was an especially festive occasion; Joe Thompson remarked that "somebody was bound to have a dance nearly every night during Christmas," that is, the six days between 25 December and New Year's Day.[17] Most participants came from Cedar Grove or from one of the other small communities in northern Orange County—Caldwell or Walnut Grove—or from Hurdle Mills or Rougemont in adjacent counties. Some people, however, journeyed great distances to attend these barn dances. According to Gladys White, who used to call sets at these functions, "They used to

come from all over . . . as far away as Burlington, Yanceyville, Rox-
boro, Durham, up in Person County or Caswell [County]. Not many
would come that distance, but a few would."[18]

For the most part, these events were family oriented. The dances
were always held in people's houses, beginning at approximately 8:00
P.M. and lasting until about midnight. Blacks of all ages attended barn
dances to talk, relax, and of course dance. The night's host supplied a
small amount of food and drink. Alcohol was consumed by many, but
rarely did drinking get out of hand. If a drunk did cause problems, he
or she would be quietly removed from the premises. Odell Thompson
recalls the spirit of these evenings: "The black people, why they just
did it for fun, the enjoyment, the kick they all got out of it. They
weren't out for no money, they were just out for fun. [They] cut up,
carry on, dance and go on."[19] Such events were held for two or three
months on a regular basis, until the spring farm work drew attention to
the land once more, usually sometime in February or early March.
"Chopping time" signaled the end of winter. As Joe Thompson explains, this time meant "cutting wood to cure tobacco with. Going out
into the woods and cutting wood to burn in the tobacco flue. You see,
back then, they used to cure all the tobacco using wood. Now they
cure it with oil or gas. A bunch of hands from the neighborhood would
go out and help this man cut today and that man cut tomorrow. They
went from one neighborhood to the other—that's the way they got
their wood cut."[20]

It was within this social context that blacks performed music on
fiddles, banjos, and guitars. The tune repertoire of these musicians was
remarkably uniform, the same songs being known to almost all the
musicians. Since the music was primarily performed to accompany
the dances and the sets often ran as long as fifteen or thirty minutes, the
size of a musician's repertoire was less important than his stamina. The
universality of this repertoire can also be attributed to the fact that all
the musicians learned from older musicians in their neighborhoods—
either relatives or friends.

The repertoire itself stems from two primary sources. The first
source is the stage music of medicine and minstrel shows, which at one
time crisscrossed the South, employing black entertainers as comedians
and musicians.[21] The most direct inspiration for Cedar Grove blacks
was perhaps the medicine show, the successor to the minstrel show,

Figure 12.4. String-band musicians Joe Thompson (fiddle) and Odell Thompson (banjo) of Mebane, N.C. (photo by Kip Lornell, courtesy of the Blue Ridge Heritage Archive, Ferrum College).

which continued to tour the area until the early 1970s. These shows featured musicians, often traditional performers, who played the fiddle and banjo tunes they grew up with.

A second and probably more important source for many of the tunes found among Cedar Grove musicians was the indigenous white instrumental tradition. This music was rooted in the British Isles, yet remains strong in the southern Appalachians and in certain sections of the Deep South. These tunes gradually became part of a shared repertoire from which black and white musicians equally drew, although the extent of this sharing and its ramifications are only now being explored.[22]

It is impossible, of course, to know exactly how many tunes made up this corpus, particularly because so many Cedar Grove musicians either were deceased or hadn't picked up their instruments for many years before I visited the community. During the years 1973 to 1976, I taped fifteen different tunes:

1. Ain't Gonna Rain No More
2. Alabama Gals
3. Corn Liquor
4. Donnie Got a Rambling Mind
5. Georgia Buck
6. Hook and Line
7. John Henry
8. Little Brown Jug
9. Mississippi Sawyers
10. Molly Put The Kettle On
11. Old Joe Clark
12. Old Molly Hare
13. Pumpkin Pie
14. Rya's House
15. Soldier's Joy[23]

In sum, black secular music in Cedar Grove, North Carolina, was almost exclusively string-band music performed on fiddles, banjos, and guitars for community-based square dances. These square dances were family events held during the winter months following completion of the farming cycles so important to their livelihood. Significantly, blues music was virtually absent and was rarely referred to by local musicians and residents.

The great differences between black life and music in Durham and Cedar Grove support the claim that the blues is a response to environmental conditions and racism. Although it is nearly impossible to believe that race relations were relaxed anywhere in the South during the depression, evidence suggests that in Cedar Grove blacks and whites lived together in relative harmony. In Cedar Grove, where blues was rarely played, race relations were fairly relaxed and reasonably unstrained. The blatant racism that infested most of the South was not as evident in northern Orange County. The one place where blacks were legally barred was the segregated school. Churches and other social gatherings, such as family picnics, also tended to be segregated, but many other social institutions that were traditionally segregated in the South, such as movie theaters or bus terminals, simply did not exist in Cedar Grove. Blacks and whites in the community also cooperated a great deal, helping each other with farm work and harvesting. Blacks enjoyed good relations with the white store owners, who extended them credit until the fall, when the tobacco crop provided them with cash to pay their debts. Odell Thompson, a black fiddle and banjo player, sums up race relations in Cedar Grove this way: "I never knowed of any trouble during my time. Everybody got along fine. . . . No, we never did have no trouble."[24]

The relatively good race relations in Cedar Grove stand in strong contrast to the more racist atmosphere in Durham. The institutions that embodied racism—the public bus system, restaurants, etc.—were all present in this urban setting, which meant that Durham blacks confronted the pressure of segregation and racism daily. Durham blues musician Arthur Lyons comments, "Sure it was different than in the country. Back then we couldn't go into certain retaurants, had to sit at the back of the bus and in the theaters upstairs. Things didn't change till recent times. Back then we didn't know no better."[25] Lyons implies that blacks in Durham were certainly aware of racism and were not pleased with their treatment, but they accepted the situation because they felt powerless to change it. It was in this racially biased urban setting that blacks played and listened to blues.

It is obvious, however, even from a cursory examination of the secular black music found in these two communities that to suggest racism and a difficult social climate as the only important differentiating factors is too simplistic; it ignores the complexities of the situation. Blues scholars have, in fact, generally ignored or overlooked several important differences between rural and urban communities.

When one compares Cedar Grove and Durham, the most obvious difference is the rural/urban dichotomy. During the 1930s Cedar Grove was a small rural township. It was more physically isolated than it is today: then few people owned cars, and a single paved road ran through the main crossroads.[26] Cedar Grove was also a self-contained settlement where most of the people's needs—dry goods, clothing, and education—were taken care of by the community. The town's population was quite homogeneous. Whether white or black, the Cedar Grove adult male was typically a tobacco-growing farmer. Mildred Finley, operator of the post office and a Cedar Grove resident since 1922, says, "All the people around here . . . none of them were too different. Nearly all of them, colored or white, worked at growing tobacco, and lots of them were tenant farmers too."[27]

In a number of ways, Cedar Grove conformed to Robert Red-field's ideal construct of a "folk society." It was "small, isolated, . . . and homogeneous."[28] Such a society, according to George Foster, is "relatively immobile," a community where change is slow.[29] I believe the very essence of Cedar Grove—its size, location, and population—served to make it such a conservative community. The entire community was heavily dependent upon agrarian cycles, which is musically illustrated by the fact that barn dances were held only during the winter months, when they did not interfere with farm work. As a consequence, black residents retained the older tradition of fiddle and banjo playing for square dances that had been going on in Cedar Grove for at least fifty years. Not until the early 1950s, as roads improved, opening up jobs in nearby factories, and as other passive entertainment forms such as radio and television became more commonplace, did blacks in Cedar Grove cease holding these traditional events. However, the blues, which has usually been considered an extremely widespread musical form among rural southern Afro-Americans, was rarely played in Cedar Grove. Most of my informants recall hearing blues played in Cedar Grove only between sets at the square dances.

The more turbulent life in Durham stood in extreme contrast to the conservative element of Cedar Grove. Durham was an expanding, diverse economic and social center for blacks, many of whom were living in a city for the first time. I believe that it was at least partially due to the problems of adjustment of city life, the nature of city living, and the function music had within this environment, that the blues became so important in Durham.

Afro-Americans moving to Durham from rural areas encountered a varied social world. Lured by the promise of better-paying jobs, they moved from a fairly static world, a family-oriented community, to a bewilderingly complex one. The rural/urban dichotomy has often been noted by urban sociologists and is perhaps best summarized by T. Lynn Smith: "Rural districts are essentially homogenous, [but] . . . the city person lives amid tremendous diversity, constantly in contact with people having diverse ideas, beliefs, mores, languages, economic positions, occupations, religious traditions, morals, etc."[30] This view of the rural/urban differences is supported by the observations of "Son" Mason, who moved from a farm in Chatham County to nearby Durham in 1928: "I just got tired of the country, I reckon. There was more in

Durham . . . different people and such. There weren't no factories out there, tobacco factories. Nothing but sawmills and farms, and I just got tired of that."[31]

Movement from the rural world to the intricate, complicated urban environment E. Franklin Frazier suggests, everywhere "has been accompanied by profound changes in the Negro's behavior and general outlook on life."[32] Frazier argues that the movement of blacks from rural to urban areas during the 1920s and 1930s, coupled with the harsh economic climate of the depression, helped break down the most basic social unit in American culture, the nuclear family. In rural areas, the family was the most fundamental social unit. The movement to cities frequently led to a reorganization of the familial structure into what Frazier calls a "quasi-family."[33] Even if the family unit survived, Frazier suggests, the basic structure of black society was greatly strained: "The great mass of migrants who, as a rule, manage to preserve remnants of their family organization must face in the competitive life of the city a severe struggle for survival and, at the same time, be subjected to the disintegrating forces in the urban environment."[34]

This pattern of urban social disorganization is found in the lives of any number of black musicians who moved to Durham during the 1920s or 1930s. The recollections of Sonny Terry provide one such example. Terry moved from the confines of his family's home in rural North Carolina to the violent, exciting milieu of Durham in 1931 and was forced to make a living in Durham playing harmonica and singing on the streets without the support or stability of any kin. This precarious period in his life is well documented by Kent Cooper in *The Harp Style of Sonny Terry*. The phenomenon of social disorder in urban areas is not unique to Afro-Americans, of course. The emergence of snake-handling cults in Durham in the mid-1940s responded to a comparable breakdown of social organization among whites moving from the farms to the city.[35]

Adding to the problems of social disorientation was the unaccustomed physical environment that Afro-Americans encountered when they moved to Durham from the country. The city presented many problems that rural living did not have. In Hugh Brinton's words: "Low wages, ignorance, bad housing and poor health form a vicious circle which it is not easy for the recently arrived Negro migrant to break. He comes to town with a background of little or no schooling; accustomed to the inadequate shelter of a two-roomed cabin, lacking training in even the most common rules of health. . . . In the city he meets for the first time running water, electric lights, garbage collection and many other services made necessary by the living together of masses of people."[36] The sections of Durham populated almost entirely by blacks were often poorly maintained by the city. Consequently, physical deterioration of houses was not uncommon and added to the problems of the newly arrived migrants. Brinton describes a typical street in Hayti during the late 1920s as "an unpaved street leading from the heart of the business section. There are no trees, sidewalks, nor curbs, . . . and the houses are unpainted or very badly weathered. The northern end is very rough and steep and almost impassable during the winter."[37]

This new physical and social environment produced stresses that did not exist in the country. As one reaction to the problems of urban living, blacks in Durham during this period sang and listened to blues as a means of relieving stress. This particular function of blues has been noted by other blue scholars, most notably Paul Oliver.[38] Robert Curtis Smith, in an interview with Oliver, observed, "I love the blues because the blues is the only thing that gives me relief when I gets to the place where it seems like everything go wrong."[39]

The urban environment, of course, was not an entirely negative force. Durham also opened up new opportunities for blacks that did not exist in the rural areas. The social diversity in urban culture exposed blacks to musical diversity. According to several informants, blacks in Durham had formerly held square dances, but by the early 1920s had turned to blues and jazz. There were many local groups playing jazz in Durham, and such popular performers as Fats Waller, Cab Calloway, and Duke Ellington often stopped there. In other words, diverse musical tastes existed in Durham because blacks had the opportunity to hear varied musical forms, through both records and the radio, as well as in live performances. Hence, they embraced the blues tradition at least partially because it was relatively new and popular. This music was filtered to them beginning in the 1920s by way of commercially recorded "race records" and by traveling musicians.

It seems evident, then, that the adjustment to city life is an important sociological variable in understanding why blacks in Durham played and appreciated the blues. Durham at that period was a difficult though exciting social setting for Afro-Americans. Many members of the city's Afro-American community were caught in a rather general malaise that encompassed not only economic hardships, ill treatment, and racism, but also the psychological stresses of dislocation and adjustment to urban living. Richard Trice, a bluesman who participated in this social experience, sagely observed: "It seems like back in the late thirties the blues was king in Durham! People was having hard times [and] that's all they wanted to hear."[40]

13. Why Do Duck Decoys Have Eyes?

John Forrest

In 1978 I was involved in a yearlong anthropological study of the swamplands of northeastern North Carolina. I was interviewing Amos White, a retired waterman, when we were interrupted by a visitor whom I did not know and whose appearance was not greeted with any enthusiasm by White.[1] The caller exchanged pleasantries with us for a while and then asked Amos if he had any old decoys for sale. Amos directed him toward the barn, saying that he believed there were some decoys in there if he cared to look for them. We continued our chat, and about half an hour later the visitor returned carrying two battered decoys. He offered Amos ten dollars for the pair and left. Amos explained to me that the man was an antique dealer from a city in Virginia who periodically stopped by looking for a bargain. However, Amos, who is a hoarder of junk, memorabilia, and antiques, had no intention of parting with any object that had the slightest value. Each winter, he told me, he makes a few "antique" decoys and leaves them in the barn for the dealers to discover. As it happens, he has nearly five hundred genuine antique decoys, but he keeps these carefully hidden where no prying eyes will accidentally spot them. These decoys are not for museums or mantel shelves: they are working decoys.

Amos resents the general belief among collectors that country folk do not know the value of their possessions. The collectors claim that decoys are aesthetic objects that are best preserved in glass cases so that their visual qualities can be appreciated fully. It may come as a shock to them to learn that Amos also thinks of his decoys as aesthetic objects, yet he feels that their aesthetic qualities are best displayed when they are floating in the water in front of a duck blind. For Amos and others in the North Carolina coastal swamplands, duck hunting is primarily an aesthetic act. The pragmatics of shooting ducks are minor in comparison with the elaborate aesthetic trappings that accompany the act.

In Potuck, the town where Amos lives, a man who does not hunt is considered an oddity. Hunting is the pride of the region and has been for over a century. One local duck-hunting club has been in continuous operation since 1850. However, for most local men duck hunting was not truly a sport until 1917. Prior to that date, market hunting was legal, and men hunted primarily for profit.

By late October most talk among men at the general store in town revolves around duck hunting. By this time men also begin to get their hunting equipment in order and their blinds in shape for hunting. The latter may mean repairing weather damage or simply adding a fresh shroud of cut pine saplings.

On rough days when working on blinds is difficult or dangerous, the hunter turns his attention to his decoys. Because local hunters still use old, hand-carved juniper decoys for all or part of their rig (that is, set of decoys), one of the rainy-day chores is to touch up their paint work. In some cases the paint work is quite elaborate, involving careful painting of eyes, nostrils, and tail feathers. This is all done despite the fact that all of the hunters whom I interviewed believed that a decoy does not have to be lifelike in order to attract ducks. The following statement is typical: "You could paint every one of them a grayish-black, every one of them a grayish-black and put no other color on 'em, and I swear I believe stuff'd come to 'em just as good. Doesn't make no difference. I've took cow manure—it was cold and dry—in the wintertime, and set 'em out on the edge of the ice, and had just as good shooting as I ever had in my life." Older hunters also told me of the practice called "turfing out." This involves making decoys by placing duck-sized pieces of turf in the clefts of forked sticks and driving them into the marsh around the blind. Today rough decoys for snow geese are made by filling white trash pail liners with dirt. Thus, the careful painting of old decoys is somewhat puzzling.

Most early local carvers took some pains to make their decoys resemble ducks, but given that the market hunters had to keep a rig of anywhere from two to five hundred decoys in working condition, the carver could not spend much time on any one decoy. One of these carvers' decoys was described to me as follows: "He made the rough-

Figure 13.1. Blackhead duck decoy with prominent eye, by Mitchell Fulcher of Stacy, N.C., about 1920 (photo by Stephen Matchak).

est, outlandish decoys there was made in this county, I believe. But ducks would come to 'em. He could kill ducks with 'em. He just knocked the corners off a block of wood and rounded up a little bit, and nailed a head on it. And it didn't make any difference what size head it was." Despite the fact that "ducks would come to 'em," this hunter added, "I've got a few of his decoys here and I expect to work 'em over with a spokeshave [drawknife] and make 'em a decent decoy." In other words, a "decent" decoy is not one that attracts ducks, but one that looks good to the hunter.

Almost all of the wooden decoys still in use are painted to resemble one of three species: canvasback, redhead, or widgeon. During the market-gunning days canvasback and redhead were prime ducks, fetching up to seven dollars per pair. It takes little artistry to paint a decoy to resemble roughly a canvasback or redhead. A canvasback decoy, for example, is painted with a white body, a black bill, breast, and tail, and a red head. Even though it is now illegal to shoot canvasback because of the carnage wrought on them by the market hunters, decoys of these species are still very common. Widgeon decoys are far less common, but given the difficulty of painting one, it is surprising that any were made at all. The head is gray with a black-speckled pattern on the sides and picked out in green and white on top. Various feather configurations are marked on the tail and wings in green, black, and white, and the body plumage shades from grayish-brown on top to white underneath. Given also that gunners believe that a lump of gray wood will attract ducks, the painting is surprising.

Because goose decoys were cumbersome and the long neck was easily broken, market and early sport gunners did not use them. Modern hunters hunting on freshwater sounds frequently use a small raft of goose decoys in conjunction with their duck decoys because they think that they make the whole scene look more tranquil. Yet hunters have also explained to me that flying ducks cannot distinguish one species of decoy from another until they are within firing range. Again the decision to use goose decoys at all appears to be aesthetic.

Most modern hunters have some plastic decoys in their collections. Hunters who wish to hunt in marsh ponds buy a few plastic mallard and ringneck decoys for use there. Canvasbacks and redheads do not frequent marsh ponds, and the hunters feel that the traditional type of local decoy looks unnatural in this setting. The market hunters had little use for a marsh-duck decoy since they hunted exclusively on the sounds. Consequently, there are no wooden marsh-duck decoys for modern hunters to use. Modern hunters have no overriding objections to using rubber or plastic decoys. They are light, do not need painting, and look realistic. They have only one drawback: an errant load of number-five shot fired broadside into a raft of plastic decoys will do a lot of damage. Wooden decoys are not especially affected by such treatment.

A hunting party will set out for the blind about thirty minutes before sunrise so that hunters can be set up and ready at sunrise, the time at which one can start hunting legally. Upon reaching the blind the hunters throw out their decoys. Each hunter has his own theories about the positioning of decoys in rafts, but most end up bunching them in front of the shooting platform of the blind, with goose decoys, if used, rafted upwind from the ducks. Most hunters are aware of supposedly "scientific" placements of decoys. Each hunter owns books or subscribes to magazines that deal with how to create a lifelike setting

Figure 13.2. A hunter firing from his blind over a rig of roothead decoys, off Portsmouth Island, Carteret County, N.C., ca. 1900 (courtesy of the North Carolina Museum of Natural History and Ken Taylor).

that will bring ducks down. However, none I know bothers with such techniques. Placing decoys is difficult and time consuming. At the end of a day's hunt, picking up the decoys can be a cold and miserable affair that is best done as quickly as possible. This means that there is no time to stow the decoys in order, and also means that on the next day the decoys cannot be placed in the same order on the water. Although the hunters might prefer, aesthetically, to have the decoys look as real as possible in shape, coloration, *and* placement, the latter has to be forgone for pragmatic reasons.

After setting out the decoys, the hunters stow their boat and get themselves set up in the blind. Normally, two men hunt together for sport, but most blinds can comfortably accommodate three (fortunately for stray folklorists). Men who hunt together are usually fast friends who enjoy each other's company as much as hunting itself. During slack times they exchange stories about great hunting days in past seasons, about how far they can shoot, and so on. All the time, however, they keep an alert eye on the horizon.

When a flock that is legal to shoot is sighted, the hunter may use calls to lure it closer. Whether or not to use calls is a subject of controversy locally, so general observations are hard to make. Most hunters consider that unless one is an expert, the duck call is best left at home. The sight of an out-of-town hunter at the general store with a duck call hanging from the zipper of his hunting jacket is usually cause for a wry smile. Potuck hunters feel that this "foreigner" probably scares more ducks than he attracts with his call. The duck call is supposed to complete the illusion that the decoys are real ducks feeding, but in the wrong hands the call can destroy the illusion. Some hunters think that the call is no more than a toy to keep the hunter busy and are skeptical about its efficacy even in the best of hands. Again the call may very well be important to create an illusion for the hunters and not for the ducks.

If a group of ducks looks as if it is getting ready to decoy, the hunter gives a few greeting calls—a loud "qu-a-quack-quack-quack," followed by a feeding noise, a low jumbled "k-k-k-k" quacking. This sound is hard to produce on a call, and the hunters practice a great deal. During my fieldwork year a young hunter discovered a special call labeled a Scotch duck call. It is basically a regular duck call but has a long rubber, concertinalike bellows attached. Wagging the bellows produces a very lifelike feeding noise. The call created quite a stir at the general store, but it remained the only one in town.

After this elaborate hunting stage has been set, it remains only for the ducks to fly within firing range of the hunters. When they do, the hunters, on a prearranged signal, stand up from their cover and open fire. This process obeys certain rigidly prescribed rules:

–Never shoot at a duck that has alighted on the water.
–Never shoot a duck that will not be eaten.
–Never shoot at a large (five or more) flock of ducks.
–Never take a low-percentage shot.

This act is repeated many times until the men shoot their limit, or they get tired, or the sun goes down.

A neophyte might be forgiven for thinking that these men believe that a lifelike scene around their blinds is what brings ducks to them. As we have seen this is not true, or at least is by no means the whole truth. The counterarguments are as follows:

  –They believe that rough, uncolored blocks of wood will decoy ducks.
  –They throw decoys into the water in random bunches.
  –They are skeptical of duck calls.

There is one major reason why ducks come to the blinds, and that is not mysterious. Although the practice is outlawed, every hunter baits his blind with corn. Some hunters spread as much as fifty to a hundred pounds of corn per day in front of their blinds at the start of the hunting season. The bait in the blind attracts vast numbers of ducks, and every hunter knows this. Thus, it is difficult not to view decoys, calls, and so forth as minor hunting accessories when it comes to the business of luring ducks. They must, therefore, be primarily of aesthetic value.

The final act of hunting takes place at night. The hunters gather at the general store after supper and recount the day's events to one another. Men do not openly brag in general public about their hunting prowess, although they will recount their misfortunes unashamedly. One's hunting partner, however, may tell of his mate's successes. This is one reason why men never hunt alone. A lone hunter might have a great day's shooting, but would then be forbidden from telling of it. I should also add that there are tricks that allow hunters to brag without appearing to do so. One preferred mode is to talk of one's own skills at the expense of a universally despised group—Yankees. The following tale is typical: "I remember once guiding for this Yankee. All day he kept missing. He couldn't hit a bull in the ass with a spade. All day he kept cussin' his gun and saying he'd take it to be looked at as soon as he got back home. In the end I said, 'Let me see that gun.' Three boobies [ruddy ducks] come by and I knocked 'em down—one-two-three. 'Well,' he said, "I guess it ain't the gun.' " This story is ostensibly about how poor Yankees are at shooting. It veils the teller's bragging that he can shoot three birds with three shots.

The swamps, marshes, and freshwater sounds provide not only sport for the hunters but also their livelihood. Most of them work full-time or part-time as commercial fishermen. They fish in the winter months for rockfish, mullet, carp, shad, and other local species and in the summer for crab, eel, and catfish. The fishermen work alone or in pairs sometimes from sunrise to sunset, six days a week when the fishing is good. What is both obvious and curious about this commercial fishing is that it is almost entirely devoid of aesthetic forms. For example, in the entire year I spent in Potuck I was unable to elicit a judgment about a fishing boat that was even remotely aesthetic in character. In addition, there is no story-telling tradition that surrounds this activity and no larger community that is brought together through the shared experience of fishing.

Fishermen have little or no occupational reason to be unified as community. The work of fishing is potentially divisive. The seasons for freshwater fishing are short, and profits are contingent on factors beyond the fishermen's control. Buyers will pay prime prices for freshwater fish only until the saltwater fishing business gets under way, and northern crab buyers will make the journey to North Carolina only while the bays in Maryland and farther north remain iced up. Thus the watermen must make large catches quickly to sustain themselves financially during the long lean months. Their jobs are, therefore, inherently competitive. This also means that it is singularly disadvantageous to seek prestige and social status by stories of fishing prowess. For example, a crabber who brags about good catches is likely to find his pots surrounded by those of his fellows. If anything, turning attention away from one's prowess is beneficial.

We have two kinds of activities performed by the same men in the same environment. One—duck hunting—is socially cohesive; it is the source of social status and is surrounded by elaborate aesthetic trappings. The other—commercial fishing—is socially divisive; it is not a source of social status and is devoid of aesthetic forms. The details of duck hunting suggest that social status, social cohesion, and aesthetic production in Potuck are inextricably linked, and, in fact, this relationship is found in other aspects of Potuck life. Cohesive groups that confer social status are rich in aesthetic forms. The local church is the most obvious example of this link.

A second conclusion is that aesthetic forms are not simply social markers or expressions of other social facts, but are social facts in their own right. They can aid social cohesion and confer social status. A well-painted decoy and a well-constructed artificial landscape for hunt-

Figure 13.3. Captain Elijah Tate sitting in his battery box (sink box), surrounded by a large rig of decoys, Currituck County, N.C., ca. 1930 (courtesy of Ken Taylor).

ing confer status on the hunter. The elaborate crafting of the hunting stage has little to do with attracting ducks, but it can attract admirers. Local men speak of so-and-so as having a "pretty rig," that is, an attractive set of decoys. "Prettiness" in this context reflects the elaborateness of carving and painting. If anyone underrates the aesthetic value of the decoys, it is the out-of-town collectors and dealers who seek to remove the decoys from their appropriate context and shear them of intrinsic aesthetic attributes in the process. The hunters themselves are sensitive to the aesthetics of their activities and jealous of objects that enhance the aesthetic quality of their environs. The eyes on a decoy, like all the other fine anatomical features, such as nostrils and pin feathers, are purely aesthetic. Decoys have eyes because hunters paint them on, and they paint them on so that their decoys will be admired.

14. Tugging on Superman's Cape: The Making of a College Legend

James Wise

At Duke University in Durham, North Carolina, a certain tale about a football player is passed around in fraternity bull sessions and old-grads' reunions. The core of the story is a football player's single-handed vanquishing of a gang of would-be muggers, with detail and completeness varying greatly from one teller to the next. The story, which has been in circulation for a number of years, expresses three different sets of social oppositions that were part of the university's environment on campus and within the city of Durham.

A 1972 Duke graduate, then employed in Chapel Hill, North Carolina, recalled the essential outline of the story in the fall of 1974: "I don't know who it was—some big guy on the football team. Seven or eight spades grabbed him. They had a pipe and he got it away from them and ran them off. This was like before I showed up—ages ago."[1] A Duke graduate student also recalled the tale: "I don't know who it was—some big jock—he was walking back from East after taking a girl home and a carload of blacks pulled up and started giving him some grief. He went on for a ways, then the car pulled over and they all got out and went down on him and he ran them off. There was something about a watch, they broke his watch."[2] The graduate student recalled first hearing the story on the Duke campus, possibly in his freshman dormitory in 1966–67. When he was asked whether he had heard it again since, he replied, "Well, I've *told* it, within the last two, maybe three years."

An undergraduate recalled the following version from a session of "Dick Angier stories" in the Phi Delta Theta fraternity house during his freshman year:

There were four blacks. I don't think it happened in Durham; I think it was somewhere on Campus Drive. This happened about five years ago. I heard it two years ago. He was a quiet, real big guy. They broke his watch, that was what got him mad. They or he had a car, I don't remember which it was, for the sake of journalism say it was his car—one or the other party had a car. The blacks got in it—it was a Volkswagen—and he jumped up on top of the car and started jumping up and down on the top of it until the cops came. A cop came by and saw it, or someone heard the noise and called the cops. It was his watch—he had been an all-state football player, and he had this watch for playing in an all-star game or something. They had pipes—chains and/or sticks maybe—pipe—they were beating on the watch, that's how they broke the watch.[3]

The undergraduate recalled that there had been a name attached to the story, but did not remember what it was. Various identities are attached to the protagonist in different tellings, as well as the general "some big guy on the football team," as in an account from a Durham newsman who graduated from Duke in 1971:

It happened before I got to Duke. Can't think of the name, though there was one attached to the story when I heard it. The story was, one of the big, bad-ass football players—Angier or Valacci or one of those dudes, was downtown one Saturday night or something like that. Seems like he was in a car and maybe some words were exchanged, and he got into a thing with a fight—he whipped ass. I always wondered why I never heard of anything being done about it. I never heard any details. I hadn't thought about it in six or seven years.[4]

Asked whether race had been mentioned when he heard the story, the newsman replied, "Spades and nothing but."

A Durham landscape architect related a very similar story from Syracuse, New York:

See, Syracuse is located on this hill; and it is surrounded by the ghetto, and there was an especially rough ghetto between Syracuse, the university, and the town. And the best bars were in town. So these guys would walk on down there, especially the one dorm that the Syracuse football players lived in. So they'd go trucking down, and these little dudes, fourteen and fifteen years old, little short dudes but about fifty of them, would jump these Syracuse football players; and a couple of them almost really got their clocks cleaned, except for the people up in the dorms could look down and see them and came to the rescue. And one guy's big, sure, but, you know, just the *ants* piling on him. It was really, really incredible. Some of them got hurt. There are the stories six or seven older-type blacks jumping mean football players and the guy just taking a pipe and cleaning them out.

I remember one story that interested me, a couple guys in my dorm were walking down here and a couple of blacks jumped them. There were about four of them. The one guy was a Golden Gloves champion of Connecticut, and the other guy was probably one of the most incredible athletes I have ever met. So, these guys made a mistake jumping these two dudes. And they just wiped them out. Like when they came back they said a couple of them could have been dead there, they did such a job on them. The only thing—they got hurt, one guy got hit by a two-by-four in the head; and this was by the girl, who was there egging the blacks on to attack the dudes! You know, she came up behind them and *Boom!*[5]

This suggests that the Duke story is one version of a recurring college legend. Stories involving athletes in conflicts of one kind or another are found at practically all colleges; but the Duke story is always told as true.

Collecting revealed knowledge of the story among the university's administration and faculty: "The way I heard it, it was around midnight, and Dick Angier was walking from East to West, and a car pulled up and four or five blacks got out. And the way I heard it he just proceeded to beat the tar out of them. I don't remember any motive for it; I guess they wanted to rob him, I think robbery was the motive usually ascribed to it."[6] Some statements indicated the existence of printed sources. One suggested a locally published account:

He got jumped somewhere near campus and just wiped all of them out. It was sort of historically documented, there was a story in the *Chronicle* [student newspaper] or the Durham paper. I remember

him pointed out on campus to me. There was something about a
watch. He said something like, "I didn't really get mad until they
broke my watch." He was wearing one of these big divers' watches
or something like that. It was much talked about when it happened. I heard it from a colleague. It happened very near East
Campus or maybe just over the wall, they jumped him. . . . They
were all black. Which made the thing that much more heroic—
"Super Honky." This postdates the racial brawls that happened
around the time of the sit-in movements. There was not a specific
episode tied in, the guy wasn't out cruising for trouble. He gave a
very elaborate version of it in the story. There was something
about he got one of the guys across the hood of a car. . . . There
weren't any weapons involved. It was a football player.[7]

Another statement referred to a nationally circulated publication:

Robin Odom—in '66 or '67, maybe '68, sometime then. I know for
a fact it happened because it was written up in *Sports Illustrated*.
It was Robin Odom. It happened in early spring, after the football
banquet they have for the team every year. About eleven or twelve
at night, he was walking back from East to West, and a carload of
blacks pulls up and they jumped out and one of them had a gun.
He pointed the gun at Odom, but the gun misfired. And Robin
Odom took the gun away and beat them up with it. I did hear it
on campus, more than once or twice, and I told it myself. I usually
would hear it, or tell it, in our freshman house dormitory, shooting
the shit. It happened the year before we became freshmen, or two
years. My roommate, who was also from Durham, and I told it six
or eight times, and I heard it told during rush—of course, we em-
bellished it some. You know, at their low point the KAS [Kappa
Alpha fraternity, many members of which were football players]
lived next to the Phi Psis and one time the KAS jumped on one Phi
Psi—they didn't really beat him up or anything, but they told him
that if he told anybody about it, they'd come get him. I remember
another story of someone, Angier or Hayes, went on a rampage
swinging chairs.[8]

The story was reported in *Sports Illustrated* in June 1967.[9] The
Durham Morning Herald of 27 May 1967, carried an account of a trial

resulting from the incident, but a search of both the Durham newspapers and the *Duke Chronicle* uncovered no report of the incident itself.

According to the trial story, Robin Odom, a junior tackle on the Duke football team, was attacked about two A.M. on 14 May 1967 on Campus Drive. Ten black youths were involved, riding in two automobiles. Earlier they had been involved in an altercation at Tops, a nearby drive-in restaurant. After an exchange of words, one of the cars emptied, and after some more words during which one of the blacks likened Odom to a Ku Klux Klansman, one of the blacks hit Odom with a piece of metal pipe. The other four then began hitting him, breaking his watch, which, Odom said, "made me mad." He took the pipe away and began swinging it himself, and the blacks ran. One fell, and when Odom caught up with him, he shouted for those in the second car to "get the gun!" Odom then started beating on one of the cars with "the nozzle thing [the pipe], breaking a window glass and a radio antenna."[10] *Sports Illustrated* repeated the essential details of the newspaper story, with the addition that a "borrowed" .22 rifle was actually pointed at Odom and the trigger pulled three times, although the gun failed to fire.

The Odom story is a local rather than a migratory legend, which entered oral circulation both as a personal experience narrative (it can be assumed that Odom told the story once he got home that night) and from printed sources. The newspaper story appeared after most students had left Durham for the summer, but *Sports Illustrated* probably had much to do with spreading the story among Duke students. The students might have discovered it themselves, or they might have heard it from someone else and then looked it up. Most informants' recollections, however, indicate that the story was in oral circulation on the campus very soon after the event, well before either of the printed accounts appeared. The printed versions may have served to reinforce the oral story in the minds of people at Duke.

Whatever the paths by which the Odom story reached the individual tellers, it probably began as Odom's relation of a personal experience. But the story passed into the Duke community, and when a personal anecdote is taken into the oral tradition of a group, a process of "social censorship" begins to work upon it and to fashion it into a suitable bit of functional lore.[11] In the Odom story details have disappeared so that an easily remembered and easily transmitted core of action remains. The number of Odom's assailants has generally been reduced to make the story more believable, though sufficiently extraordinary to merit retention and telling.

As the property of a group the essential Odom story transmits information about the group that is peculiar and important to it. It embodies and resolves conflicts that are part of that group's identity, outlook, and environment. As parts of group lore, the principals in the story—Odom and his assailants—are given symbolic importance above their function in the narrative. Other details are retained or drop out as their significance to the tellers varies. In the context of Duke, to say "Robin Odom was a KA" carries implications and allusions beyond the literal identification of the man as a member of some particular fraternity. Similarly, the story carries information especially significant in the particular social contexts in which it is related, and serves to perpetuate those contexts by affirming the premises upon which they are based.

Among the attitudes that define a group's own sense of identity are its beliefs about other groups, and what it believes those other groups think of it. As representatives of particular groups, Odom and his attackers delineate oppositions and conflicts over and above the historical event of 14 May 1967. Odom was a Duke student, a white man, and a football player. His attackers were townspeople, blacks, and non–football players. The Odom story can be observed as functioning in three different sets of social oppositions that are part of the Duke environment: Duke versus Durham, white versus black, and, within the Duke student body itself, athlete versus nonathlete.

Duke versus Durham

"Town and gown" is a time-honored antagonism, and stories dramatizing the opposition are legion. Several variants of the Odom story—including *Sports Illustrated*'s—do not mention blacks at all, and one informant related a story that is expressly a Duke-versus-Durham anecdote:

> Well, for starters all I remember is that I was told this in the Ivy Room or somewhere, I never did remember where I heard it. It was back when that place was crawling with kids, back when it was

popular and noisy—back when it was that drive-in, Tops—and it got to when Duke kids went, there were these bands of little Durhamites who thought it was cool to find out if someone was a Dookie and then beat the hell out of him. It got so they'd sit out on the wall there and wait for Dookies to come by. And then one night they found a Dookie who just happened to turn out to be a football player, and he was supposed to have been actually throwing people across the street. I don't know how many of the kids there were that jumped him.[12]

This story may relate to a wholly separate incident, but its similarity to the essential Odom story suggests that it represents a fusion of other elements with the Odom theme.

The Odom story is often ascribed to other, better-remembered football players, reflecting a common circumstance in collegiate folklore.[13] One prospective informant, a Durhamite who attended Duke from 1970 to 1973, did not recall the Odom story when first questioned. However, after having the story related to him without a name attached, he exclaimed, "It was Angier!" and, though recalling no details, reported that he had heard the story both in high school and later at college, and adamantly maintained that Angier was the individual involved.

The Odom story is attached to Dick Angier more than to any other figure, and Angier has a prominent place in "town-gown" relations:

Dick Angier was the real killer-man. He was the one who when he left Duke had about fifty civil offenses against him, you know, everything from punching out officers to pissing on funeral homes. . . . I remember Angier. All the guys at Mayola's, y'know, when I was in high school, would always fantasize about coming up against Dick Angier. And it was really odd.[14]

The fusion of the Odom story with the Dick Angier image enhances it as a case of "town-gown" conflict.

However, except for one variant, the Odom story lacks much of the sense of a Duke-versus-Durham opposition. Though some informants use the term "Durhamites" in referring to the assailants, the black-versus-white theme is more common. Moreover, Duke students (and professors and administrators) use the terms "grit" or "redneck" when referring to townspeople in a negative context. These terms do not occur in any collected variant.

White versus Black

Although the incident took place after the sit-in era, racial tensions in Durham and at Duke were still high in 1967 and continued so through the next several years. Demonstrations and even rioting broke out on several occasions. The Odom story, relating a lone white man's victory over a gang of black attackers, challenged the mystique of black masculinity, and that fact undoubtedly had much to do with the story's endurance. Its reversal of stereotypes, and its "unusual and impossible elements" told for truth, provided an outlet for the "frustration" of whites facing a black militancy that threatened the institutions of white society and culture.

The story is usually set in the area between Duke's campuses, a white section of town. Thus, the presence of blacks on Campus Drive is seen as a sort of invasion, much as the black militancy of the time can be seen as an invasion of white preserves. In that context, Robin Odom becomes a defender of the white-dominated social order, successfully repelling the invasion at a time when, in fact, blacks were making strong inroads into white society. Odom is accosted on a street at night, when he is alone: the story reinforces the general idea of the unsafe nature of streets at night. It presents the blacks as unprovoked aggressors, in most versions attacking Odom for no reason other than plain meanness, thus justifying the stereotype of blacks as violent and dangerous. At a time when the mass media were promoting racial integration and equality, the Odom story stresses just the opposite.

One variant presents an interesting twist, which indicates what can happen to a story in oral circulation when it is acted upon by a complex set of attitudes and values:

Was it Steve Waits? Steve Waits—it might have been some big black football player walking along Campus Drive. Anyway, he got jumped by some Durhamites and beat them all up, and that was the end of the muggings for a while. I just remember hearing about it, I don't remember any of the details. It was in the winter sometime, it was a cold night, there was some reason why—he wouldn't normally be out walking on Campus Drive at night. I read about it in the *Chronicle*.[15]

This telling stresses the danger of the streets and mixes in elements of the Duke-versus-Durham with the white-versus-black conflict. In this variant, the blacks are identified with the university and the aggressors with Durham. Race is not one of the story's necessary elements; it may change in significance or drop out altogether.

Athlete versus Nonathlete

The Odom story is the property of the Duke community. Inquiries among Durhamites not connected with the university reveal no knowledge of the story at all, other than one individual, a self-professed "Duke fan," who thought that he remembered "something like that," but associated the story with a particular basketball player who had attended Duke in the early 1960s.

A college may be viewed as a community, but it is a divided one, with subcommunities existing in sets of various interrelations with one another. One such subcommunity is that of athletes, in particular those receiving grants-in-aid to play "major" sports—football and basketball. Although Duke policy makes no official distinction between athletes and other students, athletes do tend to group together, and certain fraternities are known for being "jock frats." In the late 1960s, those were Phi Delta Theta, Phi Kappa Sigma, Alpha Tau Omega, and Kappa Alpha.

Oppositions arise from such factors as isolation, possession by one group of special knowledge or skills, or one group's being viewed by the other as in some way admirable, favored, or awesome.[16] The image of one man overcoming a whole gang is an "awesome" one, and yet it is also an unusual element that reflects reality. The Odom story is told as true: football players are isolated from other members of the university community; they possess special skills; and are generally regarded as physically awesome.

This "awesome" jock and his "unusual" feat serve to reemphasize the difference between football players and ordinary people. The story thus justifies the social institution of separation between athletes and other students. In its retelling, it "educates" the hearer to this separation and thus encourages conformity to it. Several informants recalled hearing the Odom story during their freshman year at occasions such as dormitory bull sessions or rush parties. In that context it served as part of the newcomer's initiation into the community, introducing him to a bit of the community's stock of distinctive lore and to the ferocious image of the football player. (One informant, who joined Alpha Tau Omega, recalled hearing the story first from his freshman housemaster and, again, from football players in his fraternity—a case of initiation both into the larger university community and the subcommunity.)

On both sides of the line, the Odom story reveals and offers escape from "frustration," but in different ways. Athletes are commonly stereotyped as stupid,[17] and, along with "jock," the more pejorative term "animal" is often applied to football players at Duke. One dormitory quadrangle is known as "Animal Quad" from its habitation at one time by Kappa Alpha, considered the most animalistic of animal frats (Odom and Angier were both KAS).

One bit of KA lore was cited above in the case of the intimidated Phi Psi. Another was related by a Durham cabdriver, who heard the story from a Duke-alumnus drinking buddy. The cabdriver had never heard the Odom story, but his tale is notable for its reversals of its elements: "Carnival was telling me one night, that they [some KAS] were standing on the East, trying to hitchhike a ride, and they couldn't get the ride, because the guy—they just stood out in the middle of the road, and the guy just tried to run, just zoom, just took off, tried to run over them, it was one of the trustee's sons, and they went over and caught up with him and just broke both his legs or something."[18]

Animals are a randomly dangerous force, an ever-present threat that can be viewed as a "frustration" to nonathletes. The use of the denigrating term "animal" is in itself a method of escape, rendering the threatening object subhuman and inferior. The Odom story, to the nonathlete, can function to reinforce that prejudice, with its King Kong–like image of a raging Superjock.

Athletes, however, are aware of the attitude toward them,[19] which creates a frustrating situation for the jock. Athletes are also distinctly a

minority group among the student population. So, the Odom image—
one man set upon by a gang and whipping it—represents a symbolic
victory for "our" side, that is, athletes. Also, in perpetuating the story,
the athletes perform a sort of table turning on those who relegate them
to animal status by affirming their ferocity and animalism in their ability to stand against their oppressors.

A late-1960s basketball player who is now a development officer
for Duke said:

> Well, the way I heard it, Robin Odom was walking between the
> two campuses, and either a carload or two carloads of young kids—
> all of them were under twenty—pulled up, and they all piled out
> and came up to him and wanted his wallet. And Odom told them
> he wasn't going to give it to them. And one of them had a gun—
> or there was a gun in one of the cars, and they had a lead pipe, and
> they swung the lead pipe at Odom and he grabbed it away. I don't
> think he went after anyone in particular, he just sort of went
> around in a circle, then started just randomly delivering blows
> and put some of them on the ground and the rest started running.
> One of them went back to the car and grabbed the gun and actu-
> ally pointed it at Odom and the gun wouldn't fire, and Robin
> Odom just rushed the guy with the gun and jumped on the car
> and started beating on the car. They all got away, but two or
> three of them went to the hospital, and I think the rest of them
> were accosted later at Tops. . . . I heard it a bunch of times, and
> it seemed to get bigger each time—most people didn't seem to be-
> lieve it was really as fantastic as it was told, it seems like it got
> pared down in the later versions. . . . There was something about
> a watch, they broke his watch and that was when he really got
> mad.[20]

And an ATO who has not visited Duke since his 1971 graduation recalled in Illinois:

> It was Robin Odom—this was back in the days when you had to
> have the ladies in by—was it ten or twelve? Anyway, Odom didn't
> have a car, and his friends had left him at the door when he took
> his girlfriend back to her dorm. The buses stopped running at
> twelve so he didn't catch a bus, and he was walking back and was

jumped by two cars full of Durhamites, maybe eight guys. One car pulled up in front of him and one in back of him, and Odom didn't at first think much about it. Then, some of the guys got out, and Odom tried to make conversation with them, like, "Hi there, I see you guys been drinking a little." Then one of the guys took a swing at him, and he fended it off, and then another one came up and hit him in the back with a baseball bat. Odom said something like, "Hey, I don't want any trouble," and one of the guys took a tire iron and swung at him, and Odom threw up his left arm to protect himself, and it broke his watch. This watch that was given to him by his mother—or his father, or anyway that he had this great sentimental attachment to. And then he just said, "Now you've had it," and he put six of them in the hospital. He put six guys in the hospital, and he got the tire iron away and beat out the windows in one of the cars. And one of the guys had a rifle and he pointed it at Odom, and it misfired, and then Odom took the rifle away and beat out the windows of the other car with that, and the two he didn't put in the hospital got ninety days. The court didn't do anything to the other six, because they'd learned their lesson. But there was this one thing. At the trial, the judge asked, "Mr. Odom, did you ever consider retreat?" and Odom just looked at him and said, "What for?" This is the way it was told to me by the other football players. It was first told to me by this Sigma Chi in my freshman house, and I heard different versions of it later. The gun, there was a gun involved, and Odom didn't press charges for attempted murder, as he could have. I heard it both from this housemaster, who was a Sigma Chi, and later on from the other football players.[21]

The retention of great amounts of detail in these variants from members of two jock fraternities suggests that the occurrence, vitality, and therefore significance of the story has been greatest among the athletes themselves. By affirming Odom's ferocity, the athlete satirizes the would-be satirists—those who look upon him and his group as animals. It was in the telling of the story by these last two informants that humor was most strikingly evident; the teller pausing every few sentences to laugh and seeming to take a considerable amount of pleasure in the story. Humor was evident in some other tellings, but not to such an extent.

Although all three oppositions are significant in the Odom story, the opposition of athletes and nonathletes is the most important. It is in this paradigm that the story is found and functions on both sides of the opposition. Surprisingly, the Duke-versus-Durham opposition seems the least important.

Temporal context is important. The Odom incident occurred at a time of racial tension, and at a time when college campuses were dividing internally along establishment-versus-activist lines. Although activism in the 1960s often aggravated town-versus-gown antagonism, football players were generally identified with the establishment as opposed to their politically or psychedelically inclined fellow collegians.

The Odom story has followed the course expected for a personal experience narrative turning into a legend: the loss and confusion of detail, a merger with other stories and impressions, and "social censorship" honing an "unusual" event into a socially functioning tale. The greater the social distance of the tale from the teller, the vaguer the legend is likely to become—from the athletes' detailed accounts to a British religion professor's "I believe I have heard that, somewhere."[22]

15. The Dissembling Line: Industrial Pranks in a North Carolina Textile Mill

Douglas DeNatale

Lillie Smith had been furious. Even though the incident was long past, the anger sparked by the recollection was fresh. Some fifty years ago, a fellow worker in the textile mill at Bynum, North Carolina, had tormented Lillie and interfered with her job as a winder for a whole week. The work was difficult enough. There were hundreds of bobbins to keep spinning smoothly on the long banks of spindles, full cones of yarn had to be quickly replaced with empty ones, and all the while there was the constant checking for any broken threads to be retied. But Iola White seemed to delight in idly taunting Smith, tossing insults from the end of the alley until it was impossible to concentrate on the tedious business. In a final, brazen stroke, Iola stole Smith's knotter, the hand-held device used for joining broken threads. Recruiting a new victim, Iola approached Smith's niece, a newcomer to the mill, and dragged the unwilling accomplice into the bathroom. There she brandished the knotter before tossing it up out of sight on a window ledge. Years later, the strange incident remained vivid for both aunt and niece:

"She took me in the bathroom and throwed [the knotter] up in the window," recalled Smith's niece. "I knew where it was, but I didn't dare to tell [my aunt] for [Iola White] to jump on me and beat me. I didn't know, I didn't know whether—what to say. I was just new down there, a new hand, you know."

Smith replied, "You remember what I done? I run her out there in [the boss's] arms, wasn't it?"

Her niece answered, "Yeah, you used to run bobbins at her."

"I was going to beat her to death, just about," responded Smith.[1]

The sharp laughter at the memory was brief. Such treatment, unseen or ignored by the other workers, had proved too much for even Lillie Smith's righteous anger. In the face of such antagonism, it was little wonder that she soon found reason to leave the mill.

Folklorists are also newcomers to the factory floor, turning in recent years from the gratifying, simplistic discovery of familiar expressive items in industrial situations—"old wine in new bottles"—to more careful consideration of work technique and process.[2] Despite honest intentions and a much-needed attentiveness to workers' own words, it has sometimes proved disarmingly easy for folklorists to become unknowing accomplices to slanted views and narrow purposes through our impulse for presenting occupational folklore as a functional expression of a communal spirit. Studies of folklore in industry have provided a wealth of evidence for the resiliency of human creativity in severely restricted situations but have been less successful in illuminating the use and effect of particular expressions in particular situations. It is no coincidence that folklorists' most valuable studies have focused on those moments of severe dislocation during labor-protest movements when workers have created expressive forms in response to, but outside of, the structure of everyday industrial life.[3] In contrast, those studies that try to comprehend worker and manager alike participating in the daily routine of industrial life have sheltered uncomfortably beneath the communal mantle.

If community is a valid notion at all in everyday industrial situations, it cannot be summarized by the organizational flowchart of the manufacturing establishment, or justified by ignoring the structural nature of industrial conflict through a tight focus on small collectivities of workers. Each of these approaches stems from a limited vantage point. Workers are able to fashion new forms of expression that become an essential part of the work process and yet are in opposition to management goals. Such accomplishment argues against the long-standing and still dominant use of managerial concepts of work organization as the controlling metaphor for the social structure of work. Yet such expressive acts are unable significantly to restructure the work itself. That inability renders any study that ignores the structural power of management spurious. For each particular industrial situation, workers' expressive acts are but a constituent element in the organization of

Figure 15.1. Bynum cotton mill, before it burned in 1916 (courtesy of Mary Gattis).

work, just as the ability of management to secure its ends is a constituent.

The southern textile industry is a case in point. Long cited as the worst example of a management-dominated, closed, paternalistic enclave, the southern mill village has produced a rich body of expressive culture. Proceeding from this discovery, the communalistic impulse has led at least one folklorist to claim that the folklore of southern textile mill workers "expresses a universal outlook of togetherness, and an unmitigated sense of unity, harmony, and happiness."[4] This, despite the southern mill industry's troubled, continuing history of labor relations punctuated by bitter skirmishes over labor-union representation. Nonetheless, the statement is not without support among workers themselves. In Bynum, where Lillie Smith worked, as elsewhere, southern mill workers state that *their* mill is "just about like a family—or at least it usually is." Clearly any examination of the place of expressive culture in the southern textile industry must comprehend both the immediate profession of community and the record of conflict. Given this consideration, one form of expressive culture in the textile mill—the industrial prank—deserves particular attention, for it combines a direct appeal to the notion of community and a constant potential for conflict.

Except for music, practical joking on the job has received more attention by folklorists than any other form of occupational expression. According to Jack Santino, practical joking constitutes "one of the most pervasive themes in occupational narrative."[5] Compact, intensely dramatic, clearly related to work, occupational pranks have certainly merited scrutiny as folklorists attempt to place expressive activities in their social context. Pranks are also susceptible to widely divergent interpretation. Where some labor historians overlook or dismiss pranks for their apparent triviality, and some sociologists cite pranks as evidence of organizational deformity, even some folklorists are prone to

Figure 15.2. George Hearne at his creeler in the Durham Hosiery Mills No. 4 (now Carr Mill Mall), Carrboro, N.C., about 1915 (courtesy of Mary Gattis).

superficial readings. Because pranks appear to be self-contained dramatic acts, there is a tendency to interpret them as a direct reflection of the relationships of the workplace. If antagonism is playfully expressed within the boundaries of the prank, runs the implicit argument, then the underlying tensions are resolvable within a communal ethos. Because many pranks can be selected as examples of harmless group play, we may even fail to recognize the act that victimized Smith as a prank. Overt hostility, physical danger, and sheer aggression may be important features of acts that mill workers themselves label pranks.

Judging from the reports of other Bynum workers, Smith's experience was not an act of isolated vindictiveness, nor was it a senseless piece of malicious fun. But we would be equally misled to simply consider this and similar acts the "dark side of folklore" in the mills. Instead, there is a continuous range in the Bynum mill from benign to sharply aggressive pranks, and a systematic relation between these acts of individual risk taking and the social conventions of the workplace. The meaning of southern textile pranks derives from their place in an ongoing discourse concerning the nature of mill work. Pranks do not depict the work situation but discuss it. Iola White's prank is senseless in isolation but becomes clear in relation to the general tenor of conversation among southern textile workers.

Bynum workers' classification of pranks is similar to the typology offered in Betty Messenger's study of the Irish linen industry: "Few men and women escaped being the object of practical jokes during their working days. Most young people were subjected almost immediately to hazing aimed at the newcomer making a transition from the ranks of the unemployed to the employed, and many also fell victim to pranks directed against certain categories of persons or engaged in at certain times. The harassment of workers for the sheer sake of devilment was commonplace as well."[6] In the Bynum mill, initiation pranks, pranks based on the relationship of different categories of workers, and pranks played on fellow workers of equal status are treated as interrelated types of behavior. These are grounded in a larger etiquette that determines the appropriate victims and acceptable reactions. The interrelation of these types of pranks forms an expressive profile crucial to the social meaning of individual acts.

Among the different types of pranks, the initiation prank is most easily accommodated by a dramaturgical model. As in almost any spe-

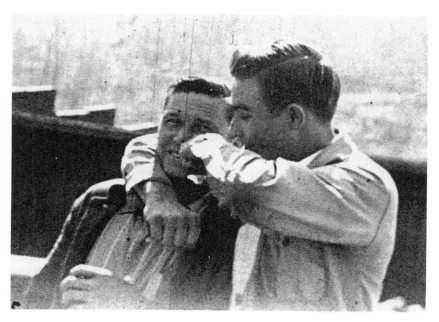

Figure 15.3. Horseplay between Bynum workers, from a film made by H. Lee Water about 1940 (courtesy of William Gerringer).

cialized occupation, the new mill worker is often subjected to torments:

> A new hand would come in down there sometimes to work, and they'd send him after a left-handed monkey wrench, and go down there and get the key to the elevator, and the bobbin-stretcher, and all that stuff. Somebody that didn't know there was no such thing. Send them to a foreman or something, and he'd send them back. They'd say, "Well, I let so-and-so have it," or something, then run him around a little bit. Some dumb folks come to work, but they'd never been in a mill or nothing, you know. They'd play stuff like that. Or, they just enjoyed themselves by doing a thing like that. But they all did seem to have a good time. It was just a happy family almost, looked like. It sure was.[7]

Such pranks are certainly not particular to the textile industry, but are adapted to the textile process. Imaginary objects such as the "bobbin-stretcher" depend on the newcomer's ignorance of the processes and tools of mill work. Workers confront the newcomer with a necessary task, but present the wrong information needed to carry it out: "Somebody new would come in, they'd tell them they'd have to go get the key to the elevator. They'd send the person to the bossman to get the key to the elevator. He'd just laugh, laugh it off."[8] "There wasn't no key, of course. There was nothing to do but start it. . . . It was run by belts, and they had a lever in the center. You'd switch that one over thataway. They'd cross, and it'd run it up. And then a straight belt on the other side'd run it down."[9] Such information, difficult to verbalize, can be gained only by demonstration, underlining the possession of technical knowledge by older hands.

A variation of this technique is to confront the newcomer with a difficult and apparently needless task, all the time insisting upon its necessity: "If you was green and you didn't know anything, they'd just try to play a little. . . . I know one time, and it was a grown man, too, . . . they told him that he'd have to move [a carding machine] and sweep under it. And you couldn't budge it with a bulldozer hardly. Well, he tried, but he finally stopped. I had come by, and he asked me. I said, 'You can't even budge that. You try to move it, just try. You know you can't move that thing.' And he said they just tried all sorts of things on him."[10]

Finally, older hands could interfere with a task surreptitiously:

We had a tank up there in the card room, that you'd draw, from the cards you'd get the sweepings and the stuff that goes in this tank. And you'd have to take that out. The man that takes out the sweepings and sweeps, he goes in this tank thing and gets all this lint and stuff from the cards, and he puts it on a sheet. And he has to carry it out to the waste room. Well, it's not very heavy, you know, by itself, oh, of course if you get, pull it out twice a night, maybe you'd get seventy-five, eighty pounds in it. And a man starts throwing it over his shoulder and go out the door with it, well, some of them would put a, maybe a fifty-pound weight in it, or a sixty-pound weight in it. And you'd start a-throwing it on your shoulder, you, it'd throw you right back on your butt. They'd do something like that. Depending on the job you got.[11]

These initiation pranks depend on the difference between the old-timer's knowledge and the new hand's ignorance. This disparity gives even the person with the lowest-status job in the mill a hierarchical advantage over the newcomer.

Initiation pranks serve a dual purpose in highlighting the distinction between mill workers and newcomers. For workers, they confirm the separate character of mill work, but do so affirmatively, stressing the technical competence necessary for mill work. Simultaneously, the initiation prank constructs a dramatic dialogue with the newcomer. The drama begins when the newcomer is set up, and reaches a climax when some old hand reveals communal knowledge of the joke: "Send a man to pick up a left-handed monkey wrench, and he'd hunt all over the mill for his left-handed wrench, you know. There was no such thing, but he didn't know the difference. And then they'd stand back and laugh."[12] The resolution comes when the newcomer demonstrates his or her reaction: "Last one I sent after anything like that, he come back, said, 'How come you tell me there was such a thing as that when there ain't?' [But] you might find one out of a hundred that gets mad about it."[13]

The manner in which newcomers react enables the old hands to assess their character. In turn, the proper resolution of the prank can result in a welcoming gesture to the newcomer. By increasing and then deflating the difficulties in learning a new job, the prank releases the inherent tension by making light of the process. The newcomer who responds correctly learns the proper form of joking relationships in the mill.[14]

The initiation prank also demonstrates to the newcomer his or her reliance on fellow workers in the manufacturing process. In this regard, it is significant that supervisors in the mill also participate in initiation pranks:

You take that boy that come down there once to work. I was learning him to doff. And he got a might nervous a little bit. Well, the superintendent lived down there at that time, you know, there's this big house in front of the church. I told him to go up there, see the superintendent, and tell him I needed a bobbin-stretcher. Well, he sent that poor boy back to the card room.

Wrote down to the supervisor down there to get the bobbin-stretcher. Said he went down there and found him. He just stood there and laughed at him. He said, "Boy, there ain't no such thing as a bobbin-stretcher."[15]

In sharing a joke with old hands at the newcomer's expense, superintendents concede the limits of their managerial roles and an overlapping of status conferred by experience:

I was a machinist down there in the winding room. I was working on the winder there one day, and they put another boy down there helping me, and he didn't know nothing about it. Didn't hardly know what a wrench was. And I told him to go upstairs and tell the bossman to send me a left-handed monkey wrench. And he took off, went up there, and found him, told him what I'd said. Well, the bossman knowed that it was a joke, so he throwed it off somewhere another to him. And the boy came back and told me he couldn't find it. Well, an hour or two after that, after I'd got it fixed—it was Frank Durham's daddy, Manly Durham, was the man—he saw me and said, "Didn't you know that they didn't make left-handed monkey wrenches?" I said, "Yeah, I knew it, but," I said, "that boy didn't."[16]

Managers are willing to play along with such pranks, but only within the confines of the workplace, and only in a manner that does not subvert their position in the job hierarchy. On one occasion, the mill superintendent was placed in a position that was questionable under community mores: "One night down there they brought in, while I was on second shift, they brought in a woman, new spinner. And I told her to go up [to the superintendent's house] after a left-handed monkey wrench. That night he come back there and told me not to send no more women up there asking nothing like that. They rode that woman high about that, that going up there after that left-handed monkey wrench."[17]

Initiation pranks thus affirm a common mill-worker identity, which can, within limits, extend even to supervisors. Yet the recognition of a job hierarchy is essential to such pranks. It is, after all, the manager's acknowledged power that gives his participation added piquancy. Managers also have their own reasons for assessing the newcomer's character: "Some of [the newcomers], you'd get a good cussing if you didn't mind, if you decided to do a little to them. Some of them were mighty meek and humble, though. Some of the best help."[18] The mill identity asserted clearly accepts the reality of hierarchical power.

These overly neat functional observations are applicable in some sense to nearly all occupations, but present several further problems for southern mill villages such as Bynum. Among workers, initiation pranks emphasize not only the distinct nature of mill work but of mill society. The Bynum native beginning mill work is warned against pranks and already knows the worst pranksters. Bynum children carry their parents' meals to the mill and are already acquainted with the mill's layout and processes.

> *DeNatale:* How about people in the village when they first went to work down there? Did they play pranks on them?
>
> *Durham:* Yes, they would, the whole lot of them. But most of them knew. Had the left-handed monkey wrench, and the key to the elevator, and the bobbin-stretcher. They'd learnt all of that.[19]

For these reasons, initiation pranks are directed primarily toward those who are newcomers to the village as well as to the mill. It is a complete outsider, like Smith, who is most vulnerable to initiation. Because such actions emphasize mill workers' distinctiveness and buttress the stereotypes applied to them by the rest of southern society, pranks have their disadvantages. But Bynum workers go beyond this—they positively assault outsiders.

In general, the victims have violated the mores of mill society in some manner. In one case, a man living near Bynum, engaged to a Bynum woman, started paying attention to another:

> There was a girl, a lady down there he was kind of wanting to fly around a little bit. And that tickled me, cause it happened, cause I didn't think he had no business down there. And he went down there to see her one night, and some of the men upstairs knew what he was up to. And he was dressed up, had on a Panama straw hat and all that, it was back when they dressed up like that. And he, they poured a bucket of dirty water on him, come right down on his Panama hat and all over him, as he started in the door of the

mill. Just soaked him. And they'd do such things as that. . . . But they knew what he was going down there for.[20]

But not all such attacks are so clearly motivated. In many instances, a visitor to the mill is vulnerable simply by virtue of being an outsider: "I've seen it down there at that mill, if somebody seen some stranger coming, he got wet. Course, back then, them windows, you could open them up. And some of them come down there, parade right around close to the mill and everything. You know what they call those fire buckets down there? They'd sit there for a long time and get stale, grease settle in them, and what have you, brother. That's all there was to it about it. I don't care who he was, he still got it if somebody seen him a-coming."[21]

It is striking that even in these pranks that were inflicted on individuals outside of the community, workers remember the management as taking their side: "We never did hear no complaints. I never did hear but one, and there weren't no complaint then. The boss says, 'I've told him to keep his what-have-you away from them windows, and he won't listen to nobody. We told four of them about getting too close to those windows. They won't listen to nobody.' "[22] As long as the victims were not in a position to retaliate, the management looked the other way.

It is not difficult to attribute an immediate function to these acts. Such pranks actively oppose the aloofness displayed by outsiders by reducing them to objects of ridicule. At times, the prank involved is a direct assault on townspeople and their snobbery:

> One time, a long time ago, the Pittsboro boys, looked like they felt they was better than the Bynum boys. My brother and a friend of his and all of them worked upstairs in the card room. And there's three or four of the boys that sort of got dressed up in their white shirts, and come down there, and we was working down there in the basement—is what it is now. . . . And they was all dressed up, and the boys upstairs looked out of the windows and seen them down there, peeping in the winding-room windows at us. And they had big old buckets of water. Had no fire extinguishers then. And that old water would get all rusty, you know. And they'd go back there in the card room, and get them big old buckets of that old iron-rust water, and just poured it right down on them. They

didn't know where it came from. Just ruined their pretty white shirts. But they never did come back over there and peep in there no more.[23]

But whatever was gained by temporary humiliation had its cost. The growing antagonism between the town and the mill village often erupted into open fights. At least one case in Bynum had to be resolved in the courts.[24] If such pranks were solely adolescent strategies for dealing with outside opinion, they were essentially self-defeating, confirming townspeople's opinion of mill workers as rough characters.

The foregoing narratives support the image of the mill as a community of mutual interest, holding a common front against the world, but the remaining pranks set elements of the mill village against each other. Among those pranks corresponding to Betty Messenger's second class there are a number that directly attack the job hierarchy in the mill. Following the observations of industrial sociologists, Roger Abrahams has suggested that such pranks "both articulate and undermine the status system, if only for a moment."[25] From this perspective, such pranks operate as a type of festive behavior for low-status workers, forming a sense of solidarity and worker community. They also allow receptive management a degree of integration with that community.

For a number of pranks in Bynum, this suggestion has some validity. Pranks directed toward managers constitute a leveling of status and a recognition of common relations and responsibility: "That old man that was boss in the winding room, he said one day, said, . . . 'I'll tell you right now, I'm gonna have to go get the Man. Y'all can't do nothing. I'm gonna have to go get the Man.' We just worried that man to death. . . . He had a little shelf up there, he'd put his old hat on it, throw it up on the shelf. We got back one day, and went to his old felt hat on the shelf. We filled that hat flat full of water and set it up there, and waited till he got there. Then he just grabbed the hat up, and turned it up, and water went all over him. We all just died."[26]

Similarly, workers who side with management can be reprimanded:

Now let me tell you something funny. This old woman, she was the queerest old woman you ever seen in your life. And she'd tell them on us, every time she could see us to. . . . She went in the bathroom [one day], and we pushed crates up against . . . the bathroom door . . . so she couldn't get out. We kept her in there

for Lord knows how long. . . . She come out, and she was the
maddest thing. She come over [to me], and: "Did you done it? I
knowed you done it! You done it." I said, "Miss Alice, I didn't do
it." "Yes you did. I knowed you did!" I didn't do it. Carl Ellis was
[the] one done it. But we was all helping him clear the pass so he
could.[27]

And I've been told about that fellow getting locked up in the
toilet. And they put a sign . . . on the door: "Snake in the
Toilet."[28]

Serious reprimands expressed in nonserious language, such pranks level
the informer through humiliation. At the same time, an opportunity to
be reintegrated with the workers is afforded the informer who grace-
fully accepts the reprimand.

Finally, on rare occasions, mill workers can use pranks to speak
directly to a perceived wrong:

I got my thumb caught in the winder and split it open. See, it's
there. And uh, they didn't want to pay me, said it was careless-
ness. . . . They didn't want to pay me for getting my hand hurt
in the winder, and it caused me to be out of the mill for a long
time. They didn't want to pay me for what time I lost. So I went
down there with mama that night, and we pulled that there thing
where you start the whole mill on, we pulled the pulley down,
tied a red ribbon around it. . . . And I pushed it up, . . . and it
stopped off, and they couldn't pull it down—I had to do it. Cause
I tied it there on account of the insurance, to get paid for my
finger getting split open and losing time out of the mill. . . . My
mama told me to do that. She was with me.[29]

Acts of sabotage such as this are extremely rare, but they can flow
easily from practical joking to practical protest. Couched in the language of pranking, open opposition to authority can carry an overtone
of community acceptance, affording the actor some measure of protection.

Jack Santino characterizes these subversions of the job hierarchy as
the most common type of occupational prank.[30] If this is the case for
most work situations, then Bynum can only be an anomaly, for such
pranks are the most uncommon there. The relations of individual

workers and individual managers in southern mills are seriously complicated by the same ties of kinship that make it possible to depict the mill village as "just like a family." The individuals the community remembers as most successful in dealing with authority are those who achieve their opposition indirectly, on memorable occasions later retold as character anecdotes: "Carl [Neal] said one time that, uh, says he was hauling yarn then, and so, says uh, the boss man told him to take that yarn and then get over there and get back. Told him, says, 'Yes Sir!' Said he reached up and turned his hat around. Says, 'What's that for?' he says, 'I'm on my way back.' "[31] The small number of such incidents does not indicate absolute consensus between labor and management but the limits of pranking in addressing the job hierarchy within the mill.

The vast majority of Bynum pranks are played on workers of equal status. I find Betty Messenger's attribution of these to the love of "sheer devilment" unconvincing, however, for it renders such acts arbitrary and poorly motivated. At first glance, one does find many pranks to which no motive besides devilment can be attached:

They picked at one another all the time. One was doing something to another all the time. . . . I was on second shift and [Ernest Williams] was on the first shift. [And he'd wear an] old piece of a shoe. I told him one day, I said, "Mr. Ernest," I said, "I'm going to nail them shoes to the floor one of these nights. . . . Well, one night I happened to think about it, and I went up there to the man's tool box, and I found a nail and a hammer. And he'd set his shoes in there on top of one another, just like that. And I took his shoes out, and I nailed them through the heel, put it, and then I set that one on top of the other one just like he had it, nailed it through that heel, then set them back under there just like he had them setting, and nailed them down that much. . . . Well, next evening when we went in, I went in just a few minutes before changing time. He seen me a-coming. And I commenced laughing just as soon as I seen him. I was right smart a little piece wrong. I went on down there to him. He said, "Doggone you, you did nail my shoes down last night, didn't you?" I said, "Well, I told you I would."[32]

[Carl Neal] had his wife to make some coffee long about eleven-thirty or twelve o'clock at night, and she'd bring him a quart of coffee down there. And he'd give me part of it. . . . He would usually pour him a cupful out, and set it up in the window and let it cool, you know, while he was going upstairs to lay some roping up. So when he'd come back it'd be cool, and he'd drink it. . . . Well, my brother was working down there. . . . He told me, he says, "I'm going to fix old Carl." I says, "What are you going to do to him?" He says, "When he gets gone," he says, "I'm going to drink that coffee. And I'm going to pour some more in there. It'll be hot when he comes back." I said, "You ought not to do that. He'll come back up here and grab that whole mouthful of that coffee, and it'll burn him." He says, "Naw, he won't." So he drinked the coffee, and poured the cup full again, and Carl come back up, picked that cup up and turned it up and got a whole mouthful of that hot coffee, and he just "PHEWWWW!!!" every which way, you know, and he looked straight at me. And my brother had left a note there. It said, "The Fox has been here." Carl said, "Yeah, and I know who the fox is!" I said, "You know it wasn't me." "Yes it was too!" I said, "Naw, it wasn't me." And he said, "Well, you know who it was then." I said, "Yeah, but I ain't going to tell you!" But that, that's the kind of trick they'd play on one another.[33]

If these are taken as self-contained acts, their gargantuan excess is evident.

It is the surface appearance of such pranks taken individually that has earned them the judgment of childishness by outsiders. Glenn Gilman, a sociologist who portrays southern mill workers and management as a homogeneous folk society, also sees pranks in this light: "The recollections of long service employees . . . even when one makes allowances for the embroidery that had been added to make a good story, support the old bromide that 'kids will be kids.' They appear to have been much more concerned with what they could get away with than with what they could accomplish."[34] In isolation, these pranks do amount to little more than having some fun, but to workers' understanding they had an intimate connection to the larger dialogue about proper worker relations. Any individual prank can appear senseless until brought in relation with similar acts. Pranks against fellow workers then find sense and purpose.

Mill workers' acceptance of such pranks relies on the recognition of an underlying tacit code. One element of this code, as expressed in the prank played on Carl Neal with his coffee, is the group concealment of a prankster. This is part of a larger etiquette of mill relations, which entail protecting an individual worker's right to decide his or her own actions: "Nobody wouldn't tell on each other."[35] Even if other mill workers should disapprove of a particular action, they protect the prankster's identity:

> One time there was a colored girl—a good one and a good cook—
> brought her lady that was spinning down there, that she was
> working for, her dinner or supper. A fellow dropped a little pa-
> per bag of water on her head, and she never would come down
> there any more. No, no, no. They advertised, somebody stuck up
> a sign there, "So-and-so wanted a water-broke cook." . . . And
> the superintendent offered a five-dollar reward to anybody that
> would tell the one that did it, because she was a nice colored lady
> and well thought of. And they didn't want them bothered, the
> folks that would bring anything in there. But the guy that did it
> was in the service in World War II. He wrote him and told him
> that he was the one done it.[36]

Despite a sizable reward at a time when wages were about a dollar a day, and despite the prankster's apparently guilty conscience, his fellow workers conspired to withhold his identity from the management.

Such protection held even against the displeasure of Arthur London, the mill owner. London, known for his bad driving, habitually made one of the workers turn his car around in the narrow, hillside parking lot of the mill:

> I was down there one day after I went to work, and my oldest
> brother, he was an oiler down in the spinning room, and he'd been
> home to get him some supper. And I went out onto the fire escape
> there to smoke. [London] looked down there, and he seen me up
> there. Well, I seen my oldest brother coming down, he had done
> been home to get supper, and [London] commenced to hollering
> for him—he wanted him to turn his car around. He didn't even
> look—he knowed what he wanted—he just went on in the mill.
> [London] looked up there and saw me. He says, "Oh boy, come

here." I went down there. He says, "Now who was that young man?" I says, "I don't know, sir, I never saw him before in my life." He meant my oldest brother![37]

With the knowledge that their own actions were thus protected, workers are less likely to retaliate against pranksters in an open fashion.

Implicit sanctions against excessive or improper pranking are another important part of the tacit code. Fellow workers can enforce these sanctions by retaliating in the proper form: another prank. Such pranks avoid a further escalation by addressing the prank rather than the prankster. As in the snake prank cited above, the answering prank should ideally invert the actions of the offending prankster, resulting in the biter bit: "I remember hearing my daddy saying one time that this guy he worked with was forever biting his ears. He'd run up behind him and bite him on his ears. So one day he thought to himself, "Well, I'm getting tired of him biting my ears." So, said he just filled his ears full of pepper. And that day he run up and bit him on the ear. Said he didn't bother him nohow. Said he got a mouthful of that pepper. I remember hearing daddy tell that. That was way back."[38] By fighting fire with fire in this manner, workers make perfectly phrased reprimands that the original offending prankster is expected to take as a good sport. Such pranks turn back on the tacit code, comment upon it, and reaffirm its validity.

Most of these pranks refer to particular social norms. One of these is the reciprocal sharing of individual resources. It is the practice in Bynum, as elsewhere, for workers to share the food and possessions they bring to the mill.[39] Individuals work toward a proper balance in the exchange of goods. Those who exceed propriety are appropriately reprimanded:

There was one played a joke on somebody with a biscuit down there one time, somebody did, and I can't remember. There was somebody that was always a-begging you to bring him a biscuit or something, and they filled it full of red pepper, and wrapped it up, and brought it, and give it to him.[40]

This fellow used to hang around here right smart on second shift. If you'd set your something to eat down and turn your back on it, he'd get it. So, this fellow brought him some chocolate pie one night to work with him. He had that thing doctored up with Ex-Lax. And that fellow eat that pie. I'll tell you one thing. It was a day or two before that fellow come back to the mill. He was busy the next day all right.[41]

Such pranks are probably the most common of all pranks in Bynum, and extend to other personal items as well. As in the pie story just quoted, the ever-popular laxative ploy is a favorite:

We used to have a boy that worked with us, me and the boy I worked with, Roy Howard. We'd just keep a big bottle of Bromo-Seltzer set up there, you know, for people that had indigestion or anything. Well, we didn't care if it got eaten, but this old boy, he would, he would go down there every few minutes and get him a big mouthful of it, and take him a drink of water. And he'd be getting, he just stayed kind of hopped up on it, you know, till one of them great big old bottles wouldn't last a day. Well, we decided we'd just fix him. We put, got a brand new bottle, poured half of it out, and poured it full of Sal Hepatica. He went down there about four times, and he went home![42]

Another incident echoes the pepper-in-the-ears trick: "We couldn't keep any [snuff]. There was another girl come to our box every time and got our snuff. One day, me and Mrs. Farrell had snuff with me. We got some red pepper and poured it in there, and stirred it up. And it wasn't but a little bit before she come back there to dip snuff, and poured out a mouthful. And she done some spitting! And she didn't bother ours or nothing any more."[43] Rabelaisean humor such as this levels the offender and allows a possible reintegration into the community of fellow workers. Such pranks share the dramatic structure of complication, climax, and resolution that links them to initiation pranks. Because they are constructed on the analogy of more benign pranks, workers can insist to the offended party that these retaliatory acts belong to the domain of "just having a little fun."

In addition to these direct responses to individual offenses, there are other, more subtle pranks of this sort. In these instances, workers take offense at the violation of more general behavioral norms. Such acts break faith through ostentation: "[Bruce Ward] had bought him a little old, when they first come out with one of them little old Aus-

tins. He bought one. He went and stopped there at Mr. Carey's store.
And us boys picked it up and put it on four crates. He come out and
got in that thing. Went 'rrr-RRRRRR!!!' And he got out and looked
around, and he seen it was on crates. Said, 'I'll kill you!' "[44]

Even the simple act of separating one's work identity from one's
outside identity is open to retaliation:

> An old man used to work here. . . . He used to wear these old
> man comforts, just them old sandals like you slip on, you know,
> then with an elastic here in the side. He'd leave them down there.
> And come in, first thing he'd do, he'd get them things and put
> them on. And some of the boys down there, they, and I don't
> know, I still don't know who done it, took a forty-penny nail and
> drove through both of them shoes, and nailed them into the post.[45]

> Fixed that joker up. He'd bring a pair of shoes over there and he
> would work in them, you know. Bring another pair he was going
> to wear away from there. . . . He got hot about that, but I don't
> reckon he found out who done it.[46]

Anonymous acts of personal sabotage, these pranks once again under-
line the distinctiveness of the mill identity but point beyond this to the
reciprocal responsibilities such an identity entails.

In her study of the folklore in a North Carolina hosiery mill, Camilla Collins correctly characterizes pranks played on workers of equal
status as being involved with behavioral norms in the mill, but she
downplays the antagonistic force of the pranks.[47] A number of the
pranks she cites as examples of harmless devilment go well beyond simple fun. Hiding wasps in socks so inspectors will get stung, tying socks
together so fellow knitters will lose time untying them, and telling a
"mentally impaired" worker in the dye house to fill a dyeing tub with
muddy branch water—ruining "several hundred dozens of socks"—
hardly constitute harmless fun.[48] Any prank played on a fellow worker
in a piece-rate setting is an economic assault, for it limits the amount
that can be produced. The serious overtones of such pranks, along with
their acceptance by fellow mill workers, point to a more powerful
motive.

It should be clear from comparing these with the "harmless" pranks
cited that even the most playful and benign practical jokes have the

more serious purpose of maintaining a complicated language of indi-
rect reprimand. The same type of prank that is used in harmless devilment can be loaded with a barbed point. The meaning of an individual
act depends on how it is performed. According to the tacit code, a personal assault can be answered only if the response is made in fun, in
the guise of a prank. The interpretation of harmlessness can be made
only in reference to truly harmless pranks. Beneath their playful exterior, pranks can be very serious business. Pranks occur against a background of community, but we should be wary of a tendency to assume
community as a given. "Community" is the semantic domain of these
acts, not a given state of affairs. Some people are never integrated. Discourse breaks down. Pranks backfire. Tragedy intervenes: "I vaguely
remember something that, uh, this wasn't a, it was a prank to start with,
because they used to have air hoses in there, you know, and uh, it was
either some, this happened in Bynum cotton mill, or something happened in another cotton mill up the river somewhere, that some guy
was, uh, grabbed the air hose and rammed it into some guy's rectum
and he blowed air in him and really, caused him a lot of damage, you
know. I don't know if he died from it or not."[49]

A worker in another North Carolina mill recounted for an inter-
viewer of the Federal Writers' Project: "Ira and me was doffers and
the other doffers played tricks on us. You know how they always is
about new hands. We was awful green without no learnin' nor nothin'.
One day Ira got mad at the way they picked on him and had it out
with another boy at dinnertime. That little boy—he won't [sic] but
twelve year old—stuck a knife in Ira's heart and he was dead before
the doctor got there."[50] In order to prevent such disasters, it is crucial
that antagonisms be played out on the level of what the management
and workers see as "a little fun."[51]

If the accidents that can arise from pranking shock us with the
hostile power coiled within, we have a problem that Bynum workers
do not share. Acts that are an outright assault, that do not fit a dramaturgical model of complication, climax, and resolution, are also considered pranks. The question remains: why are such acts necessary? A
number of reasons have already been given, but all of these have been
subsumed under a functionalist answer: the establishment of a mill
identity and a particular code of behavior. This answer remains par-
adoxical, for why should mill workers want to maintain an identity

that feeds outsiders' stereotypes? With this question, we return to the relationship of work process and expressive activity.

The assaultive actions that workers label pranks are intimately connected with the train of production. The Bynum mill produces thread by carding the raw cotton, twisting the fibers on spinning frames, then rewinding the thread onto cones on winding frames. Wages vary according to the job: spinners are paid at an hourly rate, and winders by the pound. The train of production makes workers mutually dependent. Any worker is in a position to harm another. If, for example, the bobbins on the spinning frames are removed too early, the winders cannot produce as much during their shift. If winders do not remove their work by the end of the shift, the next shift suffers a delay before they can begin. Because such actions restrict another's income, they can be taken as an individual assault. It is not a proper response to bring one's complaint to management, for this too is an antisocial violation of the tacit code: "If I got a bad bobbin, I wound it and kept my mouth shut. You just as well to, it don't do no good. I found that out a long time ago. . . . If you complained, sometimes they'd only get worse, you know, just to spite I have an idea. I won't say that they did it for spite, but I always figured that was it. So I learned to not say nothing, because you get along better if you don't."[52]

The appropriate response is to do exactly the same thing to the offending individual—appropriate because the action has to be accepted as a prank: "I'm sure there's been some bad feelings, you know. Following a man up on a shift, a man that's running, just like I run a set of frames, and I followed this man up, if he wanted to he could leave me in a bad hole, and start me off where there weren't no way for me to make production, you know. I'd just have to work, work at it so hard. . . . Just go on and do the best they could. And the next time if I got a chance, I'd try to leave him in the hole. The same way. If he left me in the hole, I'd try to make it hard on him, try to do the same thing to him if I got a chance. . . . We just took it as a joke."[53] The rationale for such acts goes beyond individual interest. In order to avoid impinging on another worker's ability to meet a production quota during the next shift, a worker has to sacrifice measures that would make his or her own job easier.

Individual interest is insufficient motive for this discourse of indirection. Bynum workers—all southern textile workers—are up against a classic problem, made more complex by the bonds of kinship. The mill management seeks increased production, and the prospect of personal gain in hard times is a powerful inducement for workers to comply. From management's perspective, it might even be advantageous for one shift to leave the next shift in the hole, for the second shift would be induced to work harder to catch up. Older hands fear the possible results: "Aw, they'd jump on them, they'd just, they wanted everybody to uh, kind of go along about the same production. . . . They'd go up on the production, so that everybody would have to make that amount. Course some of [the workers] really couldn't make it. That's the only thing they'd say anything about it. . . . Well, they figured, see, if, say maybe I was making, maybe five or ten more, or fifteen more hanks in a night, and uh, for eight or ten hours, than the next man was, that he was goofing off or something. And then maybe he was older than I am, and he couldn't go along as fast."[54]

Pacing work in this manner, or establishing a stint, is a tactic to which labor historians have drawn attention in the industrial North. Yet its appearance in southern mills goes unnoticed in the labor history of southern textiles. This is a crucial tactic by mill workers who have no direct control over the mill process. By these acts they seek a degree of autonomy achieved through a discourse of indirection.

The individual mill worker has to sacrifice potential economic good in hard times for the sake of other low-status workers. It is this tacit understanding that incited the conflict between Lillie Smith and Iola White, and the attendant theft of Mrs. Smith's knotter. Here is Lillie Smith's problem: she had unwittingly offended her fellow worker simply by working too hard, by not taking breaks with the rest: "[Iola] made it up, all the things, made it up and have a fuss with anybody she wanted to. . . . But wanting me to go out and sit out on that thing, I reckon. I thought that's what it was, on that back porch and smoke. I didn't smoke. . . . They was taking a break. . . . Might have caught up with bobbins, they didn't care. . . . I don't know what she got mad at me. Cause I was working, I reckon. I don't know what."[55] The theft of Smith's knotter was powerfully appropriate, for it was a mechanical tool introduced by mill management that was designed to speed up the winding process. Without it, she was reduced to the slow chore of retying broken threads by hand.

The community of workers is not uniform. As an ideal to which individual mill workers subscribe, it is threatened by the pressures of management goals allied with individual interest. Cooperation is not a given but an ongoing achievement, supported by a discourse articulated in acts such as pranks and the narratives about them. The common reference thus established is a proper bearing in work, a delicate balance of individual autonomy, mutual responsibility, and assertion of common right: "They used to have a code over there. Well, it wasn't a code, it was uh, mostly just the people, as long as they come over there and act like somebody had some principle, nobody said nothing to them. If they come over there and tried to show off, or try to take over, you know, the boys didn't stand for it. They'd do something to them, if they didn't do nothing but drop a bag of water on their head. And there's been a lot of them got it, too."[56]

David Montgomery discusses how this proper bearing laid the foundations of trade unionism in the nineteenth century.[57] The union struggles of the Southeast, which came later and were instigated from outside, were dominated by the dramatic national counterpoint of the late 1920s and 1930s. It is easy to miss the quiet development of southern workers' own concept of a proper bearing, continually reassessed in the discourse of their actions.

Here is the eloquence of a seemingly trivial form of expression. If we link expressive act to act, it is possible to regain the rationale of that discourse, and gather new respect for the creativity of southern mill workers in meeting the problems of their common life. Their achievement, however limited, confounds solicitude and stereotype alike.

Notes

Introduction

1 Untitled, stapled pamphlet in the Southern Folklife Collection, Wilson Library, University of North Carolina at Chapel Hill.

2 *Charlotte Observer*, 31 October 1979, B1.

3 Ruel W. Tyson, James L. Peacock, and Daniel W. Patterson, eds., *Diversities of Gifts*, Folklore and Society Series (Urbana, Ill.: University of Illinois Press, 1988).

4 Ralph Steele Boggs, "Reminiscences on the Prenatal Care and Birth of the Curriculum," *Curriculum in Folklore Newsletter, 1981* (Chapel Hill, N.C.: University of North Carolina), 1–2.

5 John Ashworth Papers, PC.1577.1, North Carolina State Archives, Raleigh, N.C.

6 Church Records, Buffalo Presbyterian Church, Session Minutes, 1777–1788, Reel R.046/08003, North Carolina State Library, Raleigh, N.C.

7 3 June 1838, Methodist Episcopal Church South, South/North Carolina and Virginia Conferences, Salisbury and Yadkin districts, Iredell Circuit, No. 2939, Quarterly Conference Minutes, 1823–1951, Manuscripts Department, Duke University Library, Durham, N.C.

8 James Lee Love Papers, "Memoirs—Random Records—Recollections," MS 4139, vol. 3, Southern Historical Collection, Wilson Library, University of North Carolina at Chapel Hill.

9 John Lawson, *A New Voyage to Carolina*, ed. Hugh T. Lefler (Chapel Hill, N.C.: University of North Carolina Press, 1967).

10 Harden Taliaferro, *Fisher's River (North Carolina) Scenes and Characters* (New York: Harper and Brothers, 1859).

11 See Daniel W. Patterson, "William Hauser's *Hesperian Harp* and *Olive Leaf:* Shape-Note Tunebooks as Emblems of Change and Progress," *Journal of American Folklore* 101 (January–March 1988): 23–36.

12 William F. Allen, Charles Pickard Ware, and Lucy McKim Garrison, *Slave Songs of the United States* (1867; reprint, New York: Peter Smith, 1919), x, xii.

13 Cecil Sharp, *English Folk Songs from the Southern Appalachians*, 2 vols., ed. Maud Karpeles (London: Oxford University Press, 1932), 1: xii–xiii.

14 For information about Greer and a transcript of one of his presentations see Daniel W. Patterson, ed., "North Carolina Folk Songs and Ballads Presented by Isaac G. Greer," *The Bookmark*, no. 36, University of North Carolina Library (July 1966): 3–14.

15 See Loyal Jones, *Minstrel of the Appalachians: The Story of Bascom Lamar Lunsford* (Boone, N.C.: Appalachian Consortium Press, 1984).

16 The best known are Richard Chase's two tale collections *The Jack Tales* (Boston: Houghton-Mifflin, 1943), and *The Grandfather Tales* (Boston: Houghton-Mifflin, 1948).

17 See the account of the Warner's friendship with such North Carolina musicians as the Hicks and Proffitt families on Beech Mountain and the Tilletts at Wanchese in *Traditional American Folk Songs from the Anne and Frank Warner Collection*, ed. Anne Warner (Syracuse, N.Y.: Syracuse University Press, 1984).

18 See Neil V. Rosenberg and Debora G. Kodish, *"Folk Songs of America": The Robert Winslow Gordon Collection, 1922–1932*, Library of Congress Records L68.

19 John A. Lomax, *Adventures of a Ballad Hunter* (New York: Macmillan, 1947), 295, makes brief mention of his work in this state.

20 Mercedes Steely, "The Folk-Songs of Ebenezer Community" (Ph.D. diss., University of North Carolina at Chapel Hill, 1936).

21 Louis W. Chappell, *Folk-Songs of Roanoke and the Albemarle* (Morgantown, W.Va.: The Ballad Press, 1939).

22 See Daniel W. Patterson, "A Woman of the Hills: The Work of Maude Minish Sutton" in *Long Journey Home: Folklife in The South*, ed. Allen E. Tullos, special issue of *Southern Exposure* 5 (Summer–Fall 1977): 105–10.

23 Wayland D. Hand, "Preface," *The Frank C. Brown Collection of North Carolina Folklore* (Durham, N.C.: Duke University Press, 1961), 6:ix.

24 Newman I. White, "General Introduction," *Brown Collection* (1952), 1:13.

25 Ibid., 1:19.

26 Ibid., 1:20.

27 Ibid., 1:27.

28 Archer Taylor, ed., "Riddles," *Brown Collection*, 1:320.

29 White, "General Introduction," *Brown Collection*, 1:9.

30 Reprinted together as James Mooney, *Myths of the Cherokee and Sacred Formulas of the Cherokee from the 19th and 7th Annual Reports B. A. E.* (Nashville, Tenn.: Charles and Randy Eller, 1982).

31 See Lynn Moss Sanders, "A Study of Howard W. Odum's 'New Regionalism' and Its Effect on the Collecting, Study, and Literary Use of Folklore at the University of North Carolina: 1920–1935" (Ph.D. diss., University of North Carolina at Chapel Hill, 1986).

32 These four books were issued from the University of North Carolina Press in 1925, 1926, 1930, and 1929 respectively.

33 Dan Ben-Amos, "Toward a Definition of Folklore in Context," in *Toward New Perspectives in Folklore,* ed. Américo Paredes and Richard Bauman, Publications of the American Folklore Society, Bibliographical and Special Series 23 (Austin and London: University of Texas Press, 1972), 13.

34 Roger Abrahams, "Introductory Remarks to a Rhetorical Theory of Folklore," *Journal of American Folklore* 81 (April–June 1968): 146.

35 See Francis James Child, ed., *The English and Scottish Popular Ballads,* 5 vols. (1882–1898; reprint, New York: Cooper Square Publishers, 1962).

36 White, "General Introduction," *Brown Collection*, 1:26.

37 Isabel Gordon Carter, "Mountain White Folk-Lore: Tales from the Southern Blue Ridge," *Journal of American Folklore* 38 (July–September 1925): 340–74; Chase, *The Jack Tales.*

38 See, for example, Jan Harold Brunvand, *The Vanishing Hitchhiker: American Urban Legends and Their Meanings* (New York: W. W. Norton, 1981).

39 See Mary Seelhorst, " 'The Assailant in Disguise': Old and New Functions of Urban Legends About Women Alone in Danger," *North Carolina Folklore Journal* 34 (Winter–Spring 1987): 29–37.

40 James W. Clay, Douglas M. Orr, Jr., and Alfred W. Stuart, eds., *North Carolina Atlas: Portrait of a Changing Southern State* (Chapel Hill, N.C.: University of North Carolina Press, 1975), 34.

41 See Robert H. Byington, ed., *Working Americans: Contemporary Approaches to Occupational Folklife*, Smithsonian Folklife Series, No. 3 (Washington, D.C.: Smithsonian Institution Press, 1978); reprinted from *Western Folklore* 37 (July 1978): 143–245.

42 Henry Glassie, *Pattern in the Material Folk Culture of the Eastern United States* (Philadelphia: University of Pennsylvania Press, 1968).

43 See Jules David Prown, "Mind in Matter: An Introduction to Material Culture Theory and Method," *Winterthur Portfolio* 17 (Spring 1982): 1–19.

44 See, for example, Carl Lounsbury, *Alamance County Architectural Heritage* ([Graham, N.C.]: Alamance County Historic Properties Commission, 1980).

45 Doug Swaim, ed., *Carolina Dwelling*, The Student Publication of the School of Design, vol. 26 (Raleigh, N.C.: North Carolina State University, 1978).

46 John Bivens, *The Moravian Potters in North Carolina* (Chapel Hill, N.C.: University of North Carolina Press, 1972).

47 Charles G. Zug III, *Turners and Burners: The Folk Potters of North Carolina* (Chapel Hill, N.C.: University of North Carolina Press, 1986). For descriptions of seventeen contemporary North Carolina potteries see Nancy Sweezy, *Raised in Clay: The Southern Pottery Tradition* (Washington, D.C.: Smithsonian Institution Press, 1984).

48 Daisy Wade Bridges, ed., *Potters of the Catawba Valley, North Carolina* (Charlotte, N.C.: The Mint Museum, 1980).

49 Charles G. Zug III, *The Traditional Pottery of North Carolina* (Chapel Hill, N.C.: The Ackland Art Museum, 1980).

50 See John Bivins, Jr., and Paula Welshimer, *Moravian Decorative Arts in North Carolina* (Winston-Salem, N.C.: Old Salem, Incorporated, 1981).

51 *Artistry in Quilts* (Raleigh: The North Carolina Museum of History, 1974).

52 *North Carolina Country Quilts: Regional Variations* (Chapel Hill, N.C.: The Ackland Art Museum, 1978).

53 Charles G. Zug III, *Five North Carolina Folk Artists* (Chapel Hill, N.C.: The Ackland Art Museum, 1985).

54 "The Federal Cylinder Project," *Folklife Center News* 9 (January–March 1986): 14–15, and "Omaha Indian Music," *Folklife Center News* 8 (July–September 1985): 4–5.

55 Many of these recordings may be heard on the album *Unto Brigg Fair: Joseph Taylor and Other Traditional Lincolnshire Singers Recorded in 1908 by Percy Grainger*, ed. Bob Thomson, Leader Records LEA-4050.

56 White, "General Introduction," *Brown Collection*, 1:19.

57 See Archie Green, "Hillbilly Music: Source and Symbol," *Journal of American Folklore* 78 (July–September 1965): 204–28.

58 Guy B. Johnson, "Some Thoughts on South Carolina Folklore Research Fifty Years Ago" (Paper read at the conference Fifty Years of Folk-

lore Research in South Carolina, 3 October 1986, typescript in the Southern Folklife Collection, Wilson Library, University of North Carolina at Chapel Hill), 5.

59 To identify North Carolina performers who can be heard in long-playing recordings, see Beverly B. Boggs and Daniel W. Patterson, *Index to Selected Folk Recordings* (Chapel Hill, N.C.: University of North Carolina Curriculum in Folklore, 1984), geographic list; but this covers only five hundred important albums.

60 William Clements, "Religious Folklife Recordings," *Journal of American Folklore* 96 (October–December 1983): 500.

61 Archie Green, *Babies in the Mill*, Testament Records T-3301.

62 See for example *Piedmont Blues*, vol. 2, Flyright Records LP-107; *Carolina Slide Guitar: Guitar Shorty*, Flyright LP-500; *Blues Come to Chapel Hill*, Flyright LP-504; *Orange County Special*, Flyright LP-506; and *The Last Medicine Show*, Flyright LP-508/509.

63 Bruce Bastin, *Red River Blues*, and Norm Cohen, *Long Steel Rail* (Urbana, Ill.: University of Illinois Press, 1987 and 1981 respectively).

64 Photographic Archive, North Carolina Collection, Wilson Library, University of North Carolina at Chapel Hill.

65 John R. Kemp, ed. *Lewis Hine, Photographs of Child Labor in the New South* (Jackson and London: University of Mississippi Press, 1986).

66 Southern Historical Collection, Wilson Library, University of North Carolina at Chapel Hill.

67 See Margaret Ruth Little, "Sticks and Stones: A Profile of North Carolina Gravemarkers through Three Centuries" (Ph.D. diss., University of North Carolina at Chapel Hill, 1984); and Daniel W. Patterson, "Upland North and South Carolina Stonecarvers: A Report on Research in Progress," Southern Tombstones Issue, ed. Ruth Little-Stokes, *Newsletter of the Association for Gravestones Studies* 6 (Summer 1982): 3–4.

68 Ruth Haislip Roberson, ed., *North Carolina Quilts* (Chapel Hill, N.C.: University of North Carolina Press, 1988). The preface contains a full account of the project.

69 The Seeger tapes are on deposit in the Smithsonian Institution, and the Martin-Kalow tapes in the Southern Folklife Collection, Wilson Library, University of North Carolina at Chapel Hill.

70 For the background of this film, see John Cohen, "A Visitor's Recollections," in *Long Journey Home*, ed. Tullos, 115–18.

71 *Welcome to Spivey's Corner, N.C.* (Deerfield, Ill.: Perspective Films of Simon and Schuster Communications, 1979); and *The Angel that Stands by Me* (San Francisco: Light-Saraf Films, 1983).

72 *Ray Hicks of Beech Mountain, North Carolina* (Johnson City: East

Tennessee State University, 1974), and the more successful *Fixin' to Tell about Jack* (Whitesburg, Ky.: Appalshop Films, 1974).

73 See "George Mahon Holt," a Brown-Hudson Award commendation and overview of Holt's career, in *North Carolina Folklore Journal* 34 (Winter–Spring 1987): 9–10; *Free Show Tonite* (Wychoff, N.J.: Benchmark Films, 1984).

74 *Born for Hard Luck, Being a Joines, A Singing Stream* (Delaplane, Va.: Tom Davenport Films, 1976, 1980, and 1986 respectively).

75 *Dink* has not been commercially released but can be borrowed from the Audiovisual Services Branch of the North Carolina Department of Cultural Resources in Raleigh; *Sprout Wings and Fly* (El Cerrito, Calif.: Flower Films, 1983).

1. The North Carolina Wildfowl Decoy Tradition

1 William J. Mackey, Jr., *American Bird Decoys* (New York: E. P. Dutton, 1965), 166.

2 All material pertaining to John Austin and his family comes from interviews, some tape-recorded, conducted in Corolla, 8 March, 26 April, and 27 April 1977. The interview tapes and notes are in the author's possession.

3 John Brickell, *The Natural History of North Carolina* (Dublin: James Carson, 1737), 202.

4 John Lawson, *A New Voyage to Carolina*, ed. Hugh Talmadge Lefler (Chapel Hill, N.C.: University of North Carolina Press, 1967), 154.

5 Brickell, *Natural History of North Carolina*, 204.

6 David Stick, *The Outer Banks of North Carolina, 1584–1958* (Chapel Hill, N.C.: University of North Carolina Press, 1958), 25.

7 H. B. Ansell, "Recollections of a Life Time and More," MS 1570, Southern Historical Collection, Wilson Library, University of North Carolina at Chapel Hill, 1:5.

8 Ibid., vol. 1, prefatory notes.

9 Ibid., 1:7–8.

10 Ibid., MS 1570-B, 3:28, 30.

11 Ibid., 3:30, 32.

12 Ibid., 3:32.

13 Ibid.

14 *The Laws of North Carolina, Enacted in the Year 1822* (Raleigh, N.C.: Bell and Lawrence, 1823), 72.

15 Ansell, "Recollections of a Life Time," 3:36.

16 Ibid., 1:55.

17 Ibid., 3:42, 44.

18 Ibid., 3:46.

19 Richard Randolph Michaux, *Sketches of Life in North Carolina* (Culler, N.C.: W. C. Phillips, 1894), 127.

20 Edmund Ruffin, *Agricultural, Geological, and Descriptive Sketches of Lower North Carolina and the Similar Adjacent Lands* (Raleigh, N.C.: Institution for the Deaf and Dumb and the Blind, 1861), 153.

21 Mike Wade, tape-recorded interview with author, Knott's Island, 27 April 1977. The interview tape is in the author's possession.

22 Ansell, "Recollections of a Life Time," 3:40.

23 Thomas Gilbert Pearson, *Adventures in Bird Protection* (New York: D. Appleton-Century, 1937), 51, 118.

24 Quinton Colio, "American Decoys: Folk Art," in *American Bird Decoys*, by Mackey, 241.

25 Adele Earnest, *The Art of the Decoy: American Bird Carvings* (New York: Bramhall House, 1965), 43.

26 Mackey, *American Bird Decoys*, 166.

27 George Ross Starr, *Decoys of the Atlantic Flyway* (New York: Winchester Press, 1974), 291.

28 Mackey, *American Bird Decoys*, 168–69.

29 Earnest, *The Art of the Decoy*, 185.

30 Mackey, *American Bird Decoys*, 172.

31 William Neal Conoley, Jr., *Waterfowl Heritage: North Carolina Decoys and Gunning Lore* (Wendell, N.C.: Webfoot, 1982).

2. The Emergence of the New River Valley String Band, 1875–1915

1 See Eric Davidson and Paul Newman, *Traditional Music from Grayson and Carroll Counties*, Folkways Records FS-3811, and *Bluegrass from the Blue Ridge: A Half Century of Change*, Folkways Records FS-3832. Numerous other recordings exist from the region, see in particular, *Round the Heart of Old Galax*, 3 vols., County Records 533, 534, 535.

2 Alan Jabbour's seminal field collection of southern fiddling (AFS 13,031-13,050) is available at the Archive of Folk Culture, Library of Congress, Washington, D.C.

3 See Thomas R. Carter, "Joe Caudill: Traditional Fiddler from Alleghany County, North Carolina" (Master's thesis, University of North Carolina at Chapel Hill, 1973), 14–25.

4 For a thorough discussion of the string-band repertoire, see Thomas Carter and Blanton Owen, brochure notes for *Old Originals: Old-Time Instrumental Music Recently Recorded in North Carolina and Virginia*, 2 vols., Rounder Records 0057 and 0058.

5 A good introductory survey of the string-band style is found in Davidson and Newman, brochure notes for *Bluegrass from the Blue Ridge*, 4–5.

6 Carter, "Joe Caudill," 20.

7 Davison and Newman, *Bluegrass from the Blue Ridge*, 4–5.

8 Carter, "Joe Caudill," 17–18.

9 Hus Caudill, tape-recorded interview with Thomas Carter and Blanton Owen, Spata, North Carolina, 11 September 1973.

10 See Alan Dundes, "The Devolutionary Premise in Folklore Theory," *Analytic Essays in Folklore* (The Hague: Mouton, 1975), 17–27.

11 Thomas Carter, brochure notes for *Emmett W. Lundy: Fiddle Tunes from Grayson County, Virginia*, String Records 802, 5.

12 See Dan Ben-Amos, "Toward a Definition of Folklore in Context," in *Toward New Perspectives in Folklore*, ed. Américo Paredes and Richard Bauman (Austin, Tex.: University of Texas Press, 1972), 3–15; Richard Bauman, *Verbal Art as Performance* (Rowley, Mass.: Newbury House, 1977), 3–60; and Henry Glassie, *Folk Housing in Middle Virginia* (Knoxville, Tenn.: University of Tennessee Press, 1975), 66–113.

13 The settlement history of the area is outlined in Davyd Foard Hood, "The Architecture of the New River Valley," in *Carolina Dwelling: Toward Preservation of Place: In Celebration of the North Carolina Vernacular Landscape*, ed. Doug Swaim, The Student Publication of the School of Design, vol. 26 (Raleigh, N.C.: North Carolina State University, 1978), 202–15.

14 This history of the Lundys is largely taken from "Lundy Generations," a genealogy prepared by Anita Lundy Tiller, 29 July 1974, which is in the author's possession. Additional information was obtained in an interview with Kelly J. Lundy by Thomas and Ann Carter, 23 July 1974, Galax, Virginia.

15 See Davidson and Newman, brochure notes for *Traditional Music from Grayson and Carroll Counties*, 3.

16 Biographical information on Green Leonard was provided in a personal communication from Andy Cahan and Alice Gerrard, November 1983.

17 Emmett Lundy, interview by Elizabeth Lomax, AAFS 4938, Archive of Folk Culture, Library of Congress, Washington, D.C.

18 The earliest collection of Virginia fiddling is George P. Knauff's *Vir-*

ginia Reels, 4 vols. (Baltimore: George Willig, Jr., c. 1839). See also Winston Wilkinson, "Virginia Dance Tunes," *Southern Folklore Quarterly* 6 (March 1942): 1–10. The problems in comparing early American fiddling with that of the British Isles are treated by Alan Jabbour in the brochure notes to *The Hammons Family: A Study of a West Virginia Family's Traditions,* Library of Congress Records, L65-L66, 2.

19 "Belles of Lexington," AAFS 4938, Archive of American Folk Culture, Library of Congress, Washington, D.C.; and "Kitty's Wedding," in *The Dance Music of Ireland,* ed. Francis O'Neill (Chicago: Lyon and Healy, 1907), 146.

20 Alan Jabbour, "Fiddle Tunes of the Old Frontier: In Search of a Fresh Intercultural Model" (Paper delivered at a conference on Music and Dance in Nineteenth-Century America, Museums at Stony Brook, Stony Brook, New York, 9 August 1984).

21 "Highlander's Farewell," AAFS 4939, Archive of Folk Culture, Library of Congress, Washington, D.C.

22 A conjectural reconstruction of Emmett Lundy's repertoire is found in Carter, *Emmett W. Lundy,* 6–7.

23 Emmett Lundy, "Ducks on the Millpond," AAFS 4945 Archive of Folk Culture, Library of Congress, Washington, D.C.

24 Luther Davis, "Ducks on the Millpond," recorded by Thomas Carter and Blanton Owen, Galax, Virginia, 8 February 1974.

25 Joe Caudill, "Geese on the Millpond," recorded by Thomas Carter and Bill Hicks, Ennice, North Carolina, 21 January 1973.

26 The best discussion of Tommy Jarrell's music is found in Barry Poss's brochure notes for *Sail Away Ladies,* County Records 756, 2. For general information on the music of the Round Peak area, see Ray Alden, "Music of Round Peak," *Sing Out* 21 (November–December 1972): 1–11; and Richard Nevins, brochure notes for *Da Costa Woltz's Southern Broadcasters 1927,* County Records 524. Records featuring the music of the Round Peak area include *Down to the Cider Mill,* County Records 713; *Back Home in the Blue Ridge,* County Records 723; and *Stay All Night and Don't Go Home,* County Records 741.

27 See Carter, "Joe Caudill," 33–40, and *Emmett W. Lundy,* 2–5.

28 Robert B. Winans, "The Folk, the Stage, and the Five-String Banjo in the Nineteenth Century," *Journal of American Folklore* 89 (October–December 1976): 420–30.

29 Cecelia Conway, "The Afro-American Traditions of the Folk Banjo" (Ph.D. diss., University of North Carolina, 1980), 110. See also Dena Epstein, "The Folk Banjo: A Documentay History," *Ethnomusicology* 19 (September 1975): 347–71; and Robert B. Winans, "The Black Banjo-

Playing Tradition in Virginia and West Virginia," *Folklore and Folk-life in Virginia* 1 (1979): 7–27.

30 Conway, "Afro-American Traditions," chap. 3.

31 The clawhammer technique is described in Davidson and Newman, *Traditional Music from Grayson and Carroll Counties*, 4.

32 Emmett Lundy, "Forked Deer," AAFS 4435, Archive of Folk Culture, Library of Congress, Washington, D.C.; and Sidna Myers, "Forkey Deer," *High Atmosphere: Ballads and Banjo Tunes from Virginia and North Carolina*, Rounder Records 0028.

33 The various local banjo tunings are listed in Davidson and Newman, *Traditional Music from Grayson and Carroll Counties*, 4–5.

34 Conway, "Afro-American Traditions," 133–49.

35 Davidson and Newman, *Bluegrass from the Blue Ridge*, 7, and Conway, "Afro-American Traditions," 135. Conway observes, "Folk banjo tunings limit the number of possible fingering patterns appropriate for a tune and are thus the most stable and crucial ingredient of a folk playing style." Hus Caudill considered "Waves on the Ocean" a good banjo tune, though he could no longer play the tune when he was recorded during the 1973–1974 period; see Blanton Owen's notes to the *Old Originals*, vol. 2, Rounder Records 0058, 3.

36 See Carter, *Emmett W. Lundy*, 2–6.

37 This idea is implicit in most descriptions of the string band; see for example Carter, *Emmett W. Lundy*, 4.

38 "Old Bunch of Keys," *Down to the Cider Mill*, County Records 713.

39 See James Deetz, *In Small Things Forgotten: The Archaeology of Early American Life* (Garden City, N.Y.: Anchor Books, 1977), 127–33.

40 Hood, "The Architecture of the New River Valley," 208. In the new architectural fashion, Hood notes, "The houses are all three bays wide on the front elevation, two stories in height, clad in weatherboards and have either interior or exterior gable-end chimneys. Roofs are either hipped or gable, or a combination of the two. The interior generally follows a central-hall plan with equal size rooms on either side, usually a parlor and a bedroom. The kitchen and a dining room are contained in a one- or two-story ell."

3. The Hugh Dixon Homestead

1 James Deetz, *Invitation to Archeology* (Garden City, N.Y.: Natural History Press, 1967), 12.

2 Henry Glassie, *Pattern in the Material Folk Culture of the Eastern*

United States (Philadelphia: University of Pennsylvania Press, 1968), 16.

3 Carl Lounsbury, *Alamance County Architectural Heritage* ([Graham, N.C.]: Alamance County Historic Properties Commission, 1980), 1.

4 Sixth U.S. Census, Population Schedule, Alamance County, North Carolina, 1840.

5 North Carolina Yearly Meeting, *The Discipline of the Society of Friends of North Carolina Yearly Meeting, Revised 1869* (Greensboro, N.C.: Patriot Office, 1870), 54.

6 Jules Karlin, *Joseph M. Dixon of Montana: Part I: Senator and Bull-moose Manager, 1867–1917* (Missoula, Mont.: University of Montana Press, 1974), 4.

7 Seventh U.S. Census, Agricultural Schedule, Chatham County, Upper Regiment, North Carolina, 1850.

8 Lounsbury, *Almanance County Architectural Heritage*, 2–3.

9 Ibid., 14–15.

10 McKeldon Smith discusses the equal prevalence of the hall-parlor and Quaker-plan houses in Guilford County and the advent of the central passageway in the antebellum period. See his article "Guilford County: The Architectural Traditions in an Exclusively Vernacular Landscape," in *Carolina Dwelling: Toward Preservation of Place: In Celebration of the North Carolina Vernacular Landscape*, ed. Doug Swaim, The Student Publication of The School of Design, vol. 26 (Raleigh, N.C.: North Carolina State University, 1978), 150–59.

11 "Hugh W. Dixon," *The Guilford Collegian* 12 (February 1900): 152.

12 Hugh Woody Dixon, ledger book for the Ore Hill Co., 114 (owned by Sarah Kimball, Snow Camp, N.C.).

13 Amos Rapoport, *House Form and Culture* (Englewood Cliffs, N.J.: Prentice-Hall, 1969), 74.

14 Wade Hampton Hadley, *Chatham County 1771–1971* (Durham, N.C., Moore, 1976), cites sources that describe a Quaker settlement in the western section of the county not very far from Snow Camp. A number of Quaker homes were built near a 1751 meetinghouse, each of which had a walled spring and springhouse. This Pennsylvania penchant for stone, found in Chatham, lends credence to the idea of a pre-1866 homesite on the Dixon property complete with stone springhouse.

15 Sarah Kimball, tape-recorded interview, Snow Camp, N.C., 15 March 1980. The interview tape is in the author's possession.

16 I am following Doug Swaim's lead in using his term "Georgian plan" to categorize certain double-pile central-hallway houses regardless of construction era, in distinction to the term "Georgian." Swaim's term denotes not only this floor plan but also the specific features of a dis-

tinct eighteenth-century architectural style found in both England and the colonies. See Swaim, "North Carolina Folk Housing," in *Carolina Dwelling*, 38.

17 The Moses Pike house in Snow Camp, circa 1856, is a well-built Quaker-plan house. Located on the road between Hugh Dixon's house and the Cane Creek Meeting, it is a structure that he would likely have known well.

18 Lounsbury, *Alamance County Architectural Heritage*, 72.

19 Lounsbury dated these additions between 1866 and 1900. For the reasons described above and the 1901 date of Hugh Dixon's death, it seems reasonable to place the construction date in the earlier part of this period.

4. Economic and Cultural Influences on German and Scotch-Irish Quilts

1 The best examples of recent quilt scholarship are the publications of the American Quilt Study Group and closely documented exhibition catalogues such as *North Carolina Country Quilts: Regional Variations* (Chapel Hill, N.C.: The Ackland Art Museum, 1978); *Black Belt to Hill Country: Alabama Quilts from the Robert and Helen Cargo Collection* (Birmingham, Ala.: Birmingham Museum of Art, 1982); *Kentucky Quilts, 1800–1900* (Louisville, Ky.: The Kentucky Quilt Project, 1982); and *Social Fabric: South Carolina's Traditional Quilts* (Columbia, S.C.: McKissick Museum, 1985).

2 Carl Bridenbaugh, *Myths and Realities: Societies of the Colonial South* (Baton Rouge, La.: Louisiana State University Press, 1952), 55, 120–21.

3 Robert W. Ramsey, *Carolina Cradle: Settlement of the Northwest Carolina Frontier, 1747–1762* (Chapel Hill, N.C.: University of North Carolina Press, 1964), 12, 17.

4 Sally Garoutte, "Early Colonial Quilts in a Bedding Context," in *Uncoverings 1980*, ed. Sally Garoutte (Mill Valley, Calif.: American Quilt Study Group, 1981), 20–21.

5 *Western Carolinian* (Salisbury, N.C.), 19 September 1820.

6 Ibid., 28 January 1823.

7 Ibid., 26 June 1827.

8 Ibid., 3 June 1842.

9 Ibid., 18 July 1820.

10 Ibid., 10 December 1822.

11 *Carolina Watchman* (Salisbury, N.C.), 22 April 1843.

12 James G. Leyburn, *The Scotch-Irish: A Social History* (Chapel Hill, N.C.: University of North Carolina Press, 1962), 323.

13 Clement Eaton, *A History of the Old South* (New York: Macmillan, 1949), 146.

14 Henry James Ford, *The Scotch-Irish in America* (Princeton, N.J.: Princeton University Press, 1915), 199.

15 Ibid., 529–30.

16 James S. Brawley, *The Rowan Story, 1753–1953: A Narrative History of Rowan County, North Carolina* (Salisbury, N.C.: Rowan Publishing, 1953), 137.

17 Florence M. Montgomery, *Printed Textiles: English and American Cottons and Linens, 1700–1850* (New York: Viking Press, 1970), 120.

18 A group of similar quilts from neaby Mecklenburg County was also made by women associated with Presbyterian Churches. See Ellen F. Eanes, "Nine Related Quilts of Mecklenburg County, North Carolina, 1800–1840," in *Uncoverings 1982*, ed. Sally Garoutte (Mill Valley, Calif.: American Quilt Study Group, 1983), 25–42.

19 Montgomery, *Printed Textiles*, 356, fig. 420.

20 Patsy and Myron Orlofsky, *Quilts in America* (New York: McGraw-Hill, 1974), 326.

21 Richard H. Shryock, "British Versus German Traditions in Colonial Agriculture," *Mississippi Valley Historical Review* 26 (June 1939): 46.

22 William L. Saunders, ed., *The Colonial Records of North Carolina* (Raleigh, N.C.: Josephus Daniels, Printer to the State, 1887), 5:356.

23 Brawley, *The Rowan Story*, 142.

24 Harry Roy Merrens, *Colonial North Carolina in the Eighteenth Century: A Study in Historical Geography* (Chapel Hill, N.C.: University of North Carolina Press, 1964), 59.

25 Brawley, *The Rowan Story*, 191.

26 Orlofsky, *Quilts in America*, 59.

27 Ibid., 58–59.

5. The Development of the Bright-Leaf Auctioneer's Chant

1 Warren C. Roberts, "Folk Crafts," *Folklore and Folklife*, ed. Richard Dorson (Chicago and London: University of Chicago Press, 1973), 234.

2 I am grateful to the following informants for information used in this paper: Herman Crawford, auctioneer and instructor in High Point, N.C.; Joe Currin, retired tobacco buyer of Angier, N.C.; T. H. Cur-

rin, warehouse manager and former auctioneer in Oxford, N.C.; Stewart Cutts, auctioneer of Oxford, N.C.; Louis Love, retired auctioneer of Danville, Va.; Dave Mitchell, warehouse manager of Oxford, N.C.; Charles K. Waddell, warehouse manager of Danville, Va.: and Ray Wilkinson, agricultural reporter for the Tobacco News Network of Raleigh, N.C. All research notes are in the author's possession.

3 Daniel Steed, "To Be an Auctioneer, You've Got to Get It in Your Blood," *Kentucky Folklore Record* 20 (April–June 1974): 42.

4 Ibid.

5 R. W. Patten, "Tatworth Candle Auction," *Folklore* 81 (Summer 1970): 132–35.

6 Ralph Cassady, *Auctions and Auctioneering* (Berkeley and Los Angeles: University of California Press, 1967), 60.

7 Ibid., 90.

8 *100 Years of Progress* (Danville, Va.: Danville Tobacco Association, 1967), 2.

9 Cassady, *Auctions and Auctioneering*, 124.

10 Ibid., 110.

11 Lloyd T. Weeks and E. Y. Floyd, *Producing and Marketing Flue Cured Tobacco* (Raleigh, N.C.: The Technical Press, 1941), 5.

12 *100 Years of Progress*, 55.

13 Nannie May Tilley, *The Bright-Leaf Tobacco Industry, 1860–1929* (Chapel Hill, N.C.: University of North Carolina Press, 1948), 200.

14 Joseph Clarke Robert, *The Story of Tobacco in America* (New York: Alfred A. Knopf, 1949), 194.

15 Tilley, *Bright-Leaf Tobacco Industry*, 206.

16 Edward Pollock, *Sketch Book of Danville, Va.* (Petersburg, Va.: Published by the author, 1885), 127.

17 Tilley, *Bright-Leaf Tobacco Industry*, 227.

18 Christopher Sykes, *Nancy: The Life of Lady Astor* (New York: Harper and Row, 1972), 20.

19 Frederic Bancroft, *Slave Trading in the Old South* (New York: Frederic Unger, 1967), has numerous accounts of slave auctions; and Joseph Clark Robert, *The Tobacco Kingdom: Plantation, Market, and Factory in Virginia and North Carolina, 1800–1860* (Durham, N.C.: Duke University Press, 1938), mentions some "pre-Langhorne" tobacco auctions, but neither of these accounts describes any distinct auction styles.

20 Tilley, *Bright-Leaf Tobacco Industry*, 205.

21 Ibid., 239.

22 Duval Porter, ed., *Men, Places and Things as Noted by Benjamin Simpson* (Danville, Va.: Dance Bros., 1891), 356.
23 Herman E. Crawford, "The Tobacco Auctions," in *The Auction Encyclopedia*, ed. R. W. Bewed and S. G. Martin (Kansas City, Mo.: Auction Research and Education Press, 1980), 209.
24 Tilley, *Bright-Leaf Tobacco Industry*, 240–1.
25 Ibid., 204.
26 *100 Years of Progress*, 72.
27 Tilley, *Bright-Leaf Tobacco Industry*, 204.

6. A Greek-American's Recollections of *Panáretos*

1 See my unpublished papers " 'Just Blowing Up the Ball for the Second Half': Some Ethnic Jokes and Stereotypes among Greeks in the United States," 20 pp., and "Saint, Images, and Icons: A Functionalist Interpretation of Miracles and Folk Belief," 21 pp., in the Southern Folklife Collection, Wilson Library, University of North Carolina at Chapel Hill.
2 Quoted material regarding the life history of Harry Chepriss is used courtesy of the Southern Highlands Research Center, University of North Carolina at Asheville, where the interview tapes and transcripts are on deposit.
3 Some of the actors' names have remained with Harry: Kolovós, Satás, Papaoikonómou, Hatziyannákis, Apostolópoulos. To Harry's mind, when these men died, performances of the play ceased. This may be true, but the hiatus proved to be only temporary. A current resident of Karpenísi, Panayiótis Tsakaníkas, has informed me by letter (15 April 1980) that he revived the play in 1972 and subsequently staged it in 1976 and 1979.
4 In the interest of presenting the play in its most complete form, I have assembled here a conflated version of the text, which I have translated into English. A complete version in the original Greek is available from the Southern Folklife Collection, Wilson Library, University of North Carolina at Chapel Hill.
5 Lines 1–6 were spoken by Harry on but one occasion, as a kind of prologue. Their tentative cadences and lack of regular meter strongly suggest improvization.
6 Lines 9–10 appear to be improvizations.
7 Lines 28–30 are clearly paraphrases.
8 Lines 46–47 are paraphrases.

9 Line 53 seems to be a paraphrase.

10 Lines 71–72 are paraphrases.

11 Harry still recalls the names of some of these people: Manzanás, Yia-trídes, Tsiatsaraíos, Hantzákis.

12 Personal communication, 24 January 1979. Mr. Meraclés is professor of folklore at the University of Yánnina, in Greece. Although there is dis-agreement as to the exact date of composition of *Erofíli*, it seems most prudent to defer to the judgment of Línos Polítis, who in his authoritative *A History of Modern Greek Literature* (Oxford: Clarendon Press, 1973), 56, puts all three of Hortátzis's major works—*Erofíli*, *Katzoúrbos*, and *Gýparis*—in the period from 1585 to 1600.

13 From the preface to *Erofíli: A Tragedy by Yiórgios Hortátzis*, ed. Stéphanos Xanthoudídos (Athens: P. D. Sakellarios, 1928).

14 Polítis, *A History of Modern Greek Literature*, 56.

15 Yiórgios Zóras, *Panáretos: A One-Act Folk Adaptation of Erofíli* (Athens: Institute for Byzantine and Modern Greek Studies, 1957), introduction.

16 Polítis, *A History of Modern Greek Literature*, 70.

17 C. A. Trypánis, *Medieval and Modern Greek Poetry* (Oxford: Clarendon Press, 1951), xliv.

18 See Zóras's line-by-line comparison of a 1957 text of *Panáretos*, collected in Amfilohía, Greece, to Hortátzis's *Erofíli*, which thoroughly demonstrates the former's autonomy in language and phrasing, as well as significant differences in plot and characters.

19 Zóras, *Panáretos*.

20 Ibid., 13.

7. A Study of "High Sheriff," Dink Roberts's Man-against-the-Law Song

1 William Attmore, *Journal of a Tour to North Carolina, 1787*, ed. Lida Tunstall Rodman (Chapel Hill, N.C.: University of North Carolina Press, 1922), 43.

2 Dink Roberts, tape-recorded interview, Haw River, Alamance County, 21 February 1974. The interview tape is in the author's possession.

3 For Ashley, see Harry Smith, *Anthology of American Folk Music*, vol. 3, "Songs," Folkways Records FA-2953A; for Smith, see George Armstrong, *Hobart Smith*, Folk-Legacy Records FSA-17; for Cocker-ham, see Charles Faurot, *More Clawhammer Banjo Songs and Tunes from the Mountains*, County Records 717; for Hammons, see Carl Fleischauer and Alan Jabbour, *The Hammons Family: A Study of a*

West Virginia Family's Traditions, Library of Congress Records L65-L66; for Crisp, see Margot Mayo, *Rufus Crisp*, Folkways Records FA-2342; for Holcomb, see John Cohen, *Roscoe Holcomb and the High Lonesome Sound*, Folkways Records FA-2368; for Boggs, see Mike Seeger, *Doc Boggs*, vol. 3, Asch Records AH-3903; and field tapes in the author's collection, including one of Lucius Smith recorded by Allen Tullos in 1976. See also Mike Seeger, *A Survey of Rural Music of the Southeastern United States*, privately issued as LP-3329.

4 Field collector Robert W. Gordon hinted of this genre in his article "Banjo Tunes," first published in the *New York Times Magazine* on 1 January 1928. "Banjo songs," he believed, differed "sufficiently from the fiddle songs to be classified as a type apart." *Folk-Songs of America* (New York: National Service Bureau, 1938), 78, 84.

5 For a discussion of these, see my study "The Afro-American Traditions of the Folk Banjo" (Ph.D. diss., University of North Carolina at Chapel Hill, 1980), 188–90. In revising chapter 5 into this essay, I was greatly assisted by an ACLS research fellowship, an award given to recent recipients of the Ph.D.

6 There are much longer variants of these songs; for example, three texts of "John Hardy" appear in *The Frank C. Brown Collection of North Carolina Folklore*, vol. 2, *Folk Ballads from North Carolina*, ed. Henry M. Belden and Arthur Palmer Hudson (Durham, N.C.: Duke University Press, 1952), 563–66. Although the relation of the legendary John Hardy celebrated in song to any particular historical person is uncertain, there is an order for the execution of a John Hardy, a black man, on file in the courthouse in Welch, McDowell County: "State of West Virginia vs. John Hardy. Felony. This day came again the state by her attorney and the prisoner who stands convicted of murder in the first degree. . . . It is therefore considered by the court that the prisoner, John Hardy, is guilty . . . and that said John Hardy be hanged by the neck until dead . . . on Friday the 19th day of January 1894. (Smith, album notes for *Anthology of American Folk Music*, vol. 3, no. 5). Smith adds that a "witness of the trial states that Hardy worked for the Shawnee Coal Company."

7 "Charles Guiteau" (E 11) on the subject of President Garfield's assassination, "John Hardy" (I 2), "Jesse James" (E 1), and "John Henry" (I 1), in G. Malcolm Laws, *Native American Balladry* (Philadelphia: American Folklore Society, 1964).

8 Roger D. Abrahams asserts that "there is a strong attraction . . . on the part of New-World negro groups toward play genres; both conversational and fictive genres gravitate" toward play. "In contrast . . . one

can discern the opposite among rural American whites, where the performer in this group commonly creates as great a sense of removal as possible while singing, playing, or telling a story." See "The Complex Relations of Simple Forms," *Folklore Genres,* ed. Dan Ben-Amos (Austin and London: University of Texas Press, 1976), 210–11.

9 Robert Duncan Bass, "Negro Songs from the Pedee Country," *Journal of American Folklore* 44 (October–December 1931): 423.

10 On the relationship between motor imagery and empathy, see Richard Harter Fogle, *The Imagery of Keats and Shelley* (Chapel Hill, N.C.: University of North Carolina Press, 1949), 146.

11 Bill Monroe performs the following text acquired from Paul Clayton. It seems very Afro-American, for it is quite close to Peg's text, and Clayton had done fieldwork with black banjo players from Caldwell County, North Carolina:

> High Sheriff riding after me
> riding after me
> coming after me
> High Sheriff and Police riding after me
> And I feel like I gotta travel on.

12 Printed in J. Rosamond Johnson's collection of arranged folk songs, *Rolling Along in Song: A Chronological Survey of American Negro Music* (New York: Viking, 1937), 170.

13 Although the omission of present participles discounts the characteristic of the threat as something *continuing,* this variant does repeat the appearance of the threat and maintain a sense of immediacy with the words "come" and "this morning."

14 See Ralph Freedman, *The Lyrical Novel* (Princeton, N.J.: Princeton University Press, 1963).

15 On paratactic structure see Barbara Hernstein Smith, *Poetic Closure: A Study of How Poems End* (Chicago and London: University of Chicago Press, 1968).

16 A participant persona is a common vehicle for the lyricism of Afro-American secular songs. In a discussion of black folk music from 1800 to 1867, Dena J. Epstein devotes one chapter to secular song. Of seventeen texts documented for that period only two do not use first-person point of view. See *Sinful Tunes and Spirituals* (Urbana, Ill.: University of Illinois Press, 1977), 161–83.

17 Peg's response does not indicate that he will be physically passive: "I better be on my way, yes!" But his movements will be away from, rather than into confrontation with, his antagonist.

18 Lawrence W. Levine, *Black Culture and Black Consciousness: Afro-American Folk Thought from Slavery to Freedom* (New York: Oxford University, 1977), 194.

19 Some black scholars, like James Weldon Johnson, have noted that the story of the plight of the Jews in the Old Testament "fired . . . listeners into a firm faith that as God saved Daniel in the lion's den, so would He save them." See *The Book of American Negro Spirituals*, ed. James Weldon Johnson, musical arrangements by Rosamond Johnson (New York: Viking, 1925), 20.

20 See the discussion of the banjo-song variants of "Garfield" in my dissertation.

21 "John Henry" identifies the new-fangled threat of industrialism, for the worker challenges the company system in his competitive race against the steam drill. John Henry died with his hammer in his hand; the black persona became a man of action at great cost.

8. The Narrative Style of Marshall Ward, Jack-Tale-Teller

1 The biographical information in this paragraph comes from Marshall Ward's autobiography, recorded in the summer of 1969 under the supervision of Thomas Burton and Ambrose Manning and stored in the archives of East Tennessee State University, Johnson City, Tennessee. In subsequent paragraphs and throughout the remainder of this article all biographical information and remarks by Ward come from two tape-recorded interviews I had with him at his home in Banner Elk in July 1974, unless otherwise noted. The interview tapes are in the author's possession.

2 For his genealogy and kinship with other Jack-tale-tellers, see James W. Thompson, "The Origins of the Hicks Family Tradition," *North Carolina Folklore Journal* 34 (Winter–Spring 1987): 21.

3 Richard Chase, *The Jack Tales* (Boston: Houghton Mifflin, 1943), vii.

4 This description of Ward's facial expressions and gestures is based on my observations during the July 1974 interviews and tale-telling sessions and on a videotape of Ward telling "Jack and His Heifer Hide" provided to me by Thomas Burton. The only significant difference in Ward's style in these two sources is that in the videotape he appears still and nervous for the first few minutes but then warms up to his usual animated style.

5 Tapes in the Burton-Manning Collection, East Tennessee State University, collected in summer 1969.

6 See *Ray Hicks of Beech Mountain, North Carolina, Telling Four Traditional "Jack Tales,"* Folk-Legacy Records FTA-14, and *Jack Tales Told by Mrs. Maud Gentry Long of Hot Springs, North Carolina,* 2 vols., Library of Congress AAFS L47, L48.

7 All quotations from Ward's tales in this article are from tapes in the Burton-Manning Collection recorded in the summer of 1969, unless otherwise indicated.

8 Ward, of course, drew upon traditional motifs in composing these tales.

9 Richard Chase, *The Grandfather Tales* (Boston: Houghton Mifflin, 1948), 65–73, 81–87.

10 Chase, *Jack Tales,* xi.

11 For a fuller discussion of these traits of the hero Jack see my essay "The Jack Tale: A Definition of a Folk Tale Sub-Genre," *North Carolina Folklore Journal* 26 (September 1978), 85–110.

12 Daniel Joseph Sobol explores a similar reshaping of Jack tales by a teller who became a Methodist minister. See his "Everyman and Jack: The Storytelling of Donald Davis" (Master's thesis, University of North Carolina at Chapel Hill, 1987).

13 Autobiography on Burton-Manning tapes.

14 Wilbur Zelinsky, *The Cultural Geography of the United States* (Englewood Cliffs, N.J.: Prentice-Hall, 1973), 103–4. See map on p. 104 showing state-by-state "age-adjusted homicide rate, white population." The southern Appalachian states have notably high homicide rates, especially in Kentucky. Zelinsky suggests that homicide rates are related to both socioeconomic attainment and regional culture.

9. Afro-American Funeral-Ribbon Quilts

1 All information on Laura Lee comes from tape-recorded interviews on 13 April 1982, 15 April 1982, and 11 December 1983 at her home in Gorgus, near Moncure, Chatham County, North Carolina. The interview tapes are in the author's possession.

2 I looked for mention of funeral-ribbon quilts in many sources: John F. Szwed and Roger D. Abrahams, *Afro-American Folk Culture: An Annotated Bibliography of Materials from North, Central and South America and the West Indies* (Philadelphia: Institute for the Study of of Human Issues, 1978); Wayland D. Hand, ed., *The Frank C. Brown Collection of North Carolina Folk*lore, vol. 6, *Popular Beliefs and Superstitions from North Carolina* (Durham, N.C.: Duke University Press, 1961); Newbell Niles Puckett, *Folk Beliefs of the Southern*

Negro (1926; reprint, New York: Dover, 1969); John Michael Vlach, *The Afro-American Tradition in Decorative Arts* (Cleveland, Ohio: The Cleveland Museum of Art, 1978); and Mary Arnold Twining, "An Examination of African Retentions in the Folk Culture of the South Carolina and Georgia Sea Islands" (Ph.D. diss., Indiana University, 1977).

3 Maude S. Wahlman enumerates these characteristics and a few others in her essay "The Aesthetics of Afro-American Quilts," in *Something to Keep You Warm*, ed. Roland L. Freeman (Jackson: Mississippi Department of Archives and History, 1981), 6–8.

4 All information on Bessie Lee comes from a tape-recorded interview on 15 April 1982, an untaped interview on 14 December 1982, and general conversation at her home in Gorgus, near Moncure, Chatham County. The interview tapes are in the author's possession.

5 All information on Jennie Burnett comes from tape-recorded interviews on 4 December 1982 and 21 November 1983 at her home near Pittsboro, Chatham County. The interview tapes are in the author's possession.

6 Laura Lee's oral version of her family history has been researched and largely confirmed by Yvonne V. Jones. She examines the homecoming in the Gorgus community in "Kinship Affiliation through Time," *Ethnohistory* 27 (Winter 1980): 49–66.

7 Laura Lee mentions the quilt often in all taped interviews.

8 Vlach, *The Afro-American Tradition*, 139.

9 Sarah H. Torian, "Ante-Bellum and War Memories of Mrs. Telfair Hodgson," *Georgia Historical Quarterly* 27 (December 1943): 352.

10 Vlach, *The Afro-American Tradition*, 139–40, quotes the Georgia Writers' Project, *Drums and Shadows: Survival Studies among the Georgia Coastal Negroes* (Athens, Ga.: University of Georgia Press, 1940), 136.

11 Vlach, *The Afro-American Tradition*, 139–47.

12 Professor Daniel Patterson, "Folklore in the South," University of North Carolina at Chapel Hill, spring 1982, class notes.

10. Environmental Art as Creative Process

1 Many authors have conceptualized similar built environments as "folk art": Herbert Hemphill, Jr. and Julia Weissman, *Twentieth Century American Folk Art and Artists* (New York: E. P. Dutton, 1974); Elinor Lander Horwitz, *Contemporary American Folk Artists* (Philadelphia and New York: J. B. Lippincott Company, 1975); Lynette I.

Rhodes, *American Folk Art from the Traditional to the Naive* (Cleveland, Ohio: Cleveland Museum of Art, 1978); Anna Wadsworth, *Missing Pieces: Georgia Folk Art 1770–1976* (Atlanta: Georgia Council for the Arts and Humanities, 1976).

2   John Michael Vlach, "Quaker Tradition and the Paintings of Edward Hicks: A Strategy for the Study of Folk Art," *Journal of American Folklore* 94 (April–June 1981): 164, 158.

3   Robert Crease and Charles Mann, "Backyard Creators of Art that Says, 'I Did It, I'm Here,' " *Smithsonian* 14 (August 1983): 91.

4   Daniel Franklin Ward, ed., *Personal Places: Perspectives on Informal Art Environments* (Bowling Green, Ohio: Bowling Green State University Popular Press, 1984). Also of note: Mary Anne McDonald, "White Rock Village: Folk Art on Route 86?" *North Carolina Folklore Journal* 30 (Fall–Winter 1982): 99–108; I. Sheldon Posen and Daniel Franklin Ward, "Watts Towers and the *Giglio* Tradition," in *Folklife Annual 1985*, ed. Alan Jabbour and James Hardin (Washington, D.C.: Library of Congress, 1985), 142–57.

5   All quotations credited to Clyde Jones have been excerpted from conversations between Clyde and the author at his home in Bynum between July 1983 and August 1984. The interview tapes are in the author's possession.

6   Varick A. Chittenden, "Veronica Terrillion's 'Woman Made' House and Garden," in *Personal Places*, 50.

7   Tom Stanley has found that the works of many similar individuals he surveyed in North and South Carolina "were an extension of the artists' vocations." Tom Stanley, "Two South Carolina Folk Environments," in *Personal Places*, 62.

8   Crease and Mann, "Backyard Creators of Art," 84.

9   Horwitz, *Contemporary American Folk Artists*, 21–22.

10 Ibid., 133.

11 Roger Cardinal, *Outsider Art* (New York and Washington, D.C.: Praeger Publishers, 1972), 172.

12 Ibid.

13 Posen and Ward, "Watts Towers," 142–57 passim.

14 Horwitz, *Contemporary American Folk Artists*, 127.

15 Cardinal, *Outsider Art*, 68.

16 Mary Ann Anders has also commented on the commentators' focus on these artworks as visionary statements, finding that Ed Galloway's informal art environment was not as much an expression of a vision as "a personal artistic attempt to fulfill a creative drive and perhaps to

arouse viewer interest and praise as well as delight." Mary Ann Anders, "Celebrating the Individual: Ed Galloway's Park," in *Personal Places*, 131.

17 Horwitz, *Contemporary American Folk Artists*, 23.

18 Annette Jordan, "Wooden 'Varmints' In Yard Get Motorists' Attention," *Durham Morning Herald*, 10 April 1984, 11A. I would like to thank Charles G. Zug III for bringing this article to my attention.

19 Horwitz, *Contemporary American Folk Artists*, 78.

20 Ibid., 76–77.

21 Ibid., 117.

22 Crease and Mann, "Backyard Creators of Art," 83.

11. Primitive Baptist Tradition in an Age of Change

1 This and subsequent quotations are from tape-recorded interviews in the Southern Folklife Collection, Wilson Library, University of North Carolina at Chapel Hill. I have chosen to protect the privacy of the informants by withholding their names.

2 D. H. Goble, ed., *Primitive Baptist Hymn Book for All Lovers of Sacred Song* (1887; Greenfield, Ind.: D. H. Goble Printing, 1887), 221.

3 Elder Cushing Biggs Hassell, *History of the Church of God, from the Creation to A.D. 1885; including Especially the History of the Kehukee Primitive Baptist Association* (Middletown, N.Y.: Gilbert Beebe's Sons, 1886).

4 The practice has its Scriptural foundation in 1 Cor. 14:34, "Let your women keep silence in the churches: for it is not permitted unto them to speak."

5 Benjamin Lloyd, ed., *The Primitive Hymns, Spiritual Songs, and Sacred Poems*, Stereotype Edition (1841; Rocky Mount, N.C.: The Primitive Hymn Corporation, 1978).

6 George Pullen Jackson, *White Spirituals in the Southern Uplands* (Chapel Hill, N.C., University of North Carolina Press, 1933). See any of Jackson's song collections for specific examples.

7 See, for example, "Jesus Is a Rock," in Brett Sutton and Pete Hartman, *Primitive Baptist Hymns of the Blue Ridge*, University of North Carolina Press, American Folklore Recordings series.

8 For examples of lining out, see "Dunlap" (black) and "Devotion" (white) in album notes to *Primitive Baptist Hymns of the Blue Ridge*.

9 *Primitive Baptist Hymns of the Blue Ridge* documents both the similarities and the differences between the black and white Primitive Baptist repertoires. See in particular pp. 14–16 of the album booklet.

10 Jeremiah Ingalls, *Christian Harmony* (Exeter, N.H.: Henry Ranlet, 1805.)

11 Singing schools using gospel songbooks in seven-shape notation were being offered in southwestern Virginia and northwestern North Carolina as early as 1878. See A. B. Funk, "A Letter from Grayson Co.," *The Musical Million and Fireside Friend* 9 (1878): 9.

12 Golden Harris recorded "Dunlap" and "Parting Hand" at Columbia studios in New York City. They were released on the Indian Valley label. See Kip Lornell, "My Christian Friends in Bonds of Love: The Story of Elder Golden P. Harris," *Old Time Music* 39 (1984): 19–21.

12. Banjos and Blues

1 Hugh P. Brinton, "The Negro in Durham" (Ph.D. diss., University of North Carolina at Chapel Hill, 1930), iv, vii; and U.S. Bureau of the Census, *Characteristics of the Population, North Carolina 1940*, 16th Census, Population, Second Series (Washington, D.C.: U.S. Government Printing Office, 1941), 164.

2 Michael Haralambos, *Right On: From Blues to Soul in Black America* (New York: Drake, 1975), 69.

3 Bruce Bastin, "The Emergence of a Blues Tradition in the Southeastern States" (Master's thesis, University of North Carolina at Chapel Hill, 1973), 111. The fullest discussion of the blues scene in Durham and the rest of North Carolina is that given in chapters 12–16 of Bastin's *Red River Blues: The Blues Tradition in the Southeast* (Urbana and Chicago: University of Illinois Press, 1986). Bastin has also issued major collections of re-recordings of early Piedmont blues on his Flyright, Heritage, and Travellin' Man labels.

4 Paul Oliver, *Conversation with the Blues*, (New York: Horizon Press, 1961), 23–24, 170.

5 Oliver, *The Story of the Blues* (New York: Chilton, 1969), chapters 1 and 2; Leroi Jones, *Blues People* (New York: William Morrow, 1963), chapters 5 and 6.

6 Glenn Hinson, "The Bull City Blues," *The Guide*, Station WDBS, Durham, N.C. (November 1975): 4–5.

7 Willie Trice, tape-recorded interview, Orange County, N.C., 12 February 1976. This and all subsequent interview tapes are in the author's possession.

8 Arthur Lyons, tape-recorded interview, Durham, N.C., 10 May 1976.

9 Sonny Terry quoted in *The Harp Styles of Sonny Terry*, by Kent Cooper (New York: Oak Publications, 1975), 20.

10 Jessie Pratt, tape-recorded interview, Durham, N.C., 13 May 1976.

11 George P. Vuckan, "An Atlas for Orange County, North Carolina" (Chapel Hill: Institute for Research in Social Science, 1948), 61 (Typescript in the North Carolina Collection, Wilson Library, The University of North Carolina at Chapel Hill).

12 U.S. Bureau of the Census, *Characteristics of the Population, 1940,* 121.

13 Vuckan, "An Atlas for Orange County," 85.

14 U.S. Bureau of the Census, *Characteristics of the Population, 1940,* 121.

15 Vuckan, "An Atlas for Orange County," 85.

16 Odell Thompson, tape-recorded interview, Cedar Grove, N.C., 15 May 1976.

17 Joe Thompson, tape-recorded interview, Cedar Grove, N.C., 15 May 1976.

18 Gladys White, tape-recorded interview, Mebane, N.C., 16 May 1976.

19 Odell Thompson, tape-recorded interview, Cedar Grove, N.C., 15 May 1976.

20 Joe Thompson, tape-recorded interview, Cedar Grove, N.C., 15 May 1976.

21 See Brooks McNamara, *Step Right Up* (Garden City, N.Y.: Doubleday, 1976).

22 Cecelia E. Conway, "The Afro-American Traditions of the Folk Banjo" (Ph.D. diss., University of North Carolina at Chapel Hill, 1980) is one example of this scholarship.

23 Some of these have been issued by Kip Lornell, *Ain't Gonna Rain No More: Blues and Pre-Blues from Piedmont North Carolina,* Rounder Records 2016.

24 Odell Thompson, tape-recorded interview, Mebane, N.C., 13 June 1976.

25 Arthur Lyons, tape-recorded interview, Durham, N.C., 16 June 1976.

26 Vuckan, "An Atlas for Orange County," 61.

27 Mildred Finley, tape-recorded interview, Cedar Grove, N.C., 10 June 1976.

28 Robert Redfield, "The Folk Society," *The American Journal of Sociology* 52 (January 1947): 297.

29 George Foster, "What Is Folk Culture?" *American Anthropologist* 55 (April–June 1953): 160.

30 T. Lynn Smith, *The Sociology of Urban Life* (New York: Dryden Press, 1951), 50.

31 Son Mason, tape-recorded interview, Raleigh, N.C., 20 Feb. 1976.

32 E. Franklin Frazier, "The Impact of Urban Civilization upon Negro Family Life," *Cities and Society*, ed. Paul K. Hatt and Albert J. Reiss, Jr. (Glencoe, Ill.: Free Press, 1957), 490.

33 Ibid., 499.

34 Ibid.

35 Weston La Barre, *They Shall Take Up Serpents* (Minneapolis, Minn.: University of Minnesota Press, 1962), 163–75.

36 Brinton, "Negro in Durham," 192.

37 Ibid., 203.

38 Oliver, *Story of the Blues*, 6.

39 Oliver, *Conversation with the Blues*, 23.

40 Richard Trice, tape-recorded interview, Durham, N.C., 15 June 1976.

13. Why Do Duck Decoys Have Eyes?

1 Reported in my doctoral dissertation "Sights of the Sound: An Ethnography of an Aesthetic Community" (Ph.D. diss., University of North Carolina at Chapel Hill, 1980). In that work and this essay all names of persons and places have been changed. All quotations hereafter are from my tape-recorded interviews and field notes.

14. The Making of a College Legend

1 William Price, Duke undergraduate, 1968–72, an independent from Monroe, North Carolina, conversation with author. Price remembered hearing the story during his freshman year but not the source. Except as otherwise noted, the oral texts in this paper were taken from conversation notes and collected in November 1974 at various locations in the Durham area.

2 Laird Ellis, Duke student, 1966–69 and 1972–75, an independent from Tampa, Florida, conversation with author. The "East" referred to is the university's East Campus, slightly more than a mile from the larger West Campus and conected to it by Campus Drive. The East Campus is located at the western edge of downtown Durham.

3 Dan Hull, Duke student, 1971–75, a Phi Delta Theta from Cincinnati, Ohio, conversation with author. "Dick Angier" is a fictitious name for a certain Duke football player who played slightly later than "Robin Odom." To avoid possible embarrassment, the names of persons given in the various oral accounts have been fictionalized, although those of informants have not.

4 John Huff, Duke student, 1967–71, an independent from Greenville, South Carolina, conversation with author.

5 Will Hooker, an upstate New Yorker who attended Syracuse in the early 1960s, tape-recorded conversation, Durham, 24 October 1974.

6 Roland Wilkins, a university development officer since 1966, conversation with author. Wilkins "thought" he had heard the story from colleague Glen Smiley (see note 20).

7 Reynolds Price, Duke English department faculty member, 1958–present, conversation with author.

8 Charles Umberger, Duke undergraduate, 1968–72; employed at the university's alumni office at the time this account was collected, member of Phi Kappa Psi fraternity, conversation with author.

9 *Sports Illustrated*, 12 June 1967, 72.

10 George Lougee, "Five Youths Receive Suspended Sentences," *Durham Morning Herald*, 27 May 1967.

11 Linda Dégh and Andrew Vázsonyi, "The Memorate and the Proto-Memorate," *Journal of American Folklore* 87 (July–September 1974): 225–39.

12 John Swetnam, Duke undergraduate, 1964–68, now living in Durham, an independent from Oklahoma, conversation with author.

13 Anonymous, "Scatological Lore on Campus," *Journal of American Folklore* 75 (July–September 1962): 260.

14 A 1972 Duke alumna, daughter of a Duke professor, who did not know the Odom story in any form. This text was taken from a tape recording. Mayola's was a restaurant and beer joint close to both Duke and Durham High School, frequented by a number of DHS toughs as well as by Duke's athlete-dominated fraternities in the late 1960s. The author recalls a story current at Duke at approximately the same time as the Odom incident, about "Dick Angier" being arrested for beating up a policeman; this coincidence of events would increase the tendency for the Odom story to be attached to the better-known Angier.

15 Clayton Owens, Duke student, 1966–70; independent from Elizabeth City, North Carolina, conversation with author. At the time his account was collected, Owens was employed in a Duke library.

16 William Hugh Jansen, "The Esoteric-Exoteric Factor in Folklore," *Fabula* 2 (1959): 205–11.

17 Richard M. Dorson, "The Folklore of Colleges," *American Mercury* 68 (June 1949): 673.

18 John Snyder, a Durham resident for about five years who associates with a number of former Duke students. Carnival, who told Snyder the story about the KAS and the trustee's son, had never heard the

Odom story, although he had attended Duke when the story was in oral circulation. This text is from a tape recording.

19   James Wise, "The Other Side of the Sidelines," *Duke Alumni Register* (June 1971): 6–11.

20   Glen Smiley, Duke student and basketball player, 1966–70, employed at the university, 1971–present, member of Phi Kappa Sigma fraternity, from Montana, conversation with author. Smiley recalled reading the stories in the newspaper and *Sports Illustrated*.

21   David Swarts, Duke undergraduate, 1967–71, telephone conversation with author, 4 November 1974. Swarts now lives in Wheaton, Illinois, and has not visited Duke since his graduation.

22   Roger J. Corless, member of the religion faculty at Duke, 1970–present, conversation with author.

15. Industrial Pranks in a North Carolina Textile Mill

1   Lillie Smith and Ann Franklin, tape-recorded interview, Bynum, 16 July 1982, 40–42. Most of the quoted material in this essay is from a series of tape-recorded interviews with Bynum residents deposited in the Southern Oral History Program Papers, Southern Historical Collection, University of North Carolina at Chapel Hill. Subsequent citations will contain the name of the interviewee, the date, and the page number of the transcript. Unless otherwise noted, all interviews were conducted in Bynum by the author.

2   The latter approach has been advanced by Robert McCarl and Robert Byington. See Robert H. Byington, ed., *Working Americans: Contemporary Approaches to Occupational Folklife*, Special Issue, *Western Folklore* 37 (July 1978); reprint, Smithsonian Folklife Studies, no. 3 (Washington, D.C.: Smithsonian Institution Press, 1978). A survey of approaches to occupational folklore by Archie Green, "Industrial Lore: A Bibliographic-Semantic Query," may also be found in that volume.

3   See, for example, Archie Green, *Only a Miner: Studies in Recorded Coal-Mining Songs* (Urbana, Ill.: University of Illinois Press, 1972).

4   Camilla Collins, "Twenty-four to a Dozen: Occupational Folklore in a Hosiery Mill" (Ph.D. diss., Indiana University, 1978), 145.

5   Jack Santino, "Characteristics of Occupational Narrative," in *Working Americans*, ed. Byington, 213–44.

6   Betty Messenger, *Picking Up the Linen Threads: A Study in Industrial Folklore* (Austin, Tex.: University of Texas Press, 1978), 169.

7   Frank Durham, 10 September 1979, 26.

8   Pauline Williams, 17 June 1981, 4.

9 Frank Durham, 17 September 1981, 61.
10 Ibid.
11 Bill Ellis, 23 June 1981, 45–46.
12 Helen Andrews, Mebane, N.C., 10 July 1981, 2.
13 Jimmie Elgin, 20 October 1979, 2b.
14 See Pamela Bradney, "The Joking Relationship in Industry," *Human Relations* 10 (May 1957): 186.
15 Jimmie Elgin, 20 October 1979, 2a.
16 J. V. Suitts, 25 June 1981, 21–22.
17 Jimmie Elgin, 20 October 1979, 2a.
18 Frank Durham, 17 September 1979, 61.
19 Ibid.
20 Mary Gattis, 21 August 1979, 3b.
21 Jimmie Elgin, 20 October 1979, 1b.
22 Ibid.
23 Mozelle Riddle, 15 June 1981, 1–2.
24 Reported in the *Chatham Record*, 20 February 1930.
25 Roger D. Abrahams, "Towards a Sociological Theory of Folklore: Performing Services," in *Working Americans*, ed. Byington, 167–68.
26 Eula Durham, 1 March 1979, 2–3.
27 Ibid.
28 Jimmie Elgin, 20 October 1979, 1b–2a.
29 Ann Franklin, 16 July 1982, 44–45.
30 Santino, "Characteristics of Occupational Narrative," 201.
31 J. V. Ellis, 19 July 1982, 9–10.
32 J. V. Suitts, 25 June 1981, 17–18.
33 J. V. Ellis, 19 July 1982, 10–11.
34 Glenn Gilman, *Human Relations in the Industrial Southeast: A Study of the Textile Industry* (Chapel Hill, N.C.: University of North Carolina Press, 1956), 161.
35 Bill Ellis, 23 June 1981, 18.
36 Frank Durham, 10 September 1979, 26.
37 J. V. Ellis, 27 June 1981, 32.
38 Helen Howard, 22 October 1979, 2a.
39 Collins, "Twenty-four to a Dozen," 78–80.
40 Mary Gattis, 21 August 1979, 3b.
41 Jimmie Elgin, 20 October 1979, 1b.
42 J. V. Ellis, 27 June 1981, 27.
43 Mildred Johnson and J. V. Suitts, 25 June 1981, 21.
44 J. V. Ellis, 27 June 1981, 27–28.
45 J. V. Ellis, 19 July 1982, 12.

46 Jimmie Elgin, 20 October 1979, 1b.
47 Collins, "Twenty-four to a Dozen," 98–100, 144.
48 Ibid., 93–116.
49 Willis Beal, 13 July 1982, 9.
50 Mrs. Walter R. Rowe interview with Ethel Deal, Newton, N.C., 19 June 1939, Federal Writer's Project Papers, Southern Historical Collection, University of North Carolina at Chapel Hill.
51 Frank Durham, 17 September 1979, 60.
52 Carrie Lee Gerringer, 11 August 1979, 40–41.
53 Bill Ellis, 23 June 1981, 19–20.
54 J. V. Ellis, 19 July 1982, 7–8.
55 Lillie Smith, 14 July 1982, 25–26.
56 J. V. Ellis, 19 July 1982, 7.
57 David Montgomery, *Workers' Control in America* (Cambridge: Cambridge University Press, 1980).

Contributors

Thomas Carter took his graduate degrees in folklore from the University of North Carolina at Chapel Hill and Indiana University. He is an architectural historian with the Utah Division of State History and an adjunct assistant professor in the University of Utah's Graduate School of Architecture. He has published extensively on both traditional architecture and music and edited many albums of traditional music, including *The Old Oirginals: Instrumental Folk Music Recently Recorded in North Carolina and Virginia* (Rounder Records, 1977), *The Old Virginia Fiddlers: The Spanglers from Meadows of Dan, Virginia* (County Records, 1977), *Emmett Lundy: Fiddle Tunes from Grayson County, Virginia* (String Records, 1977), and *Eck Robertson: Famous Cowboy Fiddler* (County Records, forthcoming). His essay is based on research funded by a National Endowment for the Humanities Youth Grant. Blanton Owen collaborated in the fieldwork for this essay, and Dell Upton and Gary Stanton read earlier versions of it; their comments were useful in shaping the final product.

Kathleen Condon has studied folklore at George Washington University and the University of North Carolina at Chapel Hill. She has held a variety of public-sector folklife posts and now works as staff folklorist for BACA/The Brooklyn Arts Council. She has recently edited *Made by Hand, Played by Heart: Folk Arts in Queens*, soon to be published by Queens Council on the Arts.

Cecelia Conway holds graduate degrees in English from Duke University and the University of North Carolina at Chapel Hill, the latter with a doctoral concentration in folklore. She teaches in the department of English at Appalachian State University. Recipient of ACLS, NEA, and other grants, she has directed folklore media projects and produced and codirected the internationally exhibited award-winning films *Dink: Pre-Blues Musician* (1975) and *Sprout Wings and Fly: A Portrait of Fiddler Tommy Jarrell* (1983).

Douglas DeNatale holds graduate degrees in folklore from the University of North Carolina at Chapel Hill and the University of Pennsylvania. He has held many public-sector folklife positions, most recently being project coordinator for the Lowell Folklife Project of the American Folklife Center. Among his publications are an essay on "Reynardine" in *Western Folklore*, the album *Native Virginia Ballads* (Blue Ridge Institute, 1980), *Between the Branches: Folk Art of Delaware County, New York* (Delaware County Historical Association, 1985), *Two Stones for Every Dirt: The Story of Delaware County, New York* (Purple Mountain Press, 1987), and *The Origins of Southern Mill Culture* (forthcoming from the University of North Carolina Press). The research for his essay grew out of work with the Southern Oral History Program at the University of North Carolina at Chapel Hill.

John Forrest, associate professor of anthropology at the State University of New York at Purchase, studied at Oxford University and took graduate degrees in folklore and anthropology at the University of North Carolina at Chapel Hill. His essay developed from research for his doctoral dissertation, which Cornell University Press published under the title *Lord I'm Coming Home: Everyday Aesthetics in Tidewater North Carolina*. His related essay "The Devil Sits in the Choir" appears in *Diversities of Gifts* (University of Illinois Press, 1988). Forrest also has a particular interest in dance research and is the author of *Morris and Matachin: A Study in Comparative Choreography*, a joint publication of Sheffield University and the English Folk Dance and Song Society.

Charlotte Paige Gutierrez holds graduate degrees in folklore and anthropology from the University of North Carolina at Chapel Hill. She wrote a thesis on Jack tales and a dissertation on Cajun food ways. Her essay on Marshall Ward won the Cratis D. Williams Prize awarded by the North Carolina Folklore Society, and she has an essay on Cajuns in *Ethnic and Regional Foodways in the United States* (University of Tennessee Press, 1984). Currently a free-lance consultant and publisher, she has carried out numerous folklife projects in Biloxi, Mississippi.

Laurel Horton has master's degrees in library science and folklore and has held a variety of public-sector folklife positions. Laurel is both a professional quilt maker and a well-known student of American quilts. She serves on the national board of directors for the American Quilt Study Group and has carried out a number of field-research projects with quilts in North and South Carolina. She is currently affiliated with the McKissick Museum at the University of South Carolina, which published her exhibition catalog *Social Fabric: South Carolina's Traditional Quilts*.

Kip Lornell has a master's degree in folklore from the University of North Carolina at Chapel Hill and a doctorate in ethnomusicology from Memphis State University. He has taught at the University of Virginia and carried out many folklife projects, particularly for the Blue Ridge Institute. Kip has edited more than a dozen phonograph albums of blues, gospel, country, and other forms of traditional music. His extensive publications on folk music include *"Happy in the Service of the Lord": Afro-American Gospel Quartets in Memphis* (University of Illinois Press, 1988), and *Virginia's Blues, Country, and Gospel Records 1902–1943: An Annotated Discography* (University Press of Kentucky, 1989). In 1988 and 1989 he held a Smithsonian Institution postdoctoral fellowship for work on a book to be entitled "Folk Music, American Music."

Mary Anne McDonald studied folklore at the University of Virginia and the University of North Carolina at Chapel Hill, writing a thesis on Afro-American quilt makers. She has worked with the Virginia Folklore Archives, the Southern Oral History Program in Chapel Hill, municipal and state folklife programs in Florida, Indiana, and North Carolina, and currently serves in the folklife section of the North Carolina Arts Council. Her essay "White Rock Village: Folk Art on Route 86?" won the W. Amos Abrams Prize awarded by the North Carolina Folklore Society.

Bill Mansfield did his graduate study of folklore at the University of North Carolina at Chapel Hill. But he has also undertaken study with the traditional banjoist Fred Cockerham in an apprenticeship funded by the National Endowment for the Arts. An outstanding musician himself, Mansfield has presented folk music in public-school projects of the folklife section of the North Carolina Arts Council and has held appointments as visiting artist at community colleges and technical institutes under the sponsorship of the North Carolina Arts Council and the North Carolina Department of Community Colleges.

Stephen Matchak took a master of arts degree in Celtic studies at the University College of Wales before taking two other graduate degrees at the University of North Carolina at Chapel Hill in folklore and geography. His essay is an outgrowth of his folklore thesis. He wrote a doctoral dissertation on folk housing in New England and has subsequently done research on traditions of the Connecticut River valley and mounted exhibitions for the Connecticut River Foundation. He is assistant professor of geography at Salem State College.

Rachel B. Osborn took graduate training in folklore at the University of North Carolina at Chapel Hill and has held numerous public-sector folklife positions, most recently as director of the Sun Inn Preservation Association in Bethlehem, Pennsylvania. Her essay won the Cratis D. Williams Prize awarded by the North Carolina Folklore Society. She has done an extensive architectural field survey for the North Carolina Division of Archives and History and is currently completing a book on the historic architecture of Chatham County, North Carolina.

Daniel W. Patterson is Kenan Professor of English at the University of North Carolina at Chapel Hill and has chaired the Curriculum in Folklore. He is the author of *The Shaker Spiritual* (Princeton University Press, 1979) and *Gift Drawing and Gift Song: Two Forms of Shaker Inspiration* (The United Society of Shakers, 1983), and with Ruel W. Tyson and James L. Peacock coedited *Diversities of Gifts: Field Studies in Southern Religion* (University of Illinois Press, 1988). He has also served as project director for a series of documentary films coproduced by the Curriculum in Folklore and Tom Davenport Films.

John A. Porter took his master's degree in folklore at the University of North Carolina at Chapel Hill. He has taught English and folklore at the University of North Carolina at Asheville and written for *The Arts Journal.* He has also studied and taught in Greece. Currently he is preparing himself for the ministry at the Reformed Presbyterian Seminary in Pittsburgh, Pennsylvania.

Thomas Sauber received a master of arts degree in folklore from the University of California at Los Angeles. He is a keen student of American fiddling and has produced one album, *That's Earl: Collins Family Fiddling* (Briar Records, 1975), as well as contributed musical commentary to several others, including *Great Big Yam Potatoes: Anglo-American Fiddle Music from Mississippi* (Mississippi Department of Archives and History, 1985) and *Eck Robertson: Famous Cowboy Fiddler* (County Records, forthcoming).

Brett Sutton studied folklore at the University of Illinois before coming to the University of North Carolina at Chapel Hill for graduate degrees in folklore, anthropology, and information science. The research for his essay was funded by a National Endowment for the Humanities Youth Grant. Sutton was a recipient of the Charles Seeger Prize from the Society for Ethnomusicology for an essay published in its journal, and he has other essays on Primitive Baptists in such books as *Holding on to the Land and the Lord* (University of Georgia Press, 1982), *Perspectives on the American South* (New York, 1981), and *Diversities of Gifts: Field Studies in Southern Religion* (University of Illinois Press, 1988). He has also edited folk-music recordings for the Blue Ridge Institute and the University of North Carolina Press. He is assistant professor at the University of Illinois at Champaign-Urbana.

James Wise is a graduate of Duke University and took his master's degree in folklore at the University of North Carolina at Chapel Hill. He contributed an essay on the Sons of God movement to *Diversities of Gifts: Field Studies in Southern Religion* (University of Illinois Press, 1988). Currently he serves as life-style editor for the *Morning Herald* newspaper in Durham, North Carolina.

Charles G. Zug III is professor of English at the University of North Carolina at Chapel Hill, where he has taught since 1968. At various times he has served as chairman of the Curriculum in American Studies and chairman of the Curriculum in Folklore. He has curated and written catalogues for a number of exhibitions, including *The Traditional Pottery of North Carolina* and *Five North Carolina Folk Artists*. He has also written many articles for literary and folkloristic journals, and recently completed *Turners and Burners: The Folk Potters of North Carolina*, which was published in 1986 by the University of North Carolina Press.

Index